AFRICAN AMERICAN
LITERATURE

AFRICAN AMERICAN LITERATURE

An Anthology of Nonfiction, Fiction, Poetry, and Drama

Demetrice A. Worley ◆ Jesse Perry, Jr.

Foreword by Nikki Giovanni

National Textbook Company
a division of *NTC Publishing Group* • Lincolnwood, Illinois USA

About the cover

The illustration on the cover is a detail from *Family Tree,* a quilt designed by Wini McQueen in 1987. This quilt was part of the exhibition "Stitching Memories," organized by the Williams College Museum of Art, Macon, Georgia. Ms. McQueen, an African American artist who calls herself "a storyteller working in old world methods modified by new world technology," used mixed media to create the images on the quilt, including the transfer of photographs to cloth. *Family Tree* is shown in its entirety on page 318 and is reproduced here by permission of the artist and the Museum of Arts and Sciences, Macon, Georgia.

Credits for literary selections: See page 323, which is an extension of the copyright page.

Interior design: Susan Stirling

1994 Printing

Published by National Textbook Company, a division of NTC Publishing Group.
©1993 by NTC Publishing Group, 4255 West Touhy Avenue,
Lincolnwood (Chicago), Illinois 60646-1975 U.S.A.
Library of Congress Catalog Card Number 92-61939
Manufactured in the United States of America.

4 5 6 7 8 9 0 VP 9 8 7 6 5 4 3

This book is dedicated to my friend and husband, C. Nickolas Goloff, who believes in my abilities and shares in my dreams; to my parents, Ernestine R. Worley and Thomas D. Worley, Jr., who nurtured my early desire to read and write; and to my brothers, Timothy D. Worley and Michael D. Worley, who never let me get away with anything.

D.A.W.

This volume is dedicated to my wife and best friend, Maxine Gray Perry, who supports me in every professional endeavor; to our sons, Desmond and Derrick, their wives and children; to our son, Brian, and to my sister, Mary J. Morris; to my brother, Willie, and to the memory of my late father and mother, Jesse and Caroline Perry, and to my late brother, Benny.

J.P.J.

About the Authors

Dr. Demetrice A. Worley teaches African American Literature at Bradley University, where she is also Director of Writing. Among her many interests are the importance of and use of multicultural literature in the classroom and the relationship of writing theory to writing practice.

Dr. Jesse Perry, Jr., has been very actively involved in the field of language and literature education as a teacher and administrator since 1959. His most recent position was Program Manager (K–12), English Language Arts, San Diego City Schools.

Foreword

NIKKI GIOVANNI

A few years ago, *Voyager II* crossed our galaxy heading toward the Dog Star. We don't know a lot about the light that Earth sees but we know the brightest star in the galaxy is beyond the influence of the yellow sun. Galileo would be proud. I'm a Trekkie. I like the concept of both Space and the future. I'm not big on aliens that always seem to want to destroy Earth and Earthlings. It's almost laughable that the most destructive force in the known universe, the human race, always fears something is out there trying to get them. Freud said something about projection . . . and though I would hardly consider myself a Freudian, I think he had a point.

It's not really a question of whether or not E.T. is Black, his story is the story of sojourning. It doesn't even matter whether he came to Earth to explore or was brought to Earth for less honorable pursuits. He found himself left behind with neither kith nor kin to turn to. He depended, in the words of Tennessee Williams, "upon the kindness of strangers." E.T. didn't sing, but if he had he would have raised his voice to say "Sometimes I feel like a motherless child . . . a long way from home." E.T., had he taken the time to assess his situation, may have lifted his voice to the sky to say "I'm going to fly away . . . one of these days . . . I'm going to fly away." When the men with the keys captured him, taking him to the laboratory to dissect him, to open him up in order to find what he was made of, he might have hummed "You got to walk this lonesome valley . . . you got to walk it by yourself." But E.T., like Dorothy, had friends who came to his rescue. Dorothy returned to Kansas more sensitive, more aware of her world. E.T. returned to space having, I'm sure, a mixed view of Earth. Black Americans settled here, making a stand for humanity.

It is an honorable position . . . to be a Black American. Our Spirituals teach "I've been 'buked and I've been scorned . . . I've been talked about sure as I'm born." We maintained an oral tradition and created a written one. Phillis Wheatley, a slave girl, wrote poetry while others sang our songs. We did both because both are necessary. Hammer, while different from, is not in contrast to Frederick Douglass. Two Live Crew is in a direct line with Big Mama Thornton and all the other blues singers who sang what is called the "race music." (The "good" people would not allow it in their it in their churches or homes.) But we have survived and thrived because of our ability to find the sacred in the secular. "Oh, pray my wings gonna fit me well," says the song but whether they fit ill or well we wear what we have with style.

Style has profound meaning to Black Americans. If we can't drive we will invent walks and the world will envy the dexterity of our feet. If we can't have ham we will boil chitterlings; if we are given rotten peaches we will make cobblers; if given scraps we will make quilts; take away our drums and we will clap our hands. We prove the human spirit will prevail. We will take what we have to make what we need. We need confidence in our knowledge of who we are.

America is no longer a nation of rural people. We no longer go to visit grandmother and grandfather on the farm in the summer. This is no longer a nation where the daily work is done by the body; the daily work is now performed by the mind. The distance between families is no longer a walk, or even, a short drive. Families, for that matter, are no longer clear. Biology no longer defines who we love or relate to. We are now able to make emotional choices. There is so much to be done to prepare Earth for the next century. Humans, who are so fearful of change, are in such a radical transition. The literature of Black Americans can lead the way. As we were once thrown into a physical unknown where our belief in the wonder of life helped forge a new nation, we can help lead Earth into an emotional unknown and seek acceptance for those who are unique. Our literature shows that humans can adjust to the unacceptable and yet still find a way to forgive. Our stories, which once were passed sitting on porches after dinner spitting tobacco juice at fireflies, as Alex Haley's grandmother did, are now passed through the poems, speeches, stories we have written and recorded.

While a bowl of navy beans is one of my favorite meals (with a bit of cole slaw and corn muffins on the side) I still enjoy a smorgasbord. Sometimes a bit of everything creates an appetite while satisfying a hunger. For all the trouble we now understand the voyage of Columbus to have caused, it must have been exciting to live in an age when we finally began to break into a concept of the whole Earth. For sure, we have not done a great job, but we have done a better job than if we had stayed home. This century is rolling on to a close. There is both outer space and inner space to be explored. The literature of Black Americans is, in the words of Stevie Wonder, "a ribbon in the sky." We learn and love the past because it gives us the courage to explore and take care of the future. Voyager II will not come back . . . it has gone too far away. We will not return, we can only visit. But isn't it a comforting thought to realize the true pioneer of Earth is our people? Isn't it the ultimate challenge to accept responsibility not only for ourselves but our planet? One day, some identifiable life form will come to Earth and ask: Who are these people . . . these Black Americans? And we will proudly present our songs, stories, plays, speeches and poetry. We will proudly say: We are the people who believe in the possibilities.

Nikki Giovanni

Preface

We created this book to provide an anthology of African American nonfiction, fiction, poetry, and drama that would present you with an insight into the richness of African American literature and African American culture. We created this book, also, because we believe that the study of African American literature provides you with an opportunity to better understand yourself and other cultures.

This book begins with a historical overview of African American literature and presents a variety of selections written by black American authors, covering a wide range of themes for a period of time from the mid 1770s to the late 1980s. These works are arranged thematically: Slavery—Time of Trial; Standing Ground; The Folk Tradition; On Being a Man; On Being a Woman; Relationships, Love, and Conflicts; Passing Down Heritage; and Of Dreamers and Revolutionaries. You should view these themes as *starting points* for discussing the literary and cultural issues inherent in each selection.

Each chapter begins with information on the historical and social importance of the theme. Each selection is preceded with a brief biographical note on the author. This background information should serve as the first step on your way to learning more about the themes and the authors.

After each selection, there are questions to guide you as you think about the work. These are questions you can contemplate alone or with others. In addition, at the end of each selection there are reading/writing connection activities. These activities are designed to provide you with some direction as you critically and creatively respond to the literary and cultural issues raised in each selection. A reading journal is the ideal place in which to keep your writings about what you have read. If you are using this book in an educational setting, your instructor might make a reading journal part of your work. If you are reading this book on your own, it would still be a good idea to keep a journal. Your journal will provide you with a central location in which to store ideas and concerns that you may later use when responding in writing to the literary and cultural issues raised in *African American Literature*.

Acknowledgments

I would like to acknowledge the people who helped me transform an idea into this book: my co-author, Jesse Perry, Jr., for being a co-believer in the dream; our editor, Sue Schumer, for her gentle but firm guiding hand; my English 229 Afro-American Literature classes at Bradley University for their constructive feedback on the literature as well as the "Thinking About the Selection" and "Reading/Writing Connection" activities; and my graduate research assistants, Charlene Trotman, Sandra Long, and Alan Williams, for gathering necessary information.

D.A.W.

I would like to acknowledge persons who helped to make this publication a reality: my co-author, Demetrice Worley, for her vision and support; our editor, Sue Schumer, for her ability to persuade and compromise when necessary; and former students who represent an American mosaic for their receptivity and eagerness to read and respond to literature of another people.

J.P.J.

The authors and publisher extend a special thank you to Janice Bell Ollarvia, who has served as Editorial Consultant for *African American Literature*. Ms. Ollarvia has taught English for over 20 years in the Chicago Public Schools and has held various administrative positions. Currently she is Assistant Principal for Curriculum and Instruction at Fenger High School in Chicago.

CONTENTS

3
THE FOLK TRADITION

4
ON BEING A MAN

5

ON BEING A WOMAN

6

RELATIONSHIPS, LOVE, AND CONFLICTS

7

PASSING DOWN HERITAGE

8

OF DREAMERS AND REVOLUTIONARIES

A HISTORICAL OVERVIEW OF THE AFRICAN AMERICAN LITERARY TRADITION

Slavery (1700s to 1865)

The Africans who were brought to the United States of America as slaves were faced first with the ordeal of surviving the middle passage—the voyage across the Atlantic Ocean—and then surviving within the institution of slavery. As slaves, they were denied the right to retain their languages and religions. Instead, they were forced to learn a new language, English, and a new form of religion, Christianity.

The fact that there is any evidence of African American literature written before 1865, when the Civil War ended, is remarkable. In many areas it was against the law to educate a slave. Thus, the majority of slaves were illiterate. Some slaves tricked their owners' children into teaching them to read and write. A few slaves were lucky; their owners believed in educating slaves.

We should not confuse illiteracy, however, with a lack of literature or culture. The African literary tradition that the slaves carried with them was an oral tradition. The customs, values, traditions, and history of a people were embodied in their oral literature. The earliest survivors of the African oral tradition were the work songs and field hollers that slaves called to each other as they worked in the fields. Another literary survivor was the folktale. Early African Americans shared folktales that explained the unexplainable, expressed values, and identified acceptable and unacceptable behavior. Folktales such as ''How Buck Won His Freedom'' and ''People Who Could Fly'' provided the slaves with hope and entertainment.

In the late 1700s, a limited amount of African American literature had been written or published. Early African American poetry, such as that of Phillis Wheatley and Jupiter Hammon, reflects the strong religious influences of the time. Revolutionary War–era writers like Benjamin Banneker, mathematician and astronomer, and Olaudah Equiano (Gustavus Vassa) spoke out for the equality of all people, especially African Americans.

By the early 1800s, African American literature appeared in a number of forms. White abolitionists encouraged the writing and publication of slave narratives, such as *Incidents in the Life of a Slave Girl* by Harriet A. Jacobs. Often, illiterate African American slaves were encouraged to tell their life stories to white writers who wrote them down. African American abolitionists produced nonfiction, such as Nat Turner's pamphlet *The Confessions of Nat Turner* (1831), and drama, such as William Wells Brown's *The Escape, or A Leap for Freedom* (1858), the first African American play. In 1859 Harriet E. Wilson published *Our Nig; or, Sketches from the Life of a Free Black*, the first novel published in the United States by an African American. Poets such as Frances Watkins Harper captured the horror of the institution of slavery. Other black writers, such as Frederick Douglass and David Walker, used the podium and essays to promote the right of African Americans to freedom and equality. Educated African Americans, such as Charlotte Forten Grimké, kept journals of their daily lives.

From its beginnings to the Civil War, the African American literary tradition was built and focused on a quest for freedom and equality. This quest has continued to serve as a foundation for much of the African American literary effort to this day.

Post Civil War, Reconstruction, and Reaction (1865 to 1920)

After the Civil War, the Reconstruction Act of March 1867 provided federal protection to African Americans in the South. For the first time, education—even though segregated—became a legal reality for all African Americans. However, many blacks still received little beyond a rudimentary education because of their financial need to work. By 1880 the economic and political gains that African Americans had made after the Civil War were eroded by the Ku Klux Klan, lynchings, increased unemployment, and legalized segregation of public accommodations and facilities (Jim Crow laws).

The African American literature produced between 1865 and 1920 reflects the disappointments, fears, and frustrations produced by America's failure to fulfill its promises of freedom and equality after the Civil War. Biographies and autobiographies, such as Frederick Douglass' *Narrative of the Life of Frederick Douglass, an American Slave* (1845) and Booker T. Washington's *Up from Slavery* (1901), were created. Charles W. Chesnutt became the first published short story writer and one of the first African American novelists. Paul Laurence Dunbar, whose dialect poetry was well received by whites, wrote novels such as *The Uncalled* (1898). Another excellent writer, James Weldon Johnson, author of *The Autobiography of an Ex-Coloured Man* (1912), published novels, as well as sermons in verse. This growing body of literature, however, was often ignored by white literary critics.

As the number of educated African Americans increased, so did the number of African American writers. At the beginning of the 1920s, this growing number of black writers were seeing their work published, and—more importantly—a growing number of educated African Americans were reading it.

Harlem Renaissance (Early 1920s to the Early 1930s)

Between 1915 and 1918 two events—the Great Migration and the end of World War I— contributed to the beginning of the Harlem Renaissance, a very creative literary period for African Americans. In 1915 African Americans began moving from the rural South to the urban North in search of jobs and a better life. Lured by the promise of employment, hundreds of thousands of African Americans migrated to large cities such as Chicago, Detroit, New York, and Philadelphia. After fighting in World War I to make the world safe for democracy, African Americans returned home to be confronted with racism, unemployment, and poverty. However, their racial identity had been solidified by their participation in the War. Blacks' experiences in Europe had made them more aware of this country's prejudices against them. After World War I, African Americans began to fully recognize something that racism and poverty in the United States could not take from them—their culture.

The Harlem Renaissance was a celebration of African American culture at a time in America's history when the restraints of the Victorian era were giving way to the boldness of the Roaring Twenties. The word *renaissance*, literally, means rebirth. Instead of a rebirth, however, the Harlem Renaissance was actually the first opportunity African Americans had to give birth to—and to celebrate—the uniqueness of African American culture. Both black and white readers were eager to experience a slice of African American life. The literature of the time provided that experience.

Young, educated African Americans traveled to New York City—in particular to Harlem, the cultural and artistic center of African Americans—to make a place for themselves in the literary scene. Harlem was *the* gathering place for what black leader, sociologist, and historian W.E.B. Du Bois had labeled the talented tenth: the ten percent of African American intellectuals and artists who would lead African Americans in the United States. In Harlem these intellectuals and artists argued about the future of African Americans. Some conservative African American critics believed that the literature written by blacks should "uplift" the race—show African Americans in a positive light. Younger, more radical African Americans believed that a "realistic" view of African American life had to be presented because it was art.

During the Harlem Renaissance, New York City provided a wide variety of publishing opportunities. Major publishing companies began soliciting and publishing literary works by black writers. Several agencies had magazines that published work by young black writers and sponsored writing contests. Two such periodicals were *The Crisis*, published by the National Association for the Advancement of Colored People (NAACP) and edited by W. E. B. Du Bois, and *Opportunity*, published by the Urban League and edited by Charles S. Johnson. Independent magazines, such as *The Messenger*—a militant socialist journal edited by A. Philip Randolph and Chandler Owen—published up-and-coming African American writers. Some writers, such as Wallace Thurman, Langston Hughes, Zora Neale Hurston, Aaron Douglas, John P. Davis, Bruce Nugent, and Gwendolyn Bennett, even tried to start their own literary journal—*Fire!!*—which lasted only one issue.

Many young African American writers came into prominence during the Harlem Renaissance. Four in particular were recognized as the premier writers of the time: Claude McKay, Jean Toomer, Countee Cullen, and Langston Hughes. Many others, including James Weldon Johnson, Zora Neale Hurston, Nella Larson, Sterling Brown, Georgia Douglas Johnson, Jessie Fausett, and Rudolph Fisher, received recognition for their poetry, short stories, drama, and novels. Continuing work he had begun at the beginning of the century, Du Bois produced books and essays on the position of African Americans in this country and on the steps African Americans needed to take to achieve equality.

The Harlem Renaissance writers reflected both the "uplifting" theme of the conservative African American critics and the "realistic" artist movement of the younger, more radical African American critics. Both sides succeeded in showing African Americans and the world that their culture was a worthy literary topic, that it was "beautiful"—a theme that would reemerge during the Black Power movement of the mid–1960s and early 1970s.

Social Change and Civil Rights
(Mid-1930s to the Mid-1960s)

The stock market crash in 1929 signaled the beginning of the Great Depression. African Americans, who were typically the last to be hired and the first to be fired, suffered even more extreme economic and political hardships during the 1930s. Thousands of already poor African Americans joined the soup lines that formed across the country.

Franklin D. Roosevelt, elected President of the United States in 1932, promised the country a New Deal. The Federal Writers' Project, supervised by the Works Progress Administration, was one part of President Roosevelt's New Deal. Established African American writers like Langston Hughes, Zora Neale Hurston, and Arna Bontemps participated in the Federal Writers' Project in order to earn a living while they continued their writing. New African American literary voices emerged as well, including those of Richard Wright, Robert Hayden, Frank Yerby, and Margaret Walker.

Wright is considered the major writer of the late 1930s and the 1940s. His novel *Native Son* (1940) protested the conditions under which African Americans lived in the urban North. Like Wright, novelists Chester Himes, author of *If He Hollers, Let Him Go* (1945), and Ann Petry, author of *The Street* (1946), wrote strong novels about the effect of environment on the individual.

After World War II, many African Americans were more disillusioned than ever with the state of equality in the United States. Black soldiers who had risked their lives fighting facism in Europe were denied rights upon their return home—rights that were guaranteed to all citizens under the U.S. Constitution. Some African Americans saw the end of World War II as a sign that they could and should assimilate into the dominant culture. In the 1940s a number of African American literary critics believed that black writers should emerge into the mainstream of American literature and deny that the African American experience in this country had any influence on their work.

The publication of Ralph Ellison's *Invisible Man* (1952), winner of a National Book Award, established that black authors could write social protest literature about the condition of African Americans in this country and, at the same time, write about the universal concerns of humanity. James Baldwin's first novel, *Go Tell It on the Mountain* (1953), further stressed black writers' abilities to present a uniquely African American viewpoint and the universal concern for personal identity. These works, and others by black writers such as dramatist Alice Childress, showed that African American literature did not have to fit within this country's literary mainstream to qualify as literature.

Rosa Parks' refusal in 1955 to move to the back of the bus in Montgomery, Ala., signaled the birth of the civil rights movement. Led by the Reverend Dr. Martin Luther King, Jr., African Americans began to protest the denial of their rights as U.S. citizens. By the late 1950s and the early 1960s, black writers were responding to the fight for civil rights. Such poets as Gwendolyn Brooks, who won a Pulitzer Prize in 1950 for *Annie Allen* (1949), Robert Hayden, Melvin Tolson, Margaret Danner, Langston Hughes, Mary Elizabeth Vroman, and Sterling Brown registered their awareness of that fight in their poetry. Other writers, such as Lorraine Hansberry, Mari Evans, Paule Marshall, William Melvin Kelley, and Ernest Gaines, expressed their views in plays, short stories, and novels.

Black Power Movement (Early 1960s to the Early 1970s)

During the 1960s, the African American fight for civil rights was in full force—from the peaceful demonstrations led by Dr. King to the more militant call for action in the early works of Malcolm X. Major battles were won in the middle and late 1960s. The Civil Rights Acts of 1964 and 1968 prohibited discrimination in public accommodations, schools, and employment. The Voting Rights Act of 1965 prohibited discrimination in voting because of color, religion, or national origin. A new wind was blowing across the country. In this wind, African Americans heard "Black Is Beautiful" and "Black Power."

For the first time since the Harlem Renaissance, a movement was underway that emphasized the beauty and uniqueness of the African American culture. Unlike the Harlem Renaissance, which took place primarily in New York City, the Black Power movement took place throughout the country. African Americans openly celebrated and incorporated into their lives the songs, stories, and customs of their African ancestors.

After the riots in the urban ghettos in the mid-1960s, African American poetry became a political weapon. Such poets as Amiri Baraka (LeRoi Jones), Nikki Giovanni, Haki Madhubuti (Don L. Lee), Sonia Sanchez, Dudley Randall, Lucille Clifton, and Etheridge Knight used their poetry to speak not for themselves as individuals, but in a dramatic voice for all African Americans. The Black Power movement made an impact also on African American novelists, such as William Melvin Kelley (*dem*, 1967). Powerful autobiographies and biographies appeared, including *The Autob raphy of Malcolm X* (1964) by Malcolm X with Alex Haley, *Soul on Ice*

(1968) by Eldridge Cleaver, and *I Know Why the Caged Bird Sings* (1970) by Maya Angelou. Playwrights, such as Amiri Baraka (*Dutchman*, 1964), Douglas Turner Ward (*Day of Absence*, 1965), and Charles Gordone (*No Place to Be Somebody*, 1967) brought the new awareness to the stage. The movement was expressed in the short stories of Paule Marshall and Ernest Gaines and in the books by Julius Lester.

In 1968 Amiri Baraka and Larry Neal published *Black Fire, An Anthology of Afro-American Writing*. In the foreword, the editors explained that a new day had arrived for African American art. Their anthology served as the birthplace of the Black Arts movement. Larry Neal explained that this movement was opposed to any concept that separated African American artists from their community. He felt that African American art was directly related to the quest of African Americans for self-determination. Many African American writers and critics embraced the ideas of the Black Arts movement. Other more conservative African American critics argued against it. The Black Arts movement attracted much attention to African American literature. More and more, independent African American and white publishers began to seek out and publish literature by black writers. The increased availability of this literature allowed the number of readers, both African American and white, to grow.

Building on the Tradition (Mid-1970s to the Present)

In the early and mid-1970s, the civil rights movement began to wane. Attention shifted from gaining equal rights for African Americans as a whole to achieving individual rights. Blacks had made some economic and political gains through the civil rights and Black Power movements; across the country—however—unemployment, poverty, and discrimination still plagued African Americans.

The literary texts of African American writers in the middle and late 1970s reflected this shift in national focus. Writers like Nikki Giovanni and Haki Madhubuti moved from writing only black power poetry to writing poetry about the political and economic conditions of people of color throughout the world. Ishmael Reed's "Hoo Doo" fiction satirized America's culture. Throughout all of these works runs a theme that continues to be prominent in African American literature in the 1980s and 1990s: the importance of African Americans' knowledge of their history. August Wilson's dramas *Fences* (1987, Pulitzer Prize-winner) and *Piano Lesson* (1990) and Charles Johnson's National Book Award-winner, *Middle Passage* (1990), illustrate the power of one's history.

The civil rights movement increased awareness of the inequality of women. America's growing interest in women's issues has helped female African American writers gain prominence. The literature produced by African American women often stresses the interconnectedness of family, home, and community as well as a black woman's ability to survive. In these works, characters name themselves and the world in which they live. This "specifying" of the African American women's experience can be seen in such works as Ntozake Shange's choreographed poem *For Colored Girls Who Have Considered Suicide/When the Rainbow Is Enuf* (1977) and in novels by Alice Walker (*The Color Purple*, 1982), Gloria Naylor (*The Women of Brewster Place*, 1983), and Paule Marshall (*Praisesong for the Widow*, 1984). Rita Dove's Pulitzer Prize–winning book of poetry *Thomas and Beulah* (1986) and Toni Morrison's Pulitzer Prize–winning novel *Beloved* (1989) are powerful examples of women's literary voices. Fiction writers and poets such as Terry McMillan, Paulette Childress White, and Ai have firmly established themselves in the African American literary tradition.

At the close of the twentieth century, African American literature continues to build on the foundation established in the eighteenth century: the quest for freedom and equality. This quest has taken African Americans from the chains of slavery through war and peace, prosperity and poverty. African American literature has recorded the defeats and the triumphs. It contains the fears and the dreams. Its strength lies in its ability to present the truth, whether ugly or beautiful. The validity of African American literature, like the rights of African Americans as individuals and as citizens of this country, cannot be denied. In the following lines from "Still I Rise," Maya Angelou, speaking in the collective voice of African Americans, describes their eternal spirit:

Out of the huts of history's shame
I rise
Up from a past that's rooted in pain
I rise
I'm a black ocean, leaping and wide,
Welling and swelling I bear in the tide.

Leaving behind nights of terror and fear
I rise
Into a daybreak that's wonderously clear
I rise
Bringing the gifts that my ancestors gave,
I am the dream and the hope of the slave.
I rise
I rise
I rise.

AFRICAN AMERICAN LITERATURE

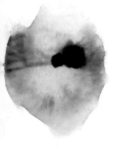

Design by Doug Burnett. Reprinted courtesy of the National Council of Teachers of English. The copy of the recently discovered manuscript of Phillis Wheatley is used courtesy of Baker Library at Dartmouth College.

1

SLAVERY— TIME OF TRIAL

Slavery is a condition in which one human being owns another human being. Those who are owned have no rights and their lives depend on the owner. Slaves are considered the material property of their owner. Today in our society, the idea that one human being can be the property of another human being is not acceptable. However, for over two hundred years slavery existed in the United States of America. Beginning in the early 1600s, Africans were brought to America as slaves. Those who survived the unspeakable conditions on the slave ships were sold on America's shores to the highest bidder. The institution of slavery did not end in America until after Abraham Lincoln signed the Emancipation Proclamation in 1863. With the end of the Civil War and passage of the 13th Amendment to the Constitution in 1865, slavery was abolished in the United States.

The institution of slavery influenced how Americans viewed African Americans—as property to be managed and controlled. African Americans were considered by many white Americans to be unintelligent or animal-like. African American slaves could not marry in civil and religious ceremonies. Families were not allowed to stay together: family members were sold to different slave owners. Children were separated from their mothers and made to work in the fields at a young age. Before the Civil War, in many states it was against the law for African Americans to learn to read and write. This type of thinking caused many African Americans to be mistreated and killed. Survival within the institution of slavery took a tremendous amount of energy and dignity. Many African Americans did not survive, but those who did passed their strength and dignity on to others.

Those slaves who learned to read and write and who were able to obtain their freedom told American and foreign audiences through lectures and publications about the horrible conditions of slavery. Since the end of slavery in America, African Americans have continued to write about its effects. These writers, who have written about slavery from the outside, remind us of the horror of the institution so that we will not forget it, so that we will never let it be repeated.

Frances Watkins Harper

(1825–1911) was born the only child of free black parents in Baltimore, Md. She attended a school for free blacks that was owned by her uncle, William J. Watkins, a minister, craftsman, and abolitionist. She was trained in domestic arts and worked in a Baltimore bookstore. In 1850 she became an instructor of domestic science at a new school for free blacks, run by the African Methodist Episcopal Church. She later gave up her teaching career to become a lecturer. Until her retirement at nearly eighty, Harper was a writer and social reformer. She wrote and spoke against slavery until after the Civil War, when she turned to the causes of temperance and woman suffrage.

Harper was the major African American woman poet of the nineteenth century. Her audiences called her the "Bronze Muse." She published numerous books of poetry: *Poems on Miscellaneous Subjects* (1854); *Moses: A Story of the Nile* (1869); *Sketches of Southern Life* (1872); *Iola Leroy; or, Shadows Uplifted* (1892); and *Atlanta Offering, Poems* (1895).

The Slave Mother

FRANCES WATKINS HARPER

Heard you that shriek? It rose
  So wildly in the air,
It seemed as if a burdened heart
  Was breaking in despair.

Saw you those hands so sadly clasped   5
  The bowed and feeble head
The shuddering of that fragile form
  That look of grief and dread?

She is a mother, pale with fear,
  Her boy clings to her side,   10
And in her kirtle vainly tries
  His trembling form to hide.

He is not hers, although she bore
  For him a mother's pains;
He is not hers, although her blood   15
  Is coursing through his veins!

He is not hers, for cruel hands
  May rudely tear apart
The only wreath of household love
  That binds her breaking heart.   20

---

11. *kirtle*: a woman's gown; a skirt or outer petticoat.

Thinking About the Poem

1. Which line in the poem is the most important? Why?

2. The poem is written in four-line **stanzas**. Each **quatrain** expresses a complete idea. How do the quatrains work together to create a vivid description of this aspect of slavery?

3. Why do you think slave owners would separate mothers and children? Speculate on what inspired Harper to write "The Slave Mother" and how she used her writing in the antislavery movement.

Reading/Writing Connections

1. In your journal describe a time when you felt as though you did not have control over your life. How did you feel? What did you do to help yourself through that difficult time?

2. Write a poem in which a five- or six-year-old describes being separated from his or her mother to work in a field from sunrise to sunset. Try using the same stanzaic form, the quatrain, as Harper did in her poem.

3. The poem begins with the sound of a shriek, but in the last stanza, the speaker states that

> He is not hers, for cruel hands
>   May rudely tear apart
> The only wreath of household love
>   That binds her breaking heart.

Notice that the speaker or **persona** in the poem uses the word *may*. Has something actually been taken away from the mother? Or is she responding to the possibility that her son will be taken away?

Phillis Wheatley

(1753?–1784) was brought to America on a slave ship in 1761. She was purchased by John Wheatley of Boston as a gift for his wife. Phillis Wheatley was given a classical education: She read the Bible, Alexander Pope, and Homer, and became proficient in grammar and in understanding style. Her favorite poet was John Milton, a seventeenth-century English poet. Wheatley's level of education was rare in colonial society, especially for young women. She was a devout Christian and a member of the Old South Meeting House. In 1772 Wheatley traveled to London, where a collection of her poems was published: *Poems on Various Subjects, Religious and Moral, By Phillis Wheatley, Negro Servant to Mr. John Wheatley of Boston*. In 1773 the Wheatleys freed her; in 1778 Phillis Wheatley married John Peters, a free black Bostonian. She had three children, all of whom died in infancy.

During her lifetime, Wheatley wrote poetry for specific occasions, such as the poem "To His Excellency General Washington," which she sent to George Washington in honor of his being appointed commander of the American armies in 1775. Her use of **heroic couplets**, an emotional detachment from the subject being discussed, and Biblical references all reflect the **neoclassical** literary style of the time.

On Being Brought from Africa to America

PHILLIS WHEATLEY

'Twas mercy brought me from my pagan land,
Taught my benighted soul to understand
That there's a God, that there's a Saviour too:
Once I redemption neither sought nor knew.
Some view that sable race with scornful eye: 5
"Their colour is a diabolic dye."
Remember, Christians, Negroes black as Cain
May be refined and join the angelic train.

---

2. *benighted*: being in intellectual darkness.
6. *diabolic dye*: color of or pertaining to the devil.
7. *Cain*: in the Bible, the first man to murder his brother, Abel.

Thinking About the Poem

1. Which words in the poem indicate Wheatley's **neoclassical** style of writing? What are the words' meanings and what does the use of such references reveal about the poet?

2. Is the speaker in the poem sincere when she says, " 'Twas mercy brought me from my pagan land''? Why or why not?

3. In this poem what point is being stressed about Africans and African Americans? Why would the speaker in the poem need to emphasize this point to her audience in the eighteenth century?

Reading/Writing Connections

1. In a journal entry, discuss how you handle situations in which your words might upset others. How do you feel during these situations? Does your way of handling these situations work out best for you and for others?

2. Many slaves who spoke out against slavery were punished for expressing their opinions. After researching slavery in the United States, describe in an essay how slaves used songs, coded messages, and other forms of communication to express their feelings on slavery.

3. Rewrite Wheatley's poem using words from your vocabulary to replace some of her classical wording. How do your word choices change the meaning and the **tone** of the poem?

Robert Hayden   (1913–1980) was born in Detroit and received a bachelor's degree from Wayne State University and a master's degree from the University of Michigan. He taught at Fisk University in Tennessee (1946–69) and then at the University of Michigan (1969–80).

He researched African American history for the depression-era Federal Writers' Project. He served as poetry editor for the *Baha'i World Faith Magazine* and edited an anthology, *Kaleidoscope: Poems by American Negro Poets* (1967). Hayden's collections of poetry are *Heart-Shape in the Dust* (1940), his best-known work; *The Lion and the Archer*, written in collaboration with Myron O'Higgins (1948); *A Ballad of Remembrance* (1962); *Selected Poems* (1966); *Angle of Ascent: New and Selected Poems* (1979); and *Robert Hayden: Selected Poems* (1985). He was the recipient of the Hopwood Award from the University of Michigan, a Rosenwald Literary Fellowship, and a Ford Foundation grant. *A Ballad of Remembrance* received the Grand Prize for Poetry in 1965 at the First World Festival of African American Arts, held in Dakar, Senegal. In 1976, Hayden became the first African American to be named as a poetry consultant to the Library of Congress.

Runagate Runagate

ROBERT HAYDEN

I.

Runs falls rises stumbles on from darkness into darkness
and the darkness thicketed with shapes of terror
and the hunters pursuing and the hounds pursuing
and the night cold and the night long and the river
to cross and the jack-muh-lanterns beckoning beckoning   5
and blackness ahead and when shall I reach that somewhere
morning and keep on going and never turn back and keep on going

   Runagate
     Runagate
       Runagate   10

Many thousands rise and go
many thousands crossing over

          O mythic North
       O star-shaped yonder Bible city

Some go weeping and some rejoicing   15
some in coffins and some in carriages
some in silks and some in shackles

   Rise and go or fare you well

No more auction block for me
no more driver's lash for me   20

   If you see my Pompey, 30 yrs of age,
   new breeches, plain stockings, negro shoes;
   if you see my Anna, likely young mulatto
   branded E on the right cheek, R on the left,
   catch them if you can and notify subscriber.   25
   Catch them if you can, but it won't be easy.

They'll dart underground when you try to catch them,
plunge into quicksand, whirlpools, mazes,
turn into scorpions when you try to catch them.

And before I'll be a slave   30
I'll be buried in my grave

North star and bonanza gold
I'm bound for the freedom, freedom-bound
and oh Susyanna don't you cry for me

Runagate   35

Runagate

II.

Rises from their anguish and their power,

Harriet Tubman,

woman of earth, whipscarred,
a summoning, a shining   40

Mean to be free

And this was the way of it, brethren brethren,
way we journeyed from Can't to Can.
Moon so bright and no place to hide,
the cry up and the patterollers riding,   45
hound dogs belling in bladed air.
And fear starts a-murbling, Never make it,
we'll never make it. *Hush that now,*
and she's turned upon us, levelled pistol
glinting in the moonlight: 50
Dead folks can't jaybird-talk, she says;
you keep on going now or die, she says.

Wanted   Harriet Tubman   alias The General
alias Moses   Stealer of Slaves

In league with Garrison Alcott Emerson   55
Garrett Douglass Thoreau John Brown

Armed and known to be Dangerous

Wanted Reward Dead or Alive

    Tell me, Ezekiel, oh tell me do you see
    mailed Jehova coming to deliver me?   60

Hoot-owl calling in the ghosted air,
five times calling to the hants in the air.
Shadow of a face in the scary leaves,
shadow of a voice in the talking leaves:

    Come ride-a my train   65

Oh that train, ghost-story train
through swamp and savanna movering movering,
over trestles of dew, through caves of the wish,
Midnight Special on a sabre track movering movering,
first stop Mercy and the last Hallelujah.   70

    Come ride-a my train

    Mean mean mean to be free.

Thinking About the Poem

1. In Part I of this poem written in **free verse**, the poet illustrates the slaves' flight through placing certain words in a given fashion. What are these words and how are they visually displayed?

2. Who's speaking in the following lines?

> If you see my Pompey, 30 yrs of age,
> new breeches, plain stockings, negro shoes;
> if you see my Anna, likely young mulatto
> branded E on the right cheek, R on the left,
> catch them if you can and notify subscriber.

3. In Part II, Hayden mentions Harriet Tubman and the underground railroad. Who was Tubman and what was her role in the slaves' search for freedom?

4. The slaves exhibited both fear and determination as they journeyed toward freedom. Which lines in Part II best demonstrate this duality?

Reading/Writing Connections

1. "Runagate Runagate" is a poem about flight toward freedom. In your journal, write a description of how you imagine the slaves felt upon reaching their final destination.

2. Hayden uses lines from **spirituals** or, as W. E. B. Du Bois calls them, "sorrow songs" to convey the slaves' desire for freedom. For example:

> And before I'll be a slave
> I'll be buried in my grave

Write a poem in free verse, in which you use lyrics from a popular song that express a feeling or dream you or someone else has.

3. The poet writes: "And this was the way of it, brethren brethren, / way we journeyed from Can't to Can." Write an essay in which you explain the meaning of the phrase "journeyed from Can't to Can."

Frederick Douglass (1818–1895) was born a slave in Talbot County, Md. He escaped from bondage in 1838, first to New York and later to Massachusetts. Douglass did not have a formal education. He taught himself how to read and write. In 1841 he spoke at a meeting sponsored by the abolitionists of Massachusetts; he was a powerful speaker. His height and his ability to speak often held his audiences spellbound. He made a commanding presence at such meetings with his crown of flowing hair. Douglass' fame as an orator in the anti-slavery movement preceded him to England in 1845 where he spoke to a sympathetic audience, enlisting their support in the abolition of slavery in America. His critics suggested that he could not possibly have been a slave because of the eloquence with which he spoke.

Upon his return to the United States from England, he became the leading African American spokesperson in the anti-slavery movement in 1847. He began working for the Underground Railroad, assisting many slaves to escape to the North and then to Canada. As a way of communicating to wider audiences, he published the *North Star*. It later became the most influential newspaper in the African American community. Douglass helped recruit African American males to serve during the Civil War. He served his country as Secretary of the Santo Domingo Commission, Marshal and Recorder of the Deeds for the District of Columbia, and Minister of the United States of America in Haiti.

Douglass wrote three autobiographies during his life. The most famous, *Narrative of the Life of Frederick Douglass, an American Slave*, was published in 1845; the second, *My Bondage and My Freedom*, was published ten years later. The third, *Life and Times of Frederick Douglass*, was first published in 1881.

Letter to His Master

FREDERICK DOUGLASS

Thomas Auld:

Sir—The long and intimate, though by no means friendly relation which unhappily subsisted between you and myself, leads me to hope that you will easily account for the great liberty which I now take in addressing you in this open and public manner. The same fact may possibly remove any disagreeable surprise which you may experience on again finding your name coupled with mine, in any other way than in an advertisement, accurately describing my person, and offering a large sum for my arrest. In thus dragging you again before the public, I am aware that I shall subject myself to no inconsiderable amount of censure. I shall probably be charged with an unwarrantable, if not a wanton and reckless disregard of the rights and proprieties of private life. There are those North as well as South who entertain a much higher respect for rights which are merely conventional, than they do for rights which are personal and essential. Not a few there are in our country, who, while they have no scruples against robbing the laborer of the hard earned results of his patient industry, will be shocked by the extremely indelicate manner of bringing your name before the public. . . .

I have selected this day on which to address you, because it is the anniversary of my emancipation; and knowing of no better way I am led to this as the best mode of celebrating that truly important event. Just ten years ago this beautiful September morning, yon bright sun beheld me a slave—a poor, degraded chattel—trembling at the sound of your voice, lamenting that I was a man, and wishing myself a brute. The hopes which I had treasured up for weeks of a safe and successful escape from your grasp, were powerfully confronted at this last hour by dark clouds of doubt and fear, making my person shake and my bosom to heave with the heavy contest between hope and fear. I have no words to describe to you the deep agony of soul which I experienced on that never to be forgotten morning—(for I left by daylight). I was making a leap in the dark. The probabilities, so far as I could by reason determine them, were stoutly against the undertaking. The preliminaries and precautions I had adopted previously, all worked badly. I was like one going to war without weapons—ten chances of defeat to one of victory. One in whom I had confided, and one who had promised me assistance, appalled by fear at the trial hour, deserted me, thus leaving the responsibility of success or failure solely with myself. You, sir, can never know my feelings. As I look back to them I can scarcely realize that I have passed through a scene so trying. Trying however as they were, and gloomy as was the prospect, thanks be to the Most High, who is ever the God of the oppressed, at the moment which was to determine my whole earthly career. His grace was sufficient, my mind was made up. I embraced the golden opportunity, took the morning tide at the flood, and a free man, young, active and strong, is the result. . . .

Since I left you, I have had a rich experience. I have occupied stations which I never dreamed of when a slave. Three out of the ten years since I left you, I spent as a common laborer on the wharves of New Bedford, Massachusetts. It was there I earned my first free dollar. It was mine. I could spend it as I pleased. I could buy hams or herring with it, without asking any odds of any body. That was a precious dollar to me. You remember when I used to make seven or eight, or even nine dollars a week in Baltimore, you would take every cent of it from me every Saturday night, saying that I belonged to you, and my earnings also. I never liked this conduct on your part—to say the best, I thought it a little mean. I would not have served you so. But let that pass. I was a little awkward about counting money in New England fashion when I first landed in New Bedford. I like to have betrayed myself several times. I caught myself saying phip, for fourpence; and at one time a man actually charged me with being a runaway, whereupon I was silly enough to become one by running away from him, for I was greatly afraid he might adopt measures to give me again into slavery, a condition I then dreaded more than death.

I soon, however, learned to count money, as well as to make it, and got on swimmingly. I married soon after leaving you: in fact, I was engaged to be married before I left you; and instead of finding my companion a burden; she was truly a helpmeet. She went to live at service and I to work on the wharf, and though we toiled hard the first winter, we never lived more happily. After remaining in New Bedford for three years, I met with Wm. Lloyd Garrison, a person of whom you have *possibly* heard, as he is pretty generally known among slave-holders. He put it into my head that I might make myself serviceable to the cause of the slave by devoting a portion of my time to telling my own sorrows, and those of other slaves which had come under my observation. This was the commencement of a higher state of existence than any to which I had ever aspired. I was thrown into society the most pure, enlightened and benevolent that the country affords. Among these I have never forgotten you, but have invariably made you the topic of conversation—thus giving you all the notoriety I could do. I need not tell you that the opinion formed of you in these circles, is far from being favorable. They have little respect for your honesty, and less for your religion.

But I was going on to relate something of my interesting experience. I had not long enjoyed the excellent society to which I have referred, before the light of its excellence exerted a beneficial influence on my mind and heart. Much of my early dislike of white persons was removed, and their manners, habits and customs, so entirely unlike what I had been used to in the kitchen-quarters on the plantations of the South, fairly charmed me, and gave me a strong disrelish for the coarse and degrading customs of my former condition. I therefore made an effort so to improve my mind and deportment as to be somewhat fitted to the station to which I seemed almost providentially called. The transition from degradation to respectability was indeed great, and to get from one to the other without carrying some marks of one's former condition, is truly a difficult matter. I would not have you think that I am now entirely clear of all plantation peculiarities, but my friends here, while they entertain the strongest dislike to them, regard me with that charity to which my past life somewhat entitles me, so that my condition in this respect is exceedingly pleasant. So far as my domestic affairs are concerned, I can boast of as comfortable a dwelling as your own. I have an industrious and neat companion, and four dear children—the oldest a girl of nine years and three fine boys, the oldest eight, the next six, and the youngest four years old. The three oldest are now going regularly to school—two can read and write, and the other can spell with tolerable correctness words of two syllables. Dear fellows! they are all in comfortable beds, and are sound asleep, perfectly secure under my own roof. There are no slaveholders here to rend my heart by snatching them from my arms, or blast a mother's dearest hopes by tearing them from her bosom. These dear children are ours—not to work up into rice, sugar and tobacco, but to watch over, regard, and protect, and to rear them up in the nurture and admonition of the gospel—to train them up in the paths of wisdom and virtue, and, as far as we can to make them useful to the world and to themselves. Oh! sir, a slave-holder never appears to me so completely an agent of hell, as when I think of and look upon my dear children. It is then that my feelings rise above my control. I meant to have said more with respect to my own prosperity and happiness, but thoughts and feelings which this recital has quickened unfit me to proceed further in that direction. The grim horrors of slavery rise in all their ghastly terror before me, the wails of millions pierce my heart, and chill my blood. I remember the chain, the gag, the bloody whip, the death-like gloom overshadowing the broken spirit of the fettered bondman, the appalling liability of his being torn away from wife and children, and sold like a beast in the market. Say not that this is a picture of fancy. You well know that I wear stripes on my back inflicted by your direction; and that you, while we were brothers in the same church caused this right hand, with which I am now penning this letter, to be closely tied to my left, and my person dragged at the pistol's mouth, fifteen miles, from the Bay side to Easton to be sold like a beast in the market for the alleged crime of intending to escape from your possession. All this and more you remember, and know to be perfectly true, not only of yourself, but of nearly all of the slaveholders around you.

At this moment, you are probably the guilty holder of at least three of my own dear sisters, and my only brother in bondage. These you regard as your property. They are recorded on your ledger, or perhaps have been sold to human flesh mongers, with a view to filling your own ever-hungry purse. Sir, I desire to know how and where these dear sisters are. Have you sold them? or are they still in your possession? What has become of them? are they living or dead? And my dear old grandmother, whom you turned out like an old horse, to die in the woods—is she still alive? Write and let me know all about them. If my grandmother be still alive, she is of no service to you, for by this time she must be nearly eighty years old—too old to be cared for by one to whom she has ceased to be of service, send her to me at Rochester, or bring her to Philadelphia, and it shall be the crowning happiness of my life to take care of her in her old age. Oh! she was to me a mother, and a father, so far as hard toil for my comfort could make her such. Send me my grandmother! that I may watch over and take care of her in her old age. And my sisters, let me know all about them. I would write to them, and learn all I want to know of them, without disturbing you in any way, but that, through your unrighteous conduct, they have been entirely deprived of the power to read and write. You have kept them in utter ignorance, and have therefore robbed them of the sweet enjoyments of writing or receiving letters from absent friends and relatives. Your wickedness and cruelty committed in this respect on your fellow-creatures, are greater than all the stripes you have laid upon my back, or theirs. It is an outrage upon the soul—a war upon the immortal spirit, and one for which you must give account at the bar of our common Father and Creator. . . .

I will now bring this letter to a close, you shall hear from me again unless you let me hear from you. I intend to make use of you as a weapon with which to assail the system of slavery—as a means of concentrating public attention on the system, and deepening their horror of trafficking in the souls and bodies of men. I shall make use of you as a means of exposing the character of the American church and clergy—and as a means of bringing this guilty nation with yourself to repentance. In doing this I entertain no malice towards you personally. There is no roof under which you would be more safe than mine, and there is nothing in my house which you might need for your comfort, which I would not readily grant. Indeed, I should esteem it a privilege, to set you an example as to how mankind ought to treat each other.

I am your fellow man, but not your slave.

Frederick Douglass

Thinking About the Letter

1. Initially, Douglass feels doubt and anxiety on the day of his escape from slavery. Where is this feeling expressed in his letter?

2. What is the tone of Douglass' letter to his former master?

3. What evidence is there in the letter that supports Douglass' strong love for his children?

Reading/Writing Connections

1. Douglass says to his former master: "I intend to make use of you as a weapon with which to assail the system of slavery." Write an essay in which you show how Douglass keeps his promise.

2. Assume that Douglass has received word that his former master is still holding his sisters and brother in bondage. Pretend that you are Douglass and write a letter to your relatives expressing how it feels to be free and what you wish for them.

3. Make an entry in your writing journal using the last sentence in the letter and tell what that sentence means to you.

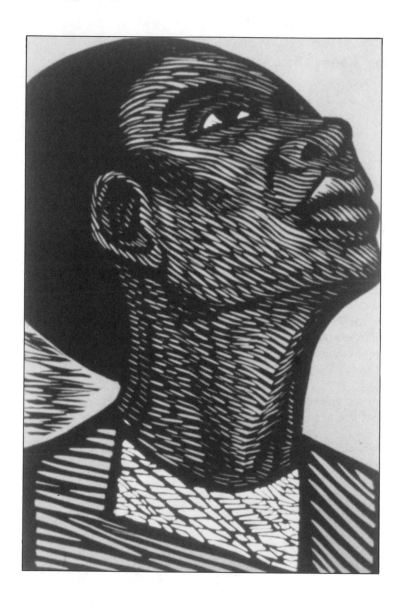

"My Right Is a Future of Equality with Other Americans" by Elizabeth Catlett.
*Medium: Linocut. Reprinted by permission of the Isobel Neal Gallery, Chicago,
Illinois.*

2

STANDING GROUND

To *stand ground* means to have a belief that you refuse to give up. No matter what conditions you are faced with, if you stand ground you will hold on to your convictions. Standing ground can be as simple as making a choice and holding firm to it or as complicated as believing in something when there is no evidence to prove it.

From the time that Africans were brought to America as slaves to the present, African Americans have had to stand ground. During slavery those who believed their servitude would end one day stood their ground when they held on to their dignity in the face of the horrors of the institution. Since slavery, African Americans have stood ground to earn the right to vote, to obtain an education, to live in decent housing, and to work in jobs where they were paid an equal salary.

African American writers stand ground when they create stories and poems that celebrate the spirit of resistance. Their work records the ability of African Americans to stand ground by taking pride in their culture and celebrating their African heritage. It records their ability to stand ground by affirming that they are entitled to the same rights as other American citizens. Finally, it records their ability to stand ground by refusing to give in when conditions are terrible. African American writers illustrate how African Americans take strength from within themselves and choose actions over which they have control.

Countee Cullen   (1903–1946) was born in Louisville, Ky., to Elizabeth Lucas. At the age of fifteen he was unofficially adopted by the Reverend Frederick Asbury Cullen and Carolyn Mitchell Cullen of the Salem Methodist Episcopal Church, in Harlem. Cullen began writing poetry at the predominantly white De Witt Clinton High School in New York City. While attending New York University, he won numerous prizes for his poetry. Cullen received a master's degree from Harvard University in 1926 and became assistant editor to Charles S. Johnson at *Opportunity* magazine. In 1928 Cullen married Nina Yolande Du Bois, daughter of W. E. B. Du Bois. The couple divorced in 1930. In 1934 Cullen became a teacher of French and English at Frederick Douglass Junior High School in New York City. In 1940 he married Ida Mae Roberson, sister of singer Orlando Roberson.

Cullen's poetry protests violations against the dignity and rights of African Americans and searches for African roots and for acceptance in America. These themes are evident in his collections of poetry—*Color* (1925), *The Ballad of the Brown Girl: An Old Ballad Retold* (1927), and *Copper Sun* (1927)—as well as in his novel, *One Way to Heaven* (1932), and his play, *St. Louis Woman*, coauthored with Arna Bontemps (1946). His children's books, *The Lost Zoo (A Rhyme for the Young, but Not Too Young)* (1940), and *My Lives and How I Lost Them* (1942) also reflect his concern for the status of African Americans.

From the Dark Tower
(To Charles S. Johnson)

COUNTEE CULLEN

We shall not always plant while others reap
The golden increment of bursting fruit,
Not always countenance, abject and mute,
That lesser men should hold their brothers cheap;
Not everlastingly while others sleep   5
Shall we beguile their limbs with mellow flute,
Not always bend to some more subtle brute;
We were not made eternally to weep.

The night whose sable breast relieves the stark,
White stars is no less lovely being dark,   10
And there are buds that cannot bloom at all
In light, but crumple, piteous, and fall;
So in the dark we hide the heart that bleeds,
And wait, and tend our agonizing seeds.

---

2. *increment*: an amount or portion added to something to increase it.
3. *countenance*: to approve or tolerate.

Thinking About the Poem

1. This poem is in the form of an **Italian sonnet**. What problem or situation does Cullen present in the **octave**, the eight line stanza? What solution or resolution is presented in the sestet, the six-line stanza?

2. The poem begins with the line "We shall not always plant while others reap." What image or images does this line bring to your mind?

3. Throughout the poem Cullen uses **metaphors** to exress his ideas. What do you think Cullen is referring to in line fourteen when the persona describes tending "agonizing seeds"?

4. How is darkness portrayed in this poem? In a negative or positive way? Use examples from the poem to support your response.

Reading/Writing Connections

1. Should groups of people who have not been treated equally by others passively wait for equality? Support your position in an essay in which you use your own opinions and evidence from other material you have read.

2. In your journal discuss an episode in your life when you waited a long time for something that was important to you. How did the waiting make you feel? Did you ever want to stop waiting?

Claude McKay

Claude McKay (1889–1948) was born to peasant farmers Thomas Francis McKay and Ann Elizabeth Edwards McKay in Jamaica. His father, a descendant of the Ashanti tribe of West Africa, told McKay African folktales. In 1912 McKay was given an award in Jamaica for two volumes of his poetry, *Songs of Jamaica* (1912) and *Constab Ballads* (1912). He then came to the United States, attended Tuskegee Institute in Alabama for two months, and transferred to Kansas State College. In 1914 he went to New York City, where he worked odd jobs and wrote poetry. By 1919 his poetry was appearing regularly in *Pearson's* and *The Liberator* magazines. McKay then left the United States and, from 1919 to 1934, lived in Europe and Russia. In 1934 he returned to live in Harlem. In the spring of 1944, McKay moved to Chicago to accept a teaching position.

McKay was one of the most radical African American writers of the **Harlem Renaissance**. His poetry fights against the idea that any group can confine another. During the Harlem Renaissance, some African American magazines would not publish his poetry because they considered it "too radical." McKay published two additional volumes of poetry: *Spring in New Hampshire* (1920) and *Harlem Shadows: The Poems of Claude McKay* (1922). He also published three novels—*Home to Harlem* (1928), *Banjo—A Story Without a Plot* (1929), and *Banana Bottom* (1933)—as well as a collection of short stories entitled *Gingertown* (1932). His autobiography, *A Long Way from Home*, was published in 1937.

If We Must Die

CLAUDE McKAY

If we must die, let it not be like hogs
Hunted and penned in an inglorious spot,
While round us bark the mad and hungry dogs,
Making their mock at our accursed lot.
If we must die, O let us nobly die,   5
So that our precious blood may not be shed
In vain; then even the monsters we defy
Shall be constrained to honor us though dead!
O kinsmen! we must meet the common foe!
Though far outnumbered let us show us brave,   10
And for their thousand blows deal one deathblow!
What though before us lies the open grave?
Like men we'll face the murderous, cowardly pack,
Pressed to the wall, dying, but fighting back!

Thinking About the Poem

1. This poem is written in the form of a **Shakespearean sonnet**. What problem or situation is presented in the three quatrains? What solution or resolution is presented in the **couplet?**

2. Throughout the poem McKay uses **similes** and **metaphors** to describe the treatment of African Americans. What do you think the speaker means in lines one through four?

3. In line eleven what is the "one deathblow" that is being discussed? How will it stop the "thousand blows"?

Reading/Writing Connections

1. In your journal, describe a real or imagined conflict in which you stand your ground and fight back with some type of physical action. How do you feel when the situation was over? Next, describe a conflict in which you stood your ground and fought back with words. How did you feel when that confrontation was over? What are the similarities and differences between these two situations?

2. In an essay defend the standing of one's ground with words instead of physical action. Why might words have a greater effect on changing a situation than physical action?

Langston Hughes

(1902–1967) was born in Joplin, Mo., to Carrie Langston Hughes and James Nathaniel Hughes. In 1903 Hughes' mother and father separated and his father moved to Mexico. Hughes went to live with his maternal grandmother, Mary Leary Langston, in Lawrence, Kans. While in high school, Hughes ran track, made the honor roll, and edited the school yearbook in addition to writing poetry. In 1921 he attended Columbia University in New York City but left after one year to work and write. In 1925, while working as a busboy at the Wardman Park Hotel, Hughes left some of his poems by Vachel Lindsay's dinner plate. The next day Hughes read in the headlines that a Negro busboy had been discovered. Hughes went to Lincoln University in Pennsylvania in 1926 and received his bachelor of arts degree in 1929. Throughout his life Hughes traveled across the United States and to Europe and Russia. Hughes felt a strong connection to the poor people he met. These people and their concerns became the material of his writing.

Hughes published a substantial amount of writing during his lifetime. He wrote books of poetry, short story collections, novels, plays, and essays. His poetry collections include *The Weary Blues* (1926), *The Negro Mother and Other Dramatic Recitations* (1931), *Lament for Dark Peoples and Other Poems* (1944), and *Selected Poems of Langston Hughes* (1959). His short stories are collected in *The Ways of White Folks* (1934), *Laughing to Keep from Crying* (1952), *Something in Common* (1963), and five volumes of sketches of his character Jesse B. Semple, or "Simple." He wrote about his life in *The Big Sea: An Autobiography* (1940) and *I Wonder as I Wander: An Autobiographical Journey* (1956).

I, Too

LANGSTON HUGHES

I, too, sing America.

I am the darker brother.
They send me to eat in the kitchen
When company comes,
But I laugh,   5
And eat well,
And grow strong.

Tomorrow,
I'll be at the table
When company comes.   10
Nobody'll dare
Say to me,
"Eat in the kitchen,"
Then.

Besides,   15
They'll see how beautiful I am
And be ashamed—

I, too, am America.

Thinking About the Poem

1. This poem is written in free verse. How does Hughes' use of single-line stanzas and no **rhyme scheme** affect the way you read the poem? The way you understand the poem?

2. In the second stanza, who or what are "They"? What role or roles do you think "they" have played in the poem's speaker's life?

3. The poem begins with the line "I, too, sing America." It ends with the line "I, too, am America." What are the similarities and differences between these two statements?

4. In the third stanza, the speaker states "Nobody'll dare / Say to me, / 'Eat in the kitchen,' / Then." What is the tone of these lines? Is this tone different from the tone in the first and second stanzas?

Reading/Writing Connections

1. Imagine that someone from another country has asked you what it means to be an "American." In an essay explain what the term "American" means to you.

2. Write a free verse poem in which you write about being an American. You may want to write about what it means to be part of American society today, with its many diverse voices.

Maya Angelou   (b. 1928) was born Marguerite Johnson in St. Louis, Mo., to Bailey and Vivian Baxter Johnson. (Angelou took her name when she began her dancing career in San Francisco.) When Angelou's parents divorced, she went to live with her maternal grandmother, Annie Henderson, in Stamps, Ark. After graduating at the top of her eighth-grade class, Angelou moved to San Francisco to live with her mother. She graduated from Mission High School in 1945. As Angelou searched to find herself, she worked at a variety of jobs— streetcar driver, cook, dancer, waitress. In the late 1950s and early 1960s, Angelou made a commitment to her writing and became a member of the Harlem Writers Guild. With the support of the group, she began to treat her writing seriously. Dr. Martin Luther King, Jr., named her the Northern Coordinator for the Southern Christian Leadership Conference. Angelou has received honorary degrees from many colleges and universities, including Smith College, Mills College, and Lawrence University.

Since 1970, Angelou has published five autobiographies: *I Know Why the Caged Bird Sings* (1970), *Gather Together in My Name* (1974), *Singin' and Swingin' and Gettin' Merry Like Christmas* (1976), *The Heart of a Woman* (1981), and *All God's Children Need Traveling Shoes* (1986). She has also written four collections of poetry: *Just Give Me a Cool Drink of Water 'Fore I Diiie* (1971), *Oh Pray My Wings Are Gonna Fit Me Well* (1975), *And Still I Rise* (1978), and *Shaker, Why Don't You Sing?* (1983). Angelou has also written many plays and screenplays, as well as a television series.

Willie

M A Y A   A N G E L O U

Willie was a man without fame
Hardly anybody knew his name.
Crippled and limping, always walking lame,
He said, "I keep on movin'
Movin' just the same."   5

Solitude was the climate in his head
Emptiness was the partner in his bed,
Pain echoed in the steps of his tread,
He said, "I keep on followin'
Where the leaders led."   10

I may cry and I will die,
But my spirit is the soul of every spring.
Watch for me and you will see
That I'm present in the songs that children sing.

People called him "Uncle," "Boy" and "Hey,"   15
Said, "You can't live through this another day."
Then, they waited to hear what he would say.
He said, "I'm living
In the games that children play.

"You may enter my sleep, people my dreams,   20
Threaten my early morning's ease,
But I keep comin' followin' laughin' cryin',
Sure as a summer breeze.

"Wait for me, watch for me.
My spirit is the surge of open seas.   25
Look for me, ask for me.
I'm the rustle in the autumn leaves.

"When the sun rises
I am the time.
When the children sing   30
I am the Rhyme."

Thinking About the Poem

1. The poem begins by the speaker saying, "Willie was a man without fame," and ends with a quote from Willie, "I am the Rhyme." How does the first line prepare you for the rest of the poem? When you reach the last line of the poem, do you still feel the same way about poem? In what ways did your thoughts change or stay the same?

2. In the second stanza, who do you think are the leaders Willie is following? Is he following an actual path or trail? Why or why not?

3. Why do you think Willie uses metaphors that refer to nature and children to describe himself?

4. How does Willie stand his ground? What belief has he refused to give up? How is this belief supported by the last stanza of the poem?

Reading/Writing Connections

1. Write a journal entry in which you create a metaphor to explain your view of life. Why is this metaphor the best one for you?

2. Write a letter to the people who called Willie "Uncle," "Boy," and "Hey" and explain why calling him by such names is disrespectful of his individuality.

Arna (Arnaud) Wendell Bontemps (1902–1973) was born in Alexandria, La., to Paul Bismark and Maria Carolina Pembroke Bontemps. His parents were Creole, and Bontemps used Creole dialect in many of his early writings. Bontemps attended San Fernando Academy in California and received an A.B. degree from Pacific Union College in 1923. At the age of twenty-one, Bontemps published his poem "Hope" in *Crisis* magazine and moved to New York City to begin teaching at the Harlem Academy. In 1926 and 1927 he won *Opportunity* magazine's Alexander Pushkin Poetry Prize. Bontemps went on to receive many other awards for his poetry and fiction. His teaching career took him from New York City to Alabama to Chicago, where he earned a master's degree in library science from the University of Chicago. From 1943 until his retirement, Bontemps was a librarian at Fisk University in Nashville, Tenn.

Bontemps was a poet, critic, novelist, playwright, librarian, and author of children's books. He influenced and was influenced by many writers including Langston Hughes (a close friend), Willa Cather, Countee Cullen, Jean Toomer, Katherine Porter, Ernest Hemingway, Claude McKay, James Weldon Johnson, Robert Lowell, and Zora Neale Hurston. The following is a brief list of some of Bontemps' published works: *God Sends Sunday* (1931), *You Can't Pet a Possum* (1934), *Drums at Dusk* (1939), *George Washington Carver* (1950), *Personals* (1963), and *Mr. Kelso's Lion* (1970).

A Summer Tragedy

ARNA BONTEMPS

Old Jeff Patton, the black share farmer,[1] fumbled with his bow tie. His fingers trembled and the high, stiff collar pinched his throat. A fellow loses his hand for such vanities after thirty or forty years of simple life. Once a year, or maybe twice if there's a wedding among his kinfolks, he may spruce up; but generally fancy clothes do nothing but adorn the wall of the big room and feed the moths. That had been Jeff Patton's experience. He had not worn his stiff-bosomed shirt more than a dozen times in all his married life. His swallow-tailed coat lay on the bed beside him, freshly brushed and pressed, but it was as full of holes as the overalls in which he worked on weekdays. The moths had used it badly. Jeff twisted his mouth into a hideous toothless grimace as he contended with the obstinate bow. He stamped his good foot and decided to give up the struggle.

"Jennie," he called.

"What's that, Jeff?" His wife's shrunken voice came out of the adjoining room like an echo. It was hardly bigger than a whisper.

"I reckon you'll have to he'p me wid this heah bow tie, baby," he said meekly. "Dog if I can hitch it up."

Her answer was not strong enough to reach him, but presently the old woman came to the door, feeling her way with a stick. She had a wasted, dead-leaf appearance. Her body, as scrawny and gnarled as a string bean, seemed less than nothing in the ocean of frayed and faded petticoats that surrounded her. These hung an inch or two above the tops of her heavy unlaced shoes and showed little grotesque piles where the stocking had fallen down from her negligible legs.

"You oughta could do a heap mo' wid a thing like that'n me—beingst as you got yo' good sight."

"Looks like I oughta could," he admitted. "But my fingers is gone democrat[2] on me. I get all mixed up in the looking glass an' can't tell wicha way to twist the devilish thing."

---

[1] *share farmer*: one who farms land as a tenant.
[2] *gone democrat*: (here) being disorderly. Historically, at the time in which Bontemps' story is set, many African Americans were members of the Republican political party. Most members of the Democratic party were aligned with monied, Southern white interest groups at that time.

Jennie sat on the side of the bed, and old Jeff Patton got down on one knee while she tied the bow knot. It was a slow and painful ordeal for each of them in this position. Jeff's bones cracked, his knee ached, and it was only after a half dozen attempts that Jennie worked a semblance of a bow into the tie.

"It got to dress maself now," the old woman whispered. "These is ma old shoes an' stockings, and I ain't so much as unwrapped ma dress."

"Well, don't worry 'bout me no mo', baby," Jeff said. "That 'bout finishes me. All I gotta do now is slip on that old coat 'n ves' an' I'll be fixed to leave."

Jennie disappeared again through the dim passage into the shed room. Being blind was no handicap to her in that black hole. Jeff heard the cane placed against the wall beside the door and knew that his wife was on easy ground. He put on his coat, took a battered top hat from the bed post, and hobbled to the front door. He was ready to travel. As soon as Jennie could get on her Sunday shoes and her old black silk dress, they would start.

Outside the tiny log house, the day was warm and mellow with sunshine. A host of wasps were humming with busy excitement in the trunk of a dead sycamore. Gray squirrels were searching through the grass for hickory nuts, and blue jays were in the trees, hopping from branch to branch. Pine woods stretched away to the left like a black sea. Among them were scattered scores[3] of log houses like Jeff's, houses of black share farmers. Cows and pigs wandered freely among the trees. There was no danger of loss. Each farmer knew his own stock and knew his neighbor's as well as he knew his neighbor's children.

Down the slope to the right were the cultivated acres on which the colored folks worked. They extended to the river, more than two miles away, and they were today green with the unmade cotton crop. A tiny thread of a road, which passed directly in front of Jeff's place, ran through these green fields like a pencil mark.

Jeff, standing outside the door, with his absurd hat in his left hand, surveyed the wide scene tenderly. He had been forty-five years on these acres. He loved them with the unexplained affection that others have for the countries to which they belong.

The sun was hot on his head, his collar still pinched his throat, and the Sunday clothes were intolerably hot. Jeff transferred the hat to his right hand and began fanning with it. Suddenly the whisper that was Jennie's voice came out of the shed room.

"You can bring the car round front whilst you's waitin'," it said feebly. There was a tired pause; then it added, "I'll soon be fixed to go."

---

[3]*scores*: groups or sets of twenty.

"A'right, baby," Jeff answered. "I'll get it in a minute."

But he didn't move. A thought struck him that made his mouth fall open. The mention of the car brought to his mind, with new intensity, the trip he and Jennie were about to take. Fear came into his eyes; excitement took his breath. Lord Jesus!

"Jeff. . . . O Jeff," the old woman's whisper called.

He awakened with a jolt. "Hunh, baby?"

"What you doin'?"

"Nuthin. Jes studyin'. I jes been turnin' things round 'n round in ma mind."

"You could be gettin' the car," she said.

"Oh yes, right away, baby."

He started round to the shed, limping heavily on his bad leg. There were three frizzly chickens in the yard. All his other chickens had been killed or stolen recently. But the frizzly chickens had been saved somehow. That was fortunate indeed, for these curious creatures had a way of devouring "poison" from the yard and in that way protecting against conjure and black luck and spells. But even the frizzly chickens seemed now to be in a stupor. Jeff thought they had some ailment; he expected all three of them to die shortly.

The shed in which the old T-model Ford stood was only a grass roof held up by four corner poles. It had been built by tremulous hands at a time when the little rattletrap car had been regarded as a peculiar treasure. And, miraculously, despite wind and downpour, it still stood.

Jeff adjusted the crank and put his weight upon it. The engine came to life with a sputter and bang that rattled the old car from radiator to tail light. Jeff hopped into the seat and put his foot on the accelerator. The sputtering and banging increased. The rattling became more violent. That was good. It was good banging, good sputtering and rattling, and it meant that the aged car was still in running condition. She could be depended on for this trip.

Again Jeff's thought halted as if paralyzed. The suggestion of the trip fell into the machinery of his mind like a wrench. He felt dazed and weak. He swung the car out into the yard, made a half turn, and drove around to the front door. When he took his hands off the wheel, he noticed that he was trembling violently. He cut off the motor and climbed to the ground to wait for Jennie.

A few minutes later she was at the window, her voice rattling against the pane like a broken shutter.

"I'm ready, Jeff."

He did not answer, but limped into the house and took her by the arm. He led her slowly through the big room, down the step, and across the yard.

"You reckon I'd oughta lock the do'?" he asked softly.

They stopped and Jennie weighed the question. Finally she shook her head.

"Ne' mind the do'," she said. "I don't see no cause to lock up things."

"You right," Jeff agreed. "No cause to lock up."

Jeff opened the door and helped his wife into the car. A quick shudder passed over him. Jesus! Again he trembled.

"How come you shaking so?" Jennie whispered.

"I don't know," he said.

"You mus' be scairt, Jeff."

"No, baby, I ain't scairt."

He slammed the door after her and went around to crank up again. The motor started easily. Jeff wished that it had not been so responsive. He would have liked a few more minutes in which to turn things around in his head. As it was, with Jennie chiding him about being afraid, he had to keep going. He swung the car into the little pencil-mark road and started off toward the river, driving very slowly, very cautiously.

Chugging across the green countryside, the small battered Ford seemed tiny indeed. Jeff felt a familiar excitement, a thrill, as they came down the first slope to the immense levels on which the cotton was growing. He could not help reflecting that the crops were good. He knew what that meant, too; he had made forty-five of them with his own hands. It was true that he had worn out nearly a dozen mules, but that was the fault of old man Stevenson, the owner of the land. Major Stevenson had the odd notion that one mule was all a share farmer needed to work a thirty-acre plot. It was an expensive notion, the way it killed mules from overwork, but the old man held to it. Jeff thought it killed a good many share farmers as well as mules, but he had no sympathy for them. He had always been strong, and he had been taught to have no patience with weakness in men. Women or children might be tolerated if they were puny, but a weak man was a curse. Of course, his own children——

Jeff's thought halted there. He and Jennie never mentioned their dead children any more. And naturally, he did not wish to dwell upon them in his mind. Before he knew it, some remark would slip out of his mouth and that would make Jennie feel blue. Perhaps she would cry. A woman like Jennie could not easily throw off the grief that comes from losing five grown children within two years. Even Jeff was still staggered by the blow. His memory had not been much good recently. He frequently talked to himself. And, although he had kept it a secret, he knew that his courage had left him. He was terrified by the least unfamiliar sound at night. He was reluctant to venture far from home in the daytime. And that habit of trembling when he felt fearful was now far beyond his control. Sometimes he became afraid and trembled without knowing what had frightened him. The feeling would just come over him like a chill.

The car rattled slowly over the dusty road. Jennie sat erect and silent with a little absurd hat pinned to her hair. Her useless eyes seemed very large, very white in their deep sockets. Suddenly Jeff heard her voice, and he inclined his head to catch the words.

"Is we passed Delia Moore's house yet?" she asked.

"Not yet," he said.

"You must be drivin' mighty slow, Jeff."

"We just as well take our time, baby."

There was a pause. A little puff of steam was coming out of the radiator of the car. Heat wavered above the hood. Delia Moore's house was nearly half a mile away. After a moment Jennie spoke again.

"You ain't really scairt, is you, Jeff?"

"Nah, baby, I ain't scairt."

"You know how we agreed—we gotta keep on goin'."

Jewels of perspiration appeared on Jeff's forehead. His eyes rounded, blinked, became fixed on the road.

"I don't know," he said with a shiver, "I reckon it's the only thing to do."

"Hm."

A flock of guinea fowls[4] pecking in the road, were scattered by the passing car. Some of them took to their wings; others hid under bushes. A blue jay, swaying on a leafy twig, was annoying a roadside squirrel. Jeff held an even speed till he came near Delia's place. Then he slowed down noticeably.

Delia's house was really no house at all, but an abandoned store building converted into a dwelling. It sat near a crossroads, beneath a single black cedar tree. There Delia, a cattish old creature of Jennie's age, lived alone. She had been there more years than anybody could remember, and long ago had won the disfavor of such women as Jennie. For in her young days Delia had been gayer, yellower, and saucier than seemed proper in those parts. Her ways with menfolks had been dark and suspicious. And the fact that she had had as many husbands as children did not help her reputation.

"Yonder's old Delia," Jeff said as they passed.

"What she doin'?"

"Jes sittin' in the do'," he said.

"She see us?"

"Hm," Jeff said. "Musta did."

That relieved Jennie. It strengthened her to know that her old enemy had seen her pass in her best clothes. That would give the old she-devil something to chew her gums and fret about, Jennie thought. Wouldn't she have a fit if she didn't find out? Old evil Delia! This would be just the thing for her. It would pay her back for being so evil. It would also pay her, Jennie thought, for the way she used to grin at Jeff—long ago, when her teeth were good.

---

[4]*guinea fowls*: a common domestic fowl with slate-colored plumage and white spots.

The road became smooth and red, and Jeff could tell by the smell of the air that they were nearing the river. He could see the rise where the road turned and ran along parallel to the stream. The car chugged on monotonously. After a long silent spell, Jennie leaned against Jeff and spoke.

"How many bale[5] o' cotton you think we got standin'?" she said.

Jeff wrinkled his forehead as he calculated.

" 'bout twenty-five, I reckon."

"How many you make las' year?"

"Twenty-eight," he said. "How come you ask that?"

"I's jes thinkin'," Jennie said quietly.

"It don't make a speck o' difference though," Jeff reflected. "If we get much or if we get little, we still gonna be in debt to old man Stevenson when he gets through counting up agin us. It's took us a long time to learn that."

Jennie was not listening to these words. She had fallen into a trance-like meditation. Her lips twitched. She chewed her gums and rubbed her gnarled hands nervously. Suddenly, she leaned forward, buried her face in the nervous hands, and burst into tears. She cried aloud in a dry, cracked voice that suggested the rattle of fodder[6] on dead stalks. She cried aloud like a child, for she had never learned to suppress a genuine sob. Her slight old frame shook heavily and seemed hardly able to sustain such violent grief.

"What's the matter, baby?" Jeff asked awkwardly. "Why you cryin' like all that?"

"I's jes thinkin'," she said.

"So you the one what's scairt now, hunh?"

"I ain't scairt, Jeff. I's jes thinkin' 'bout leavin' eve'thing like this— eve'thing we been used to. It's right sad-like."

Jeff did not answer, and presently Jennie buried her face again and cried.

The sun was almost overhead. It beat down furiously on the dusty wagon-path road, on the parched roadside grass and the tiny battered car. Jeff's hands, gripping the wheel, became wet with perspiration; his forehead sparkled. Jeff's lips parted. His mouth shaped a hideous grimace. His face suggested the face of a man being burned. But the torture passed and his expression softened again.

"You mustn't cry, baby," he said to his wife. "We gotta be strong. We can't break down."

Jennie waited a few seconds, then said, "You reckon we oughta do it, Jeff? You reckon we oughta go 'head an' do it, really?"

Jeff's voice choked; his eyes blurred. He was terrified to hear Jennie say

---

[5]*bale*: large package of goods closely pressed, wrapped, and tied with cord or copper wire.
[6]*fodder*: food for cattle.

the thing that had been in his mind all morning. She had egged him on when he had wanted more than anything in the world to wait, to reconsider, to think things over a little longer. Now she was getting cold feet. Actually, there was no need of thinking the question through again. It would only end in making the same painful decision once more. Jeff knew that. There was no need of fooling around longer.

"We jes as well to do like we planned," he said. "They ain't nothin' else for us now—it's the bes' thing."

Jeff thought of the handicaps, the near impossibility, of making another crop with his leg bothering him more and more each week. Then there was always the chance that he would have another stroke, like the one that had made him lame. Another one might kill him. The least it could do would be to leave him helpless. Jeff gasped—Lord Jesus! He could not bear to think of being helpless, like a baby, on Jennie's hands. Frail, blind Jennie.

The little pounding motor of the car worked harder and harder. The puff of steam from the cracked radiator became larger. Jeff realized that they were climbing a little rise. A moment later the road turned abruptly, and he looked down upon the face of the river.

"Jeff."

"Hunh?"

"Is that the water I hear?"

"Hm. Tha's it."

"Well, which way you goin' now?"

"Down this-a way," he said. "The road runs 'long 'side o' the water a lil piece."

She waited a while calmly. Then she said, "Drive faster."

"A'right baby," Jeff said.

The water roared in the bed of the river. It was fifty or sixty feet below the level of the road. Between the road and the water there was a long smooth slope, sharply inclined. The slope was dry, the clay hardened by prolonged summer heat. The water below, roaring in a narrow channel, was noisy and wild.

"Jeff."

"Hunh?"

"How far you goin'?"

"Jes a lil piece down the road."

"You ain't scairt, is you, Jeff?"

"Nah, baby," he said trembling. "I ain't scairt."

"Remember how we planned it, Jeff. We gotta do it like we said. Brave-like."

"Hm."

Jeff's brain darkened. Things suddenly seemed unreal, like figures in a dream. Thoughts swam in his mind foolishly, hysterically, like little blind fish in a pool within a dense cave. They rushed again. Jeff soon became dizzy. He shuddered violently and turned to his wife.

"Jennie, I can't do it. I can't." His voice broke pitifully.

She did not appear to be listening. All the grief had gone from her face. She sat erect, her unseeing eyes wide open, strained and frightful. Her glossy black skin had become dull. She seemed as thin, as sharp and bony, as a starved bird. Now, having suffered and endured the sadness of tearing herself away from beloved things, she showed no anguish. She was absorbed with her own thoughts, and she didn't even hear Jeff's voice shouting in her ear.

Jeff said nothing more. For an instant there was light in his cavernous brain. The great chamber was, for less than a second, peopled by characters he knew and loved. They were simple, healthy creatures, and they behaved in a manner that he could understand. They had quality. But since he had already taken leave of them long ago, the remembrance did not break his heart again. Young Jeff Patton was among them, the Jeff Patton of fifty years ago who went down to New Orleans with a crowd of country boys to the Mardi Gras[7] doings. They gay young crowd, boys with candy-striped shirts and rouged brown girls in noisy silks, was like a picture in his head. Yet it did not make him sad. On that very trip Slim Burns had killed Joe Beasley—the crowd had been broken up. Since then Jeff Patton's world had been the Greenbriar Plantation. If there had been other Mardi Gras carnivals, he had not heard of them. Since then there had been no time; the years had fallen on him like waves. Now he was old, worn out. Another paralytic stroke (like the one he had already suffered) would put him on his back for keeps. In that condition, with a frail blind woman to look after him, he would be worse off than if he were dead.

Suddenly Jeff's hand became steady. He actually felt brave. He slowed down the motor of the car and carefully pulled off the road. Below, the water of the stream boomed, a soft thunder in the deep channel. Jeff ran the car onto the clay slope, pointed it directly toward the stream, and put his foot heavily on the accelerator. The little car leaped furiously down the steep incline toward the water. The movement was nearly as swift and direct as a fall. The two old black folks, sitting quietly side by side, showed no excitement. In another instant the car hit the water and dropped immediately out of sight.

A little later it lodged in the mud of a shallow place. One wheel of the crushed and upturned little Ford became visible above the rushing water.

---

[7]*Mardi Gras*: Shrove Tuesday; the last day of the pre-Lenten carnival as celebrated in New Orleans.

Thinking About the Story

1. How do the time and place in which the story is set help shape the story?

2. How have the hardships that Jeff and Jennie have endured shaped them as individuals? As a married couple?

3. Why does Jeff shudder every time he thinks about the "trip" he and Jennie are planning to take?

4. At the end of the story, as Jeff and Jennie's car goes in the stream, what was your reaction? What do you assume happened? Support your responses with specific information from the story.

5. Against whom or what do you think Jeff and Jennie take a stand? Do you think their choice of action was the best one? Why or why not?

Reading/Writing Connections

1. In a one-page essay, write a description of Jeff and Jennie's life for someone who has never met them. Decide whether to focus on their lives as individuals or as a married couple.

2. In your journal, discuss in what way Jeff and Jennie's story is a "summer tragedy."

*"Watching the Good Train Go By: Cotton" by Romare Bearden. Medium:
Watercolor, gouache, and pencil on paperboard. Size: 11 ⅛ × 14 in. (18.3 ×
35.6 cm.) Reprinted by permission of the Hirschhorn Museum and Sculpture
Garden, Smithsonian Institution, Gift of Joseph H. Hirschhorn, 1966.
Photographer: Lee Stalsworth.*

*One of Bearden's projection series, this work reflects one of the historical aspects
of black life in the South—picking cotton. The train, as mentioned in the title, was
a frequently used motif for Bearden. "Watching the good trains go by" was one of
Bearden's favorite memories from his childhood in Charlotte, North Carolina.*

3

THE FOLK
TRADITION

Folklore, like other genres of literature, serves as a mirror of what we like to call the human condition. Folklore helps explain human relationships, desires, and fears, and clarify those doubts we have about life. Folktales and **mythology** have no cultural or ethnic boundaries. They are used by all the world's people to convey their culture, religion, and social customs.

Although both folklore and mythology are based on legend, there is a slight difference between them. Folklore consists of traditional tales handed down from one generation to the next by the common people. These tales may teach a lesson, impart history, or simply entertain. Myths, on the other hand, attempt to account for something that occurs in nature, and may tell about a particular country or person.

The use of folk material by African American writers began with William Wells Brown, the first African American to publish a novel in the United States. He used folk **anecdotes** in *My Southern Home* (1880). Charles Waddell Chesnutt, the father of the African American short story, also used folk material in *The Conjure Woman* (1899).

Much of the early folk literature with black themes was written not by blacks but by whites, some of whom used this invented folklore to foster negative stereotypes of African Americans, portraying them as either comic or pathetic.

African American writers found a valuable source in folk material; Paul Laurence Dunbar, for example, used it in his poetry as he wrote about everyday events in the lives of common people.

Poet and scholar Sterling Brown, who taught for many years at Howard University in Washington, D.C., enlarged the use of folk characters by depicting them in a variety of human endeavors ranging from trivial to tragic. Zora Neale Hurston, James Weldon Johnson, Langston Hughes, Jean Toomer, and Julius Lester were among those writers who utilized folk material in their literary works.

Julius Lester   (b. 1939) has worked as a newspaper columnist, folk-singer, television and radio personality, and university professor, in addition to writing seventeen books—his most recent being *How Many Spots Does a Leopard Have?*, a retelling of twelve African and Jewish folktales. An early proponent of black pride, Lester spent his youth in the Midwest and South, graduated from Fisk University, and was an organizer of the Student Nonviolent Coordinating Committee (SNCC), a civil rights organization in the U.S. during the 1960s. Currently, Lester teaches at the University of Massachusetts, Amherst.

In much of his writing, such as *To Be a Slave* (1968)—a runner-up for the Newbery Medal—and *Black Folktales* (1969), Lester used African American history and folklore to create literary works. "People Who Could Fly" is a retelling of a tale from slavery days.

People Who Could Fly

JULIUS LESTER

It happened long, long ago, when black people were taken from their homes in Africa and forced to come here to work as slaves. They were put onto ships, and many died during the long voyage across the Atlantic Ocean. Those that survived stepped off the boats into a land they had never seen, a land they never knew existed, and they were put into the fields to work.

Many refused, and they were killed. Others would work, but when the white man's whip lashed their backs to make them work harder, they would turn and fight. And some of them killed the white men with the whips. Others were killed by the white men. Some would run away and try to go back home, back to Africa where there were no white people, where they worked their own land for the good of each other, not for the good of white men. Some of those who tried to go back to Africa would walk until they came to the ocean, and then they would walk into the water, and no one knows if they did walk to Africa through the water or if they drowned. It didn't matter. At least they were no longer slaves.

Now when the white man forced Africans onto the slave-ships, he did not know, nor did he care, if he took the village musicians, artists, or witch doctors. As long as they were black and looked strong, he wanted them—men, women, and children. Thus, he did not know that sometimes there would be a witch doctor among those he had captured. If he had known, and had also known that the witch doctor was the medium of the gods, he would have thought twice. But he did not care. These black men and black women were not people to him. He looked at them and counted each one as so much money for his pocket.

It was to a plantation in South Carolina that one boatload of Africans was brought. Among them was the son of a witch doctor who had not completed by many months studying the secrets of the gods from his father. This young man carried with him the secrets and powers of the generations of Africa.

One day, one hot day when the sun singed the very hair on the head, they were working in the fields. They had been in the fields since before the sun rose, and, as it made its journey to the highest part of the sky, the very air seemed to be on fire. A young woman, her body curved with the child that grew deep inside her, fainted.

Before her body struck the ground, the white man with the whip was riding toward her on his horse. He threw water in her face. "Get back to work, you lazy nigger! There ain't going to be no sitting down on the job as long as I'm here.'' He cracked the whip against her back and, screaming, she staggered to her feet.

All work had stopped as the Africans watched, saying nothing.

''If you niggers don't want a taste of the same, you'd better get to work!''

They lowered their heads and went back to work. The young witch doctor worked his way slowly toward the young mother-to-be, but before he could reach her, she collapsed again, and the white man with the whip was upon her, lashing her until her body was raised from the ground by the sheer violence of her sobs. The young witch doctor worked his way to her side and whispered something in her ear. She, in turn, whispered to the person beside her. He told the next person, and on around the field it went. They did it so quickly and quietly that the white man with the whip noticed nothing.

A few moments later, someone else in the field fainted, and, as the white man with the whip rode toward him, the young witch doctor shouted, ''Now!'' He uttered a strange word, and the person who had fainted rose from the ground, and moving his arms like wings, he flew into the sky and out of sight.

The man with the whip looked around at the Africans, but they only stared into the distance, tiny smiles softening their lips. ''Who did that? Who was that who yelled out?'' No one said anything. ''Well, just let me get my hands on him.''

Not too many minutes had passed before the young woman fainted once again. The man was almost upon her when the young witch doctor shouted, ''Now!'' and uttered a strange word. She, too, rose from the ground and, waving her arms like wings, she flew into the distance and out of sight.

This time the man with the whip knew who was responsible, and as he pulled back his arm to lash the young witch doctor, the young man yelled, ''Now! Now! Everyone!'' He uttered the strange word, and all of the Africans dropped their hoes, stretched out their arms, and flew away, back to their home, back to Africa.

That was long ago, and no one now remembers what word it was that the young witch doctor knew that could make people fly. But who knows? Maybe one morning someone will awake with a strange word on his tongue and, uttering it, we will all stretch out our arms and take to the air, leaving these blood-drenched fields of our misery behind.

Thinking About the Story

1. How were the Africans looked upon by the slave traders in "People Who Could Fly"?

2. What do you suppose was the strange word the witch doctor uttered just before the slaves began to fly away?

3. What do you think the witch doctor whispered to the expectant mother?

Reading/Writing Connections

1. Write a journal entry in the first person in which you describe how you might feel as you fly back to your homeland.

2. The author says that one day "someone will awake with a strange word on his tongue" and, once this word is uttered, "we will all stretch out our arms and take to the air, leaving these blood-drenched fields of our misery behind." Write an essay in which you define who "we" are in the story and explain the metaphor "blood-drenched fields of our misery."

3. Suppose people really could fly. Write an essay in which you create and describe such a culture.

Julius Lester   Folktales like the others included in this chapter are seldom, if ever, written down originally. They are told as stories and handed down from generation to generation, using the **oral tradition** that is very much a part of the African and African American heritage.

"Stagolee" is a story that started out as a song about a real man. His story was likely told first in black neighborhoods in large, urban cities. This tale, as retold by Julius Lester, is of a man who grew up in a Georgia plantation. Early in his childhood Stagolee (sometimes referred to as Staggerlee) declared that he would not spend *his* life working on a plantation. He took mistreatment from no one—white or black. His legend and the retellings that grew out of it are the basis of "Stagolee," a story from Julius Lester's book *Black Folktales* that was first published in 1969. (See page 52 for biographical sketch on Lester.)

Stagolee

JULIUS LESTER

Stagolee was, undoubtedly and without question, the baddest nigger that ever lived. Stagolee was so bad that the flies wouldn't even fly around his head in the summertime, and snow wouldn't fall on his house in the winter. He was bad, jim.

Stagolee grew up on a plantation in Georgia, and by the time he was two, he'd decided that he wasn't going to spend his life picking cotton and working for white folks. Uh-uh. And when he was five, he left. Took off down the road, his guitar on his back, a deck of cards in one pocket and a .44 in the other. He figured that he didn't need nothing else. When the women heard him whup the blues on the guitar he could have whichever one he laid his mind on. Whenever he needed money, he could play cards. And whenever somebody tried to mess with him, he had his .44. So he was ready. A man didn't need more than that to get along with in the world.

By the time Stack was grown, his reputation had spread around the country. It got started one night in one of them honky-tonks down there in Alabama, and Stagolee caught some dude trying to deal from the bottom of the deck. Ol' Stack pulled out his .44 and killed him dead, right there on the spot. Then he moved the dead guy over to the center of the room and used the body as a card table. Another time, something similar happened, and Stack pulled the body over next to him, so a buddy of his, who was kinda short, would have something to sit on. Didn't take long for the word to get around that this was one bad dude! Even white folks didn't mess with Stagolee.

Well, this one time, Stagolee was playing cards with a dude they called Billy Lyons. Billy Lyons was one of them folk who acted like they were a little better than anybody else. He'd had a little education, and that stuff can really mess your mind up. Billy Lyons had what he called a "scientific method" of cardplaying. Stagolee had the "nigger method." So they got to playing, and, naturally, Stagolee was just taking all of Billy Lyons's money, and Billy got mad. He got so mad that he reached over and knocked Stagolee's Stetson hat off his head and spit in it.

What'd he do that for? He could've done almost anything else in the world, but not that. Stack pulled his .44, and Billy started copping his plea. "Now, listen here, Mr. Stagolee. I didn't mean no harm. I just lost my head for a minute. I was wrong, and I apologize." He reached down on the ground, picked up Stack's Stetson, brushed it off, and put it back on his head. "I didn't mean no harm. See, the hat's all right. I put it back on your head." Billy was tomming[1] like a champ, but Stack wasn't smiling. "Don't shoot me. Please, Mr. Stagolee! I got two children and a wife to support. You understand?"

Stack said, "Well, that's all right. The Lawd'll take care of your children. I'll take care of your wife." And, with that, Stagolee blowed Billy Lyons away. Stagolee looked at the body for a minute and then went off to Billy Lyons's house and told Mrs. Billy that her husband was dead and he was moving in. And that's just what he did, too. Moved in.

Now there was this new sheriff in town, and he had gotten the word about Stagolee, but this sheriff was a sho' nuf' cracker. He just couldn't stand the idea of Stagolee walking around like he was free—not working, not buying war bonds, cussing out white folks. He just couldn't put up with it, so, when he heard that Stagolee had shot Billy Lyons, he figured that this was his chance.

Sheriff told his deputies, said, "All right, men. Stagolee killed a man tonight. We got to get him."

The deputies looked at him. "Well, sheriff. Ain't nothing wrong with killing a man every now and then," said one.

"It's good for a man's health," added another.

"Well," said the sheriff, "that's all right for a white man, but this is a nigger."

"Now, sheriff, you got to watch how you talk about Stagolee. He's one of the leaders of the community here. You just can't come in here and start talking about one of our better citizens like that."

The sheriff looked at them. "I believe you men are afraid. Afraid of a nigger!"

Deputies thought it over for half a second. "Sheriff. Let's put it this way. We have a healthy respect for Stagolee. A long time ago, we struck a bargain with him. We promised him that if he let us alone, we'd let him alone. And everything has worked out just fine."

"Well, we're going to arrest Stagolee," the sheriff said. "Get your guns, and let's go."

The deputies stood up, took their guns, and laid 'em on the shelf. "Sheriff, if you want Stagolee, well, you can arrest him by yourself." And they went on out the door and over to the undertaker's parlor and told him to start making a coffin for the sheriff.

When all the other white folks heard what the sheriff was going to do, they ran over to talk to him. "Sheriff, you can't go around disturbing the peace." But couldn't nobody talk no sense into him.

---

[1]*tomming*: talking like "an Uncle Tom."

Now Stagolee heard that the sheriff was looking for him, and, being a gentleman, Stagolee got out of bed, told Mrs. Billy he'd be back in a little while, and went on down to the bar. He'd barely gotten the first drink down when the sheriff came stepping through the door.

He walked over to the bartender. "Barkeep? Who's that man down at the other end of the bar? You know there's a law in this town against drinking after midnight. Who is that?

Bartender leaned over the counter and whispered in his ear, "Don't talk so loud. That's Stagolee. He drinks when he gets thirsty and he's generally thirsty after midnight."

Sheriff walked over to Stagolee. Stagolee didn't even look around. Sheriff fired a couple of shots in the air. Stagolee poured himself another drink and threw it down. Finally, the sheriff said, "Stagolee, I'm the sheriff, and I'm white. Ain't you afraid?"

Stagolee turned around slowly. "You may be the sheriff, and you may be white, but you ain't Stagolee. Now deal with that."

The sheriff couldn't even begin to figure it out, no less deal with it, so he fell back in his familiar bag. "I'm placing you under arrest for the murder of Billy Lyons."

"You and what army? And it bet' not be the United States Army, 'cause I whupped them already."

"Me and this army," the sheriff growled, jabbing the pistol in Stack's ribs.

Before the sheriff could take another breath, Stagolee hit him upside the head and sent him flying across the room. Stagolee pulled out his gun, put three bullets in him, put his gun away, had another drink, and was on his way out the door before the body hit the floor.

The next day, Stagolee went to both of the funerals to pay his last respects to the sheriff and Billy Lyons, and then he settled down to living with Mrs. Billy. She really didn't mind too much. All the women knew how good-looking Stack was. And he was always respectful to women, always had plenty of money, and, generally, he made a good husband, as husbands go. Stagolee had one fault, though. Sometimes he drank too much. About once a month, Stagolee would buy up all the available liquor and moonshine in the county and proceed to get wasted, and when Stagolee got wasted, he got totally wasted.

The new sheriff waited until one of those nights when Stagolee was so drunk he was staggering in his sleep, and he was lying flat in the bed. If Judgment Day had come, the Lord would have had to postpone it until Stagolee had sobered up. Otherwise, the Lord might've ended up getting Gabriel shot and his trumpet wrapped around his head. When the sheriff saw Stagolee that drunk, he went and got together the Ku Klux Klan Alumni Association, which was every white man in four counties. After the sheriff had assured them that Stagolee was so drunk he couldn't wake up, they broke in the house just as bad as you please. They had the lynching rope all ready, and they dropped it around his neck. The minute that rope touched Stack's neck, he was wide awake and stone cold sober. When white folks saw that, they were falling over each other getting out of there. But Stack was cool. He should've been. He invented it.

"Y'all come to hang me?"

The sheriff said that that was so. Stagolee stood up, stretched, yawned, and scratched himself a couple of times. "Well, since I can't seem to get no sleep, let's go and get this thing over with so I can get on back to bed."

They took him on out behind the jail where the gallows was built. Stagolee got up on the scaffold, and the sheriff dropped the rope around his neck and tightened it. Then the hangman opened up on the trap door, and there was Stack, swinging ten feet in the air, laughing as loud as you ever heard anybody laugh. They let him hang there for a half-hour, and Stagolee was still laughing.

"Hey, man! This rope is ticklish."

The white folks looked at each other and realized that Stack's neck just wouldn't crack. So they cut him down, and Stagolee went back home and went back to bed.

After that, the new sheriff left Stagolee in peace, like he should've done to begin with.

Stagolee lived on and on, and that was his big mistake. 'Cause Stagolee lived so long, he started attracting attention up in Heaven. One day, St. Peter was looking down on the earth, and he happened to notice Stack sitting on the porch picking on the guitar. "Ain't that Stagolee?" St. Peter said to himself. He took a closer look. "That's him. That's him. Why, that nigger should've been dead a long time ago." So St. Peter went and looked it up in the record book, and sure enough, Stagolee was supposed to have died thirty years before.

St. Peter went to see the Lord.

"What's going on, St. Peter?"

"Oh, ain't nothing shaking, Lord. Well, that's not totally true. I was just checking out earth, and there's a nigger down there named Stagolee who is way overdue for a visit from Death."

"Is that so?"

"It's the truth, Lord."

"Well, we have to do something about that."

The Lord cleared his throat a couple of times and hollered out, "HEY DEATH! HEEEEY, DEATH!"

Now Death was laying up down in the barn catching up on some sleep, 'cause he was tired. Having to make so many trips to Vietnam was wearing him out, not to mention everywhere else in the world. He just couldn't understand why dying couldn't be systematized. He'd tried his best to convince God either to get a system to dying or get him some assistants. He'd proposed that, say, on Mondays, the only dying that would be done would be, say, in France, Germany, and a few other counties. Tuesday it'd be some other countires, and on like that. That way, he wouldn't have to be running all over the world twenty-four hours a day. But the Lord had vetoed the idea. Said it sounded to him like Death just wanted an excuse to eventually computerize the whole operation. Death had to admit that the thought had occurred to him. He didn't know when he was going to catch up on all the paperwork he had to do. A computer would solve everything. And now, just when he was getting to sleep, here come the Lord waking him up.

So Death got on his pale white horse. He was so tired of riding a horse he didn't know what to do. He'd talked to God a few months ago about letting him get a helicopter or something. But the Lord just didn't seem to understand. Death rode on off down through the streets of Heaven, and when folks heard him coming, they closed their doors, 'cause even in Heaven, folks were afraid of Death. And that was the other thing. Death was mighty lonely. Didn't nobody talk to him, and he was getting a little tired of it. He wished the Lord would at least let him wear a suit and tie and look respectable. Maybe then he could meet some nice young angel and raise a family. The Lord had vetoed that idea, too.

"What took you so long, Death?"

"Aw, Lord. I was trying to get some sleep. You just don't realize how fast folks are dying these days."

"Don't tell me you gon' start complaining again."

"I'm sorry, Lord, but I'd like to see you handle the job as well as I do with no help, no sleep, no wife, no nothing."

"Well, I got a special job for you today."

"Can't wait until tomorrow?"

"No, it can't wait, Death! Now hush up. There's a man in Fatback, Georgia, named Stagolee. You should've picked him up thirty years ago, and I want you to send me a memo on why you didn't."

"Well, I got such a backlog of work piled up."

"I don't want to have to be doing your job for you. You get the lists every day from the Record Bureau. How come you missed this one? If he's escaped for thirty years, who knows who else has been living way past their time. Speaking of folks living past their time, St. Peter, have the librarian bring me all the files on white folks. Seems to me that white folks sho' done outlived their time. Anyway, Death, go on down there and get Stagolee."

Death headed on down to earth. A long time ago, he used to enjoy the ride, but not anymore. There were so many satellites and other pieces of junk flying around through the air that it was like going through a junkyard barefooted. So he didn't waste any time getting on down to Fatback, Georgia.

Now on this particular day, Stagolee was sitting on the porch, picking the blues on the guitar, and drinking. All of a sudden, he looked up and saw this pale-looking white cat in this white sheet come riding up to his house on a white horse. "We ain't never had no Klan in the daytime before," Stagolee said.

Death got off his horse, pulled out his address book, and said, "I'm looking for Stagolee Booker T. Washington Nicodemus Shadrack Nat Turner Jones."

"Hey, baby! You got it down pat! I'd forgotten a couple of them names myself."

"Are you Stagolee Booker T. Wash—"

"You ain't got to go through the thing again. I'm the dude. What's going on?"

"I'm Death. Come with me."

Stagolee started laughing. "You who?"

"I'm Death. Come on, man. I ain't got all day."

"Be serious."

Death looked at Stagolee. No one had ever accused him of joking before. "I *am* serious. It's your time to die. Now come on here!"

"Man, you ain't bad enough to mess with me."

Death blinked his eyes. He'd never run up on a situation like this before. Sometimes folks struggled a little bit, but they didn't refuse. "Stagolee, let's go!" Death said in his baddest voice.

"Man, you must want to get shot."

Death thought that one over for a minute. Now he didn't know how to handle this situation, so he reached in his saddlebags and pulled out his *Death Manual*. He looked up *resistance* and read what it said, but wasn't a thing in there about what to do when somebody threatens you. Then he looked up *guns* but that wasn't listed. He looked under everything he could think of, but nothing was of any help. So he went back to the porch. "You coming or not, Stagolee?"

Stagolee let one of them .44 bullets whistle past ol' Death's ear, and Death got hot. Death didn't waste no time getting away from there. Before he was sitting in the saddle good, he had made it back to Heaven.

"Lord! You must be trying to get me killed."

"Do what? Get you killed? Since when could you die?"

"Don't matter, but that man Stagolee you just sent me after took a shot at me. Now listen here, Lord, if you want that man dead, you got to get him yourself. I am not going back after him. I knew there was some reason I let him live thirty years too long. I'd heard about him on the grapevine and, for all I care, he can live three hundred more years. I am not going back—"

"O.K. O.K. You made your point. Go on back to sleep." After Death had gone, God turned to St. Peter and asked, "We haven't had any new applications for that job recently?"

"You must be joking."

"Well, I was just checking." The Lord lit a cigar. "Pete, looks like I'm going to have to use one of my giant death thunderbolts to get that Stagolee."

"Looks that way. You want me to tell the work crew?"

The Lord nodded, and St. Peter left. It took 3,412 angels 14 days, 11 hours, and 32 minutes to carry the giant death thunderbolt to the Lord, but he just reached down and picked it up like it was a toothpick.

"Uh, St. Peter? How you spell Stagolee?"

"Lord, you know everything. You're omnipotent, omnicient, omni—"

"You better shut up and tell me how to spell Stagolee."

St. Peter spelled it out for him, and the Lord wrote it on the thunderbolt. Then he blew away a few clouds and put his keen eye down on the earth. "Hey, St. Peter. Will you look at all that killing down there? I ain't never seen nothing like it."

"Lord, that ain't Georgia. That's Vietnam."

The Lord put his great eye across the world. "Tsk, tsk, tsk. Look at all that sin down there. Women wearing hardly no clothes at all. Check that one out with the black hair, St. Peter. Look at her! Disgraceful! Them legs!"

"LORD!"

And the Lord put his eye on the earth and went on across the United States—Nevada, Utah, Colorado, Kansas, Missouri—

"Turn right at the Mississippi, Lord!"

The Lord turned right and went on down into Tennessee.

"Make a left at Memphis, Lord!"

The Lord turned left at Memphis and went on up through Nashville and on down to Chattanooga into Georgia. Atlanta, Georgia. Valdosta. Rolling Stone, Georgia, until he got way back out in the woods to Fatback. He let his eye go up and down the country roads until he saw Stagolee sitting on the porch.

"That's him, Lord! That's him!"

And the Great God Almighty, the God of Nat Turner and Rap Brown, the God of Muddy Waters and B. B. King, the God of Aretha Franklin and The Impressions, this great God Almighty Everlasting, *et in terra pax hominibus*,[1] and all them other good things, drew back his mighty arm—

---

[1]*et in terra pax hominibus*: (Latin) and on earth peace to mankind.

"Watch your aim now, Lord."

And unloosed the giant thunderbolt. BOOM!

That was the end of Stagolee. You can't mess with the Lord.

Well, when the people found out Stagolee was dead, you ain't never heard such hollering and crying in all your life. The women were beside themselves with grief, 'cause Stagolee was nothing but a sweet man.

Come the day of the funeral, and Stagolee was laid out in a $10,000 casket. Had on a silk mohair suit and his Stetson hat was in his hand. In his right coat pocket was a brand new deck of cards. In his left coat pocket was a brand new .44 with some extra rounds of ammunition and a can of Mace. And by his side was his guitar. Folks came from all over the country to Stack's funeral, and all of 'em put little notes in Stagolee's other pockets, which were messages they wanted Stagolee to give to their kinfolk when he got to Hell.

The funeral lasted for three days and three nights. All the guitar pickers and blues singers had to come sing one last song for Stagolee. All the back-sliders had to come backslide one more time for Stagolee. All the gamblers had to come touch Stack's casket for a little taste of good luck. And all the women had to come shed a tear as they looked at him for the last time. Those that had known him were crying about what they weren't going to have any more. And those that hadn't known him were crying over what they had missed. Even the little bitty ones was shedding tears.

After all the singing and crying and shouting was over, they took Stagolee on out and buried him. They didn't bury him in the cemetery. Uh-uh. Stagolee had to have a cemetery all his own. They dug his grave with a silver spade and lowered him down with a golden chain. And they went on back to their homes, not quite ready to believe that Stack was dead and gone.

But you know, it's mighty hard to keep a good man down, and long about the third day, Stagolee decided to get on up out of the grave and go check out Heaven. Stack just couldn't see himself waiting for Judgment Day. The thought of the white man blowing the trumpet on Judgment Day made him sick to his stomach, and Stagolee figured he was supposed to have his own Judgment Day, anyhow.

He started on off for Heaven. Of course it took him a long time to get there, 'cause he had to stop on all the clouds and teach the little angels to play Pittat and Coon-Can and all like that, but, eventually, he got near to Heaven. Now as he got close, he started hearing all this harp music and hymn singing. Stagolee couldn't believe his ears. He listened some more, and then he shrugged his shoulders. "I'm approaching Heaven from the wrong side. This can't be the black part of Heaven, not with all that hymn singing and harp music I hear."

So Stack headed on around to the other side of heaven, and when he got there, it was stone deserted. I mean, wasn't nobody there. Streets was as empty as the President's mind. So Stack cut on back around to the other side of Heaven. When he got there, St. Peter was playing bridge with Abraham, Jonah, and Mrs. God. When they looked up and saw who it was, though, they split, leaving St. Peter there by himself.

"You ain't getting in here!" St. Peter yelled.

"Don't want to either. Hey, man. Where all the colored folks at?"

"We had to send 'em all to Hell. We used to have quite a few, but they got to rocking the church service, you know. Just couldn't even sing a hymn without it coming out and sounding like the blues. So we had to get rid of 'em. We got a few nice colored folks left. And they nice, respectable people."

Stagolee laughed. "Hey, man. You messed up."

"Huh?"

"Yeah, man. This ain't Heaven. This is Hell. Bye."

And Stagolee took off straight for Hell. He was about 2,000 miles away, and he could smell the barbecue cooking and hear the jukeboxes playing, and he started running. He got there, and there was a big BLACK POWER sign on the gate. He rung on the bell, and the dude who come to answer it recognized him immediately. "Hey, everybody! Stagolee's here!"

And the folks came running from everywhere to greet him.

"Hey, baby!"

"What's going down!"

"What took you so long to get here?"

Stagolee walked in, and the brothers and sisters had put down wall-to-wall carpeting, indirect lighting, and best of all, they'd installed air-conditioning. Stagolee walked around, checking it all out. "Yeah. Y'all got it together. Got it uptight!"

After he'd finished checking it out, he asked "Any white folks down here?"

"Just the hip ones, and ain't too many of them. But they all right. They know where it's at."

"Solid." Stagolee noticed an old man sitting over in a corner with his hands over his ears. "What's his problem?"

"Aw, that's the Devil. He just can't get himself together. He ain't learned how to deal with niggers yet."

Stagolee walked over to him. "Hey, man. Get your pitchfork, and let's have some fun. I got my .44. C'mon. Let's go one round."

The Devil just looked at Stagolee real sadlike, but didn't say a word.

Stagolee took the pitchfork and laid it on the shelf. "Well, that's hip. I didn't want no stuff out of you nohow. I'm gon' rule Hell by myself!"

And that's just what he did, too.

Thinking About the Folktale

1. "Stagolee" is the story of a legendary African American male. As with most folktales, the author uses exaggeration as a key literary device. What do you like or not like about this tale?

2. What do you think makes Stagolee so tough?

3. How would you characterize the language used in this folktale? What was happening in the United States at the time this version of Stagolee's story was written?

Reading/Writing Connections

1. The storyteller of "Stagolee" says he was "one bad dude!" What is it in his character that makes him so? Write a one-page paper describing his character.

2. Stagolee seems to display his manhood primarily through acts of violence. Write an essay in which you defend or reject his actions. Support your point of view with evidence from your reading or personal experience.

3. It is said that "Stagolee" has heroic qualities. Write an essay in which you describe at least one heroic quality the main character displays.

Anonymous.   This short folktale from slavery days tells how a slave wins his freedom. Buck and his master make a proposition. If Buck can successfully steal the master's suit of clothes, he will be granted his freedom.

How Buck Won His Freedom

ANONYMOUS

Buck was the shrewdest slave on the big Washington plantation. He could steal things almost in front of his master's eyes without being detected. Finally, after having had his chickens and pigs stolen until he was sick, Master Henry Washington called Buck to him one day and said, "Buck, how do you manage to steal without getting caught?"

"Dat's easy, Massa," replied Buck, "dat's easy. Ah kin steal yo' clo'es right tonight, wid you aguardin' 'em."

"No, no," said the master, "you may be a slick thief, but you can't do that. I will make a proposition with you: If you steal my suit of clothes tonight, I will give you your freedom, and if you fail to steal them, then you will stop stealing my chickens."

"Aw right, Massa, aw right," Buck agreed. "Dat's uh go."

That night about nine o'clock the master called his wife into the bedroom, got his Sunday suit of clothes, laid it out on the table, and told his wife about the proposition he had made with Buck. He got on one side of the table and had his wife get on the other side, and they waited. Pretty soon, through a window that was open, the master heard the mules and the horses in the stable lot running as if someone were after them.

"Here wife," said he, "you take this gun and keep an eye on this suit. I am going to see what's the matter with those animals."

Buck, who had been out to the horse lot and started the stampede to attract the master's attention, now approached the open window. He was a good mimic, and in tones that sounded like his master's he called out, "Ol' lady, ol' lady, ol' lady, you better hand me that suit. That damn thief might steal it while I'm gone."

The master's wife, thinking that it was her husband asking for his suit, took it from the table and handed it out the window to Buck. This is how Buck won his freedom.

Thinking About the Folktale

1. How does Buck outwit his slavemaster?

2. Buck was able to sound like his master. How do you suppose he was able to do that, even though he spoke a **nonstandard dialect** of English?

3. How would you describe Master Henry Washington?

Reading/Writing Connections

1. Imagine what Buck's feelings must have been after winning his freedom. Write some of your speculations in your journal.

2. Create your own story about how a slave wins his or her freedom by outsmarting the slave master.

3. Write an essay detailing the master's reactions to Buck's ability to secure the suit from the master's wife.

A. Philip Randolph (1889–1979), who played a leading role in the struggle for black rights and was a key figure in the American labor movement, and Chandler Owen edited and published the *Messenger*, a socialist journal. In 1925 they published "The Steel Drivin' Man" in the *Messenger*. This folktale is based on the worksong "John Henry." The subject of many **ballads** and stories, the tale of John Henry was inspired by a real man by that name.

The Steel Drivin' Man

A. PHILIP RANDOLPH
and CHANDLER OWEN

. . . John Henry was a "free man." . . . While a mere lad he had saved his master from a watery grave. For this heroic act he was given his liberty, and more, the former master became his best friend. He always called the old plantation his home.

Physically, John Henry was a mighty man. He was over six feet tall. He weighted more than two hundred and fifty pounds. He could muscle and toss a hundred pound anvil with one hand. He was a pure Negro . . .

What noble deed would John Henry not do? He would give his last crust of bread to a hungry child. He would sit up all night at the bedside of a sick slave and then work hard the following day, and the work was arduous indeed, but John Henry did not care. He was the best worker in the country.

John Henry was employed by Captain Walters, a railroad contractor. The Captain was a southerner of the old school. He loved his "niggahs" as he called them, and they loved him.

The Captain also employed many slaves, hiring them from their masters until he completed his contracts. He divided his army of workers into gangs, as best suited each individual's ability. There was the "plow gang" and the "wheeler gang," the "pick-and-shovel gang" and the "skinners," and last, but most important of all, the "blasting gang," which included the steel drivers.

John Henry was a steel driver. The Captain had never seen a man drive steel as well as he did. No one on the job professed to be able to drive as well. Probably it was because he was a "free man," and was receiving into his own hand his three silver dollars per week, but . . . back on the old plantation a lassie, Lucy by name, was boss of the plantation kitchen, and John Henry was driving steel for her. John Henry loved her. He wanted her to be his wife but first he wanted her to be free, as he was. For years he had been saving his money to buy the girl, to pay for the home, and as he drove his steel into the solid rock to make the opening for the powder charge—often the echo of his hammer would speak to him his sweeheart's name,—and his "buddies" had christened his hammer "Lucy" because John Henry repeated that name so often.

John Henry loved that servant of his, his hammer. It weighed ten pounds more than any other there. It occupied a special place in the tool shanty. No one touched it but him, for had they done so they would have touched John Henry's heart.

Well, one day, the Captain landed a contract for a few miles of road through the heart of the Virginia mountains. The work began in June and John Henry was happy. It was a rough country. There was much rock. This would make overtime work compulsory and that meant for him more money. They knew he was happy for he began to sing a new song to the echo of his hammer:—

> *"Ef ah makes-huh, June, July an' Augus'-huh,*
> *Ise gwine home-huh, Ise gwine home-huh.*
> *O ef ah makes-huh, June, July an' Augus'-huh,*
> *Ise a-comin' home, Lucy-huh, Ise a-com' home-huh!"*

This would he sing as his drill went down, and he grinned much, despite the heat and the perspiration.

But one day there arrived at the camp an enemy to John Henry and to all good steel driving men. He came in the garb of a Yankee drummer, an agent for a so-called, "steam-drill." This new machine was guaranteed to drill a hole faster than any ten men could drill one in the old way with sledge hammer and steel.

That Yankee was determined to sell one to the Captain. He followed him around for days. But the old southerner was obdurate. He did not believe in the much advertised scientific improvements. It takes money to make improvements, despite their economical value in the end. Besides, he was working Negroes, and Negro labor cost him little. In those days a "nigger" was but a machine anyway—a tool to do the white man's work. Why pay for the use of brains when the use of muscle was so cheap? To rid himself of the Yankee the Captain told him:

"Suh, I have a niggah here who can take his hammah and steel and beat that three legged steam contraption of yours to a frazzle, suh. And ah'll bet yuh five hundred dollars on the spot that he can, suh."

"And I'll take your bet provided, that if I win you'll give me an order," said the wily Yankee. And thus it was settled.

The Captain was not at all afraid he would lose his money. . . . He made it his business the next day to visit the "blasting gang" just as John Henry was setting his drill. He noticed how fervently the swarthy driver gripped his sledge, and, with what apparent ease he forced the steel down into the solid rock. He saw the hot perspiration pouring from the seasoned muscles, and then, the grin illuminating the ugly features, and the old Captain chuckled. He called the driver aside.

"John, John, come here John."

"John, I've bet that fool Yankee that you and your hammer can beat that steam contraption he's got. Think you can John?"

"Yassah Cap'n, yassah, yassah."

"Well, John, we'll have the race tomorrow and you do it. You beat him and I'll give you—ah—I'll give you fifty dollars."

John Henry had never been so happy before in all his life. Fifty dollars! Fifty dollars! Why to him it meant everything. It meant that Lucy would be free. It meant that Lucy would be his wife. It meant that Lucy and he would have a home of their own. Is it any wonder then, that when night had fallen, he rubbed from his hammer every speck of dirt, placed it reverently away, and as he lay there among the jutting rocks, gazing at the stars, the melody of his songs reverberated through those rugged mountains louder and sweeter than his "buddies,"—that night in the grading camp? . . .

The Yankee did not do right . . . for he never arrived the next day until the sun was hot, and it was a day in July. But John Henry did not care. He had been singing and grinning all the morning. They chose a spot favored by the Yankee, and, as all the hands crowded around, set their drills.

The race began! It was steam against muscle; brain against brawn; progress against retrogression; Yankee against Southerner; head against heart. John Henry kissed his hammer. The Yankee opened a valve.

John Henry did not sing as he usually did when driving steel. He could not spare the breath. But he drove, ah, how he did drive! With every stroke you could almost see the drill go down and, though the Yankee used much steam, the mark on the Negro's steel was approaching the surface of the stone faster than the mark on his own. And, as the mark on John Henry's steel entered the aperture, finally becoming invisible, he poised his sledge for one more mighty stroke—to clinch the argument, as it were—to make good. The sledge descended—it struck—but dropped from his hands. He staggered and fell full length upon the rocks. He face was ashen. His lips were pale. His buddies stooped over him, fanned him and some ran for water, but he only weakly beckoned for his hammer. Some one laid it in his arms. He touched it to his lips and his kiss and his blood mingled upon the iron head.

"Lucy—Lucy—O Lucy," he whispered.

The old Captain pushed through the crowd, bent over the stricken driver, and tenderly raised his head.

"John, John," he said. "You've beat that steam contraption. You've beat the Yankee."

"We've beat him, Cap'n?"

The steel driver opened his eyes and saw the glow of victory on the contractor's wrinkled face.

"Why Cap'n, we did beat him! We beat him shor," he said and died.

Thinking About the Story

1. John Henry was a determined man; he vowed to succeed by beating the "steam-drill" to the finish line. Locate passages in the story that demonstrate this determination.

2. Name other legendary African Americans who were determined to reach their goals. Explain these goals to your classmates.

3. How would you describe the Captain's attitude toward John Henry?

Reading/Writing Connections

1. Write an essay in which you describe the mood of John Henry's friends and co-workers on the day of the race.

2. What do you think was uppermost in John Henry's mind as he drove the steel that day? Write an essay explaining what was on John Henry's mind while he was in the race.

3. John Henry was driving steel in order to make enough money to free a slave woman named Lucy. He wanted her for his wife. John Henry was a "free man." Pretend you are John Henry and write a letter to Lucy explaining to her why you have agreed to challenge the steam-drill.

"THE CRISIS for 15¢" by Phoebe Beasley. Medium: Collage. Reprinted by
permission of Isobel Neal Gallery, Chicago.

4

ON BEING
A MAN

A man who will not labor to gain his rights,
is a man who would not, if he had them,
prize and defend them.
                    —Frederick Douglass

From the moment he first stepped ashore off the first slave ship, the African American male has sought to demonstrate both his manhood and his individual identity. It was not easy then, or is it today, for an African American male to be a "man" in his country of birth. This is especially true if he is poor as well as black. Nevertheless, African American men have never given up on the ideal that, if given the opportunity, they can make a valuable contribution to the social and economic well-being of America. In their writing, African American male writers express their joy, sorrow, pain, love, and hate. Dr. Martin Luther King, Jr., expressed the essence of being a man when he said: "A man who won't die for something is not fit to live." Throughout history, men—King among them—have died for their beliefs.

The selections in this chapter are written from several different perspectives, but all focus on the male identity in the African American tradition. Hear the voices of authors Wright, Baldwin, Kelley, Gaines, Malcolm X, and Hughes as they explore what it means to be a man.

Richard Wright (1908–1960) was born near Natchez, Miss. Like most authors, he wrote from his own experience, incorporating into his work a background of poverty, family separation, prejudice, and segregation. At the age of nineteen, he went to Chicago where he worked at several menial jobs while beginning his writing career. It was in Chicago that he joined the Communist Party. He later became disenchanted with the Marxist ideology, however, and quit the party in 1944. Wright moved to Paris in 1947 and lived there until his death.

In 1938 Wright received $500 from the Federal Writers' Project for one of his short stories. In the same year he published *Uncle Tom's Children,* a collection of short stories. Publication of his first novel, *Native Son* (1940), brought Wright immediate fame. Other notable books are *Twelve Million Black Voices* (1941), the classic *Black Boy* (1945), *Savage Holiday* (1954), and *The Long Dream* (1958). Wright also published a collection of speeches entitled *White Man, Listen!* (1957) and several travel books. He received a Guggenheim Fellowship and was awarded the Spingarn Medal by the National Association for the Advancement of Colored People (NAACP) for achievement in the field of African American literature.

The Man Who Was
Almost a Man

RICHARD WRIGHT

Dave struck out across the fields, looking homeward through paling light. Whut's the usa talkin wid em niggers in the field? Anyhow, his mother was putting supper on the table. Them niggers can't understan nothing. One of these days he was going to get a gun and practice shooting, then they can't talk to him as though he were a little boy. He slowed, looking at the ground. Shucks, Ah ain scareda them even ef they are biggern me! Aw, Ah know whut Ahma do. . . . Ahm going by ol Joe's sto n git that Sears Roebuck catlog n look at them guns. Mabbe Ma will lemme buy one when she gits mah pay from ol man Hawkins. Ahma beg her t gimme some money. Ahm ol ernough to hava gun. Ahm seventeen. Almos a man. He strode, feeling his long, loose-jointed limbs. Shucks, a man oughta hava little gun aftah he done worked hard all day. . . .

He came in sight of Joe's store. A yellow lantern glowed on the front porch. He mounted steps and went through the screen door, hearing it bang behind him. There was a strong smell of coal oil and mackerel fish. He felt very confident until he saw fat Joe walk in through the rear door, then his courage began to ooze.

"Howdy, Dave! Whutcha want?"

"How yuh, Mistah Joe? Aw, Ah don wanna buy nothing. Ah just wanted t see ef yuhd lemme look at tha ol catlog erwhile."

"Sure! You wanna see it here?"

"Nawsuh. Ah wans t take it home wid me. Ahll bring it back termorrow when Ah come in from the fiels."

"You plannin on buyin something?"

Yessuh."

"Your ma letting you have your own money now?"

"Shucks. Mistah Joe, Ahm gittin t be a man like anybody else!"

Joe laughed and wiped his greasy white face with a red bandanna.

"Whut you plannin on buyin?"

Dave looked at the floor, scratched his head, scratched his thigh, and smiled. Then he looked up shyly.

"The Man Who Was Almost a Man": published in 1940 under the title "Almos' a Man."

"Ahll tell yuh, Mistah Joe, ef yuh promise yuh won't tell."

"I promise."

"Waal, Ahma buy a gun."

"A gun? Whut you want with a gun?"

"Ah wanna keep it."

"You ain't nothing but a boy. You don't need a gun."

"Aw, lemme have the catlog, Mistah Joe. Ahll bring it back."

Joe walked through the rear door. Dave was elated. He looked around at barrels of sugar and flour. He heard Joe coming back. He craned his neck to see if he were bringing the book. Yeah, he's got it! Gawddog, he's got it!

"Here, but be sure you bring it back. It's the only one I got."

"Sho, Mistah Joe."

"Say, if you wanna buy a gun, why don't you buy one from me? I gotta gun to sell."

"Will it shoot?"

"Sure it'll shoot."

"Whut kind is it?"

"Oh, it's kinda old. . . . A lefthand Wheeler. A pistol. A big one."

"Is it got bullets in it?"

"It's loaded."

"Kin Ah see it?"

"Where's your money?"

"Whut yuh wan fer it?"

"I'll let you have it for two dollars."

"Just two dollahs? Shucks, Ah could buy tha when Ah git mah pay."

"I'll have it here when you want it."

"Awright, suh. Ah be in fer it."

He went through the door, hearing it slam again behind him. Ahma git some money from Ma n buy me a gun! Only two dollahs! He tucked the thick catalogue under his arm and hurried.

"Where yuh been, boy?" His mother held a steaming dish of black-eyed peas.

"Aw, Ma, Ah just stopped down the road t talk wid th boys."

"Yuh know bettah than t keep suppah waitin."

He sat down, resting the catalogue on the edge of the table.

"Yuh git up from there and git to the well n wash yosef! Ah ain feedin no hogs in mah house!"

She grabbed his shoulder and pushed him. He stumbled out of the room, then came back to get the catalogue.

"Whut this?"

"Aw, Ma, it's jusa catlog."

"Who yuh git it from?"

"From Joe, down at the sto."

"Waal, thas good. We kin use it around the house."

"Naw, Ma." He grabbed for it. "Gimme mah catlog, Ma."

She held onto it and glared at him.

"Quit hollerin at me! Whut's wrong wid yuh? Yuh crazy?"

"But Ma, please. It ain mine! It's Joe's! He tol me t bring it back t im termorrow."

She gave up the book. He stumbled down the back steps, hugging the thick book under his arm. When he had splashed water on his face and hands, he groped back to the kitchen and fumbled in a corner for the towel. He bumped into a chair; it clattered to the floor. The catalogue sprawled at his feet. When he had dried his eyes, he snatched up the book and held it again under his arm. His mother stood watching him.

"Now, ef yuh gonna acka fool over that ol book, Ahll take it n burn it up."

"Naw, Ma, please."

"Waal, set down n be still!"

He sat down and drew the oil lamp close. He thumbed page after page, unaware of the food his mother set on the table. His father came in. Then his small brother.

"Whutcha got there, Dave?" his father asked.

"Jusa catlog," he answered, not looking up.

"Yawh, here they is!" His eyes glowed at blue and black revolvers. He glanced up, feeling sudden guilt. His father was watching him. He eased the book under the table and rested it on his knees. After the blessing was asked, he ate. He scooped up peas and swallowed fat meat without chewing. Buttermilk helped to wash it down. He did not want to mention money before his father. He would do much better by cornering his mother when she was alone. He looked at his father uneasily out of the edge of his eye.

"Boy, how come yuh don quit foolin wid tha book n eat yo suppah."

"Yessuh."

"How yuh n ol man Hawkins gittin erlong?"

"Shuh?"

"Can't yuh hear. Why don yuh listen? Ah ast yuh how wuz yuh n ol man Hawkins gittin erlong?"

"Oh, swell, Pa. Ah plows mo lan than anybody over there."

"Waal, yuh oughta keep yo min on whut yuh doin."

"Yessuh."

He poured his plate full of molasses and sopped at it slowly with a dunk of cornbread. When all but his mother had left the kitchen he still sat and looked again at the guns in the catalogue. Lawd, ef Ah only had the pretty one!

He could almost feel the slickness of the weapon with his fingers. If he had a gun like that he would polish it and keep it shining so it would never rust. N Ahd keep it loaded, by Gawd!

"Ma?"

"Hunh?"

"Ol man Hawkins give yuh mah money yit?"

"Yeah, but ain no usa yuh thinin bout thowin nona it erway. Ahm keepin tha money sos yuh kin have cloes t go to school this winter."

He rose and went to her side with the open catalogue in his palms. She was washing dishes, her head bent low over a pan. Shyly he raised the open book. When he spoke his voice was husky, faint.

"Ma, Gawd knows Ah wans one of these."

"One of whut?" she asked, not raising her eyes.

"One of these," he said again, not daring even to point. She glanced up at the page, then at him with wide eyes.

"Nigger, is yuh gone plum crazy?"

"Aw, Ma—"

"Git otta here! Don't yuh talk t me bout no gun! Yuh a fool!"

"Ma, Ah kin buy one fer two dollahs."

"Not ef Ah knows it yuh ain!"

"But yuh promised one more—"

"Ah don care whut Ah promised! Yuh ain nothing but a boy yit!"

"Ma, ef yuh lemme buy one Ahll never ast yuh fer nothing no mo."

"Ah tol yuh t git outta here! Yuh ain gonna toucha penny of tha money fer no gun! Thas how come Ah has Mistah Hawkins pay yo wages t me, cause Ah knows yuh ain got no sense."

"But Ma, we needa gun. Pa ain got no gun. We needa gun in the house. Yuh kin never tell whut might happen."

"Now don yuh try to maka fool outta me, boy! Ef we did hava gun yuh wouldn't have it!"

He laid the catalogue down and slipped his arm around her waist. "Aw, Ma, Ah done worked hard alls summer n ain ast yuh fer nothing, is Ah, now?"

"Thas whut yuh spose t do!"

"But Ma. Ah wants a gun. Yuh kin lemme have two dollah outa mah money. Please Ma. I kin give it to Pa. . . . Please, Ma! Ah loves yuh, Ma."

When she spoke her voice came soft and low.

"What yuh wan wida gun, Dave? Yuh don need no gun. Yuhll git in trouble. N ef yo Pa just thought Ah letyuh have money t buy a gun he'd hava fit."

"Ahll hide it, ma. It ain but two dollahs."

"Lawd, chil, whuts wrong wid yuh?"

"Ain nothing wrong, Ma. Ahm almos a man now. Ah wants a gun."

"Who gonna sell yuh a gun?"

"Ol Joe at the sto."

"N it don cos but two dollahs?"

"Thas all, Ma. Just two dollahs. Please, Ma."

She was stacking the plates away; her hands moved slowly, reflectively. Dave kept an anxious silence. Finally she turned to him.

"Ahll let yuh git the gun ef yuh promise me one thing."

"Whuts tha, Ma?"

"Yuh bring it straight back t me, yuh hear? It'll be fer Pa."

"Yessum! Lemme go now, Ma."

She stooped, turned slightly to one side, raised the hem of her dress, rolled down the top of her stocking, and came up with a slender wad of bills.

"Here," she said. "Lawd knows yuh don need no gun. But yer Pa does. Yuh bring it right back t me, yuh hear. Ahma put it up. Now ef yuh don, Ahma have yuh Pa lick yuh so hard yuh won ferget it."

"Yessum."

He took the money, ran down the steps, and across the yard.

"Dave! Yuuuuuuh Daaaaaave!"

He heard, but he was not going to stop now. "Naw, Lawd!"

The first movement he made the following morning was to reach under his pillow for the gun. In the gray light of dawn he held it loosely, feeling a sense of power. Could kill a man wida gun like this. Kill anybody, black or white. And if he were holding this gun in his hand nobody could run over him; they would have to respect him. It was a big gun, with a long barrel and a heavy handle. He raised and lowered it in his hand, marveling at its weight.

He had not come straight home with it as his mother had asked; instead he had stayed out in the fields, holding the weapon in his hand, aiming it now and then at some imaginary foe. But he had not fired it; he had been afraid that his father might hear. Also he was not sure he knew how to fire it.

To avoid surrendering the pistol he had not come into the house until he knew that all were asleep. When his mother had tiptoed to his bedside late that night and demanded the gun, he had first played 'possum; then he had told her that the gun was hidden outdoors, that he would bring it to her in the morning. Now he lay turning it slowly in his hands. He broke it, took out the cartridges, felt them, and then put them back.

He slid out of bed, got a long strip of old flannel from a trunk, wrapped the gun in it, and tied it to his naked thigh while it was still loaded. He did not go in to breakfast. Even though it was not yet daylight, he started for Jim Hawkins's plantation. Just as the sun was rising he reached the barns where the mules and plows were kept.

"Hey! That you, Dave?"

He turned. Jim Hawkins stood eyeing him suspiciously.

"What're yuh doing here so early?"

"Ah didn't know Ah wuz gittin up so early, Mistah Hawkins. Ah wuz fixing hitch up of Jenny n take her t the fiels."

"Good. Since you're here so early, how about plowing that stretch down by the woods?"

"Suits me, Mistah Hawkins."

"O.K. Go to it!"

He hitched Jenny to a plow and started across the fields. Hot dog! This was just what he wanted. If he could get down by the woods, he could shoot his gun and nobody would hear. He walked behind the plow, hearing the traces creaking, feeling the gun tied tight to his thigh.

When he reached the woods, he plowed two whole rows before he decided to take out the gun. Finally he stopped, looked in all directions, then untied the gun and held it in his hand. He turned to the mule and smiled.

"Know whut this is, Jenny? Naw, yuh wouldn't know! Yuhs just ol mule! Anyhow, this is a gun, n it kin shoot, by Gawd!"

He held the gun at arm's length. Whut t hell, Ahma shoot this thing! He looked at Jenny again.

"Lissen here, Jenny! When Ah pull this ol trigger Ah don wan yuh t run n acka fool now."

Jenny stood with head down, her short ears pricked straight. Dave walked off about twenty feet, held the gun far out from him, at arm's length, and turned his head. Hell, he told himself, Ah ain afraid. The gun felt loose in his fingers; he waved it wildly for a moment. Then he shut his eyes and tightened his forefinger. Bloom! The report half-deafened him and he thought his right hand was torn from his arm. He heard Jenny whinnying and galloping over the field, and he found himself on his knees squeezing his fingers hard between his legs. His hand was numb; he jammed it into his mouth, trying to warm it, trying to stop the pain. The gun lay at his feet. He did not quite know what had happened. He stood up and stared at the gun as though it were a living thing. He gritted his teeth and kicked the gun. Yuh almos broke mah arm! He turned to look for Jenny; she was far over the fields, tossing her head and kicking wildly.

"Hol on there, ol mule!"

When he caught up with her she stood trembling, walling her big white eyes at him. The plow was far away; the traces had broken. Then Dave stopped short, looking, not believing. Jenny was bleeding. Her left side was red and wet with blood. He went closer. Lawd, have mercy! Wondah did Ah shoot this mule? He grabbed for Jenny's mane. She flinched, snorted, whirled, tossing her head.

"Hol on now! Hol on."

Then he saw the hole in Jenny's side, right between the ribs. It was round, wet, red. A crimson stream streaked down the front leg, flowing fast. Good Gawd! Ah wuzn't shootin at tha mule. He felt panic. He knew he had to stop that blood, or Jenny would bleed to death. He had never seen so much blood in all his life. He chased the mule for half a mile, trying to catch her. Finally she stopped, breathing hard, stumpy tail half arched. He caught her mane and led her back to where the plow and gun lay. Then he stooped and grabbed handfuls of damp black earth and tried to plug the bullet hole. Jenny shuddered, whinnied, and broke from him.

"Hol on! Hol on now!"

He tried to plug it again, but blood came anyhow. His fingers were hot and sticky. He rubbed dirt into his palms, trying to dry them. Then again he attempted to plug the bullet hole, but Jenny shied away, kicking her heels high. He stood helpless. He had to do something. He ran at Jenny; she dodged him. He watched a red stream of blood flow down Jenny's leg and form a bright pool at her feet.

"Jenny . . . Jenny . . ." he called weakly.

His lips trembled! She's bleeding t death! He looked in the direction of home, wanting to go back, wanting to get help. But he saw the pistol lying in the damp black clay. He had a queer feeling that if he only did something, this would not be; Jenny would not be there bleeding to death.

When he went to her this time, she did not move. She stood with sleepy, dreamy eyes; and when he touched her she gave a low-pitched whinny and knelt to the ground, her front knees slopping in blood.

"Jenny . . . Jenny . . ." he whispered.

For a long time she held her neck erect; then her head sand, slowly. Her ribs swelled with a mighty heave and she went over.

Dave's stomach felt empty. He picked up the gun and held it gingerly between his thumb and forefinger. He buried it at the foot of a tree. He took a stick and tried to cover the pool of blood with dirt—but what was the use? There was Jenny lying with her mouth open and her eyes walled and glassy. He could not tell Jim Hawkins he had shot his mule. But he had to tell him something. Yeah, Ahll tell em Jenny started gittin wil n fell on the joint of the plow. . . . But that would hardly happen to a mule. He walked across the field slowly, head down.

It was sunset. Two of Jim Hawkins's men were over near the edge of the woods digging a hole in which to bury Jenny. Dave was surrounded by a knot of people; all of them were looking down at the dead mule.

"I don't see how in the world it happened," said Jim Hawkins for the tenth time.

The crowd parted and Dave's mother, father, and small brother pushed into the center.

"Where's Dave?" his mother called.

"There he is," said Jim Hawkins.

His mother grabbed him.

"Whut happened, Dave? Whut yuh done?"

"Nothing."

"C'mon, boy, talk," his father said.

Dave took a deep breath and told the story he knew nobody believed.

"Waal," he drawled. "Ah brung ol Jenny down here sos Ah could do mah plowin. Ah plowed bout two rows, just like yuh see." He stopped and pointed at the long rows of upturned earth. "Then something musta been wrong wid ol Jenny. She wouldn't ack right a-tall. She started snortin n kickin her heels. Ah tried to hol her, but she pulled erway, rearin n goin on. Then when the point of the plow was stickin up in the air, she swung erroun n twisted herself back on it. . . . She stuck herself n started t bleed. N fo Ah could do anything, she wuz dead."

"Did you ever hear of anything like that in all your life?" asked Jim Hawkins.

There were white and black standing in the crowd. They murmured. Dave's mother came close to him and looked hard into his face.

"Tell the truth, Dave," she said.

"Looks like a bullet hole ter me," said one man.

"Dave, whut yuh do wid tha gun?" his mother asked.

The crowd surged in, looking at him. He jammed his hands into his pockets, shook his head slowly from left to right, and backed away. His eyes were wide and painful.

"Did he hava gun?" asked Jim Hawkins.

"By Gawd, Ah tol yuh tha wuz a gunwound," said a man, slapping his thigh.

His father caught his shoulders and shook him till his teeth rattled.

"Tell whut happened, yuh rascal! Tell whut . . ."

Dave looked at Jenny's stiff legs and began to cry.

"Whut yuh do wid tha gun?" his mother asked.

"Come on and tell the truth," said Hawkins. "Ain't nobody going to hurt you. . . ."

His mother crowded close to him.

"Did yuh shoot tha mule, Dave?"

Dave cried, seeing blurred white and black faces.

"Ahh ddinnt gggo tt sshoooot hher. . . . Ah sssswear off Gawd Ahh ddint. . . . Ah wuz a-tryin t sssee ef the ol gggun would sshoot—"

"Where yuh git the gun from?" his father asked.

"Ah got it from Joe, at the sto."

"Where yuh git the money?"

"Ma give it t me."

"He kept worryin me, Bob. . . . Ah had t. . . . Ah tol im t bring the gun right back t me. . . . It was fer yuh, the gun."

"But how yuh happen to shoot that mule?" asked Jim Hawkins.

"Ah wuznt shootin at the mule, Mistah Hawkins. The gun jumped when Ah pulled the trigger. . . . N for Ah knowed anything Jenny wuz there a-bleedin."

Somebody in the crowd laughed. Jim Hawkins walked close to Dave and looked into his face.

"Well, looks like you have bought you a mule, Dave."

"Ah swear for Gawd, Ah didn't go t kill the mule, Mistah Hawkins!"

"But you killed her!"

All the crowd was laughing now. They stood on tiptoe and poked heads over one another's shoulders.

"Well, boy, looks like yuh done bought a dead mule! Hahaha!"

"Ain tha ershame."

"Hohohohoho."

Dave stood, head down, twisting his feet in the dirt.

"Well, you needn't worry about it, Bob," said Jim Hawkins to Dave's father. "Just let the boy keep on working and pay me two dollars a month."

"Whut yuh wan fer yo mule, Mistah Hawkins?"

Jim Hawkins screwed up his eyes.

"Fifty dollars."

"Whut yuh do wid tha gun?" Dave's father demanded.

Dave said nothing.

"Yuh wan me t take a tree lim n beat yuh till yuh talk!"

"Nawsuh!"

"Whut yuh do wid it?"

"Ah thowed it erway."

"Where?"

"Ah . . . Ah thowed it in the creek."

"Waal, c mon home. N firs thing in the mawnin git to tha creek n fin tha gun."

"Yessuh."

"Whut yuh pay fer it?"

"Two dollahs."

"Take tha gun n git yo money back n carry it t Mistah Hawkins, yuh hear? N don fergit Ahma lam you black bottom good fer this! Now march yosef on home, suh!"

Dave turned and walked slowly. He heard people laughing. Dave glared, his eyes welling with tears. Hot anger bubbled in him. Then he swallowed and stumbled on.

That night Dave did not sleep. He was glad that he had gotten out of killing the mule so easily, but he was hurt. Something hot seemed to turn over inside him each time he remembered how they had laughed. He tossed on his bed, feeling his hard pillow. N Pa says he's gonna beat me. . . . He remembered other beatings, and his back quivered. Naw, naw, Ah sho don wan im t beat me tha way no mo. . . . Dam em all! Nobody ever gave him anything. All he did was work. They treat me lika mule. . . . N then they beat me. . . . He gritted his teeth. N Ma had t tell on me.

Well, if he had to, he would take old man Hawkins that two dollars. But that meant selling the gun. And he wanted to keep that gun. Fifty dollahs fer a dead mule.

He turned over, thinking how he had fired the gun. He had an itch to fire it again. Ef other men kin shoota gun, by Gawd, Ah kin! He was still listening. Mebbe they all sleepin now. . . . The house was still. He heard the soft breathing of his brother. Yes, now! He would go down an get that gun and see if he could fire it! He eased out of bed and slipped into overalls.

The moon was bright. He ran almost all the way to the edge of the woods. He stumbled over the ground, looking for the spot where he had buried the gun. Yeah, here it is. Like a hungry dog scratching for a bone he pawed it up. He puffed his black cheeks and blew dirt from the trigger and barrel. He broke it and found four cartridges unshot. He looked around; the fields were filled with silence and moonlight. He clutched the gun stiff and hard in his fingers. But as soon as he wanted to pull the trigger, he shut his eyes and turned his head. Naw, Ah can't shoot wid mah eyes closed n mah head turned. With effort he held his eyes open; then he squeezed. Blooooom! He was stiff, not breathing. The gun was still in his hands. Dammit, he'd done it! He fired again. Bloooom! He smiled. Bloooom! Blooooom! Click, click. There! It was empty. If anybody could shoot a gun, he could. He put the gun into his hip pocket and started across the fields.

When he reached the top of a ridge he stood straight and proud in the moonlight, looking at Jim Hawkins's big white house, feeling the gun sagging in his pocket. Lawd, ef Ah had jus one mo bullet Ahd taka shot at tha house. Ahd like t scare ol man Hawkins jussa little. . . . Jussa enough t let im know Dave Sanders is a man.

To his left the road curved, running to the tracks of the Illinois Central. He jerked his head, listening. From far off came a faint hoooof-hoooof; hoooof-hoooof; hoooof-hoooof. . . . That's number eight. He took a swift look at Jim Hawkins's white house; he thought of Pa, of Ma, of his little brother, and the boys. He thought of the dead mule and heard hoooof-hoooof; hooof-hooof; hooof-hooof. . . . He stood rigid. Two dollahs a mont. Les see now. . . . Tha means itll take bout two years. Shucks! Ahll be dam! He started down the road, toward the tracks. Yeah, here she comes! He stood beside the track and held himself stiffly. Here she comes, erroun the ben. . . . C mon, yuh slow poke! C mon! He had his hand on his gun; something quivered in his stomach. Then the train thundered past, the gray and brown boxcars rumbling and clinking. He gripped the gun tightly; then he jerked his hand out of his pocket. Ah betcha Bill wouldn't do it! Ah betcha. . . . The cars slid past, steel grinding upon steel. Ahm riding yuh ternight so hep me Gawd! He was hot all over. He hesitated just a moment; then he grabbed, pulled atop of a car, and lay flat. He felt his pocket; the gun was still there. Ahead the long rails were glinting in moonlight, stretching away, away to somewhere, somewhere where he could be a man. . . .

Thinking About the Story

1. Dave thought owning a gun would make him a man. Does owning a gun make a boy a man? Why or why not?

2. How did the accidental shooting of the mule bring about a change in Dave's life?

3. Will Dave have a better chance of becoming a man after leaving home, or should he have stayed home and paid off the debt he owed for the mule's death?

Reading/Writing Connections

1. Assume you are Dave. Write a letter to your parents from your new home in Chicago. What will you tell them?

2. Imagine as a young man of seventeen, you experience humiliation from your fellow workers and possibly from your parents. Write an essay describing this humiliation. How does it make you feel? How do you react?

3. Dave frequently uses the term "Almos' a man." Assume you are his father or his mother and write a letter to him in which you give advice about how to be a man.

James Baldwin   (1924–1987) was born in New York City. He was an avid reader as a child and began writing while a student at Public School 24 in Harlem, where Countee Cullen, African American poet, was his teacher. His stepfather was a minister of a Harlem church, and Baldwin himself later became a minister. Some critics feel Baldwin always retained a preaching style in his writing.

During World War II, Baldwin moved to New Jersey where he worked in war-related industries. In 1948, he moved to Paris where he completed his first novel, *Go Tell It on the Mountain* (1953). For the rest of his life he divided his time between the United States and France. His short stories and essays have appeared in *Harper's, Esquire, Atlantic Monthly,* and *The Reporter* as well as in many other publications in the United States and abroad. Baldwin's other works include *Notes of a Native Son* (1955), *Giovanni's Room* (1956), *Nobody Knows My Name* (1961), *Another Country* (1962), *Going to Meet the Man* (1965), *Tell Me How Long the Train's Been Gone* (1968), *If Beale Street Could Talk* (1974), and *Just Above My Head* (1979). His plays, *Blues for Mr. Charlie* (1964) and *Amen Corner* (1965), were successfully produced. His book of essays, *The Fire Next Time* (1963), received critical acclaim, and many critics believe him to be one of the outstanding essayists America has ever produced.

Sonny's Blues

JAMES BALDWIN

I read about it in the paper, in the subway, on my way to work. I read it, and I couldn't believe it, and I read it again. Then perhaps I just stared at it, at the newsprint spelling out his name, spelling out the story. I started at it in the swinging lights of the subway car, and in the faces and bodies of the people, and in my own face, trapped in the darkness which roared outside.

It was not to be believed and I kept telling myself that, as I walked from the subway station to the high school. And at the same time I couldn't doubt it. I was scared, scared for Sonny. He became real to me again. A great block of ice got settled in my belly and kept melting there slowly all day long, while I taught my classes algebra. It was a special kind of ice. It kept melting, sending trickles of ice water all up and down my veins, but it never got less. Sometimes it hardened and seemed to expand until I felt my guts were going to come spilling out or that I was going to choke or scream. This would always be at a moment when I was remembering some specific thing Sonny had once said or done.

When he was about as old as the boys in my classes his face had been bright and open, there was a lot of copper in it; and he'd had wonderfully direct brown eyes, and great gentleness and privacy. I wondered what he looked like now. He had been picked up, the evening before, in a raid on an apartment downtown, for peddling and using heroin.

I couldn't believe it: but what I mean by that is that I couldn't find any room for it anywhere inside me. I had kept it outside me for a long time. I hadn't wanted to know. I had had suspicions, but I didn't name them, I kept putting them away. I told myself that Sonny was wild, but he wasn't crazy. And he'd always been a good boy, he hadn't ever turned hard or evil or disrespectful, the way kids can, so quick, so quick, especially in Harlem. I didn't want to believe that I'd ever see my brother going down, coming to nothing, all that light in his face gone out, in the condition I'd already seen so many others. Yet it had happened and here I was, talking about algebra to a lot of boys who might, every one of them for all I knew, be popping off needles every time they went to the head. Maybe it did more for them than algebra could.

I was sure that the first time Sonny had ever had horse, he couldn't have been much older than these boys were now. These boys, how, were living as we'd been living then, they were growing up with a rush and their heads bumped abruptly against the low ceiling of their actual possibilities. They were filled with rage. All they really knew were two darknesses, the darkness of their lives, which was now closing in on them, and the darkness of the movies, which had blinded them to that other darkness, and in which they now, vindictively, dreamed, at once more together than they were at any other time, and more alone.

When the last bell rang, the last class ended, I let out my breath. It seemed I'd been holding it for all that time. My clothes were wet—I may have looked as though I'd been sitting in a steam bath, all dressed up, all afternoon. I sat alone in the classroom a long time. I listened to the boys outside, downstairs, shouting and cursing and laughing. Their laughter struck me for perhaps the first time. It was not the joyous laughter which—God knows why—one associates with children. It was mocking and insular, its intent was to denigrate. It was disenchanted, and in this, also, lay the authority of their curses. Perhaps I was listening to them because I was thinking about my brother and in them I heard my brother. And myself.

One boy was whistling a tune, at once very complicated and very simple, it seemed to be pouring out of him as though he were a bird, and it sounded very cool and moving through all that harsh, bright air, only just holding its own through all those other sounds.

I stood up and walked over to the window and looked down into the courtyard. It was the beginning of the spring and the sap was rising in the boys. A teacher passed through them every now and again, quickly, as though he or she couldn't wait to get out of the courtyard, to get those boys out of their sight and off their minds. I started collecting my stuff. I thought I'd better get home and talk to Isabel.

The courtyard was almost deserted by the time I got downstairs. I saw this boy standing in the shadow of a doorway, looking just like Sonny. I almost called his name. Then I saw that it wasn't Sonny, but somebody we used to know, a boy from around our block. He'd been Sonny's friend. He'd never been mine, having been too young for me, and, anyway, I'd never liked him. And now, even though he was a grown-up man, he still hung around that block, still spent hours on the street corners, was always high and raggy. I used to run into him from time to time and he'd often work around to asking me for a quarter or fifty cents. He always had some real good excuse, too, and I always gave it to him, I don't know why.

But now, abruptly, I hated him. I couldn't stand the way he looked at me, partly like a dog, partly like a cunning child. I wanted to ask him what the hell he was doing in the school courtyard.

He sort of shuffled over to me, and he said, ''I see you got the papers. So you already know about it.''

"You mean about Sonny? Yes, I already know about it. How come they didn't get you?"

He grinned. It made him repulsive and it also brought to mind what he'd looked like as a kid. "I wasn't there. I stay away from them people."

"Good for you." I offered him a cigarette and I watched him through the smoke. "You come all the way down here just to tell me about Sonny?"

"That's right." He was sort of shaking his head and his eyes looked strange, as though they were about to cross. The bright sun deadened his damp dark brown skin and it made his eyes look yellow and showed up the dirt in his kinked hair. He smelled funky. I moved a little away from him and I said, "Well, thanks. But I already know about it and I got to get home."

"I'll walk you a little ways," he said. We started walking. There were a couple of kids still loitering in the courtyard and one of them said goodnight to me and looked strangely at the boy beside me.

"What're you going to do?" he asked me. "I mean, about Sonny?"

"Look. I haven't seen Sonny for over a year, I'm not sure I'm going to do anything. Anyway, what the hell *can* I do?"

"That's right," he said quickly, "ain't nothing you can do. Can't much help old Sonny no more, I guess."

It was what I was thinking and so it seemed to me he had no right to say it.

"I'm surprised at Sonny, though," he went on—he had a funny way of talking, he looked straight ahead as though he were talking to himself—"I thought Sonny was a smart boy, I thought he was too smart to get hung."

"I guess he thought so too," I said sharply, "and that's how he got hung. And now about you? You're pretty goddamn smart, I bet."

Then he looked directly at me, just for a minute. "I ain't smart," he said. "If I was smart, I'd have reached for a pistol a long time ago."

"Look. Don't tell *me* your sad story, if it was up to me, I'd give you one." Then I felt guilty—guilty, probably, for never having supposed that the poor bastard *had* a story of his own, much less a sad one, and I asked, quickly. "What's going to happen to him now?"

He didn't answer this. He was off by himself some place. "Funny thing," he said, and from his tone we might have been discussing the quickest way to get to Brooklyn, "when I saw the papers this morning, the first thing I asked myself was if I had anything to do with it. I felt sort of responsible."

I began to listen more carefully. The subway station was on the corner, just before us, and I stopped. He stopped, too. We were in front of a bar and he ducked slightly, peering in, but whoever he was looking for didn't seem to be there. The juke box was blasting away with something black and bouncy and I half watched the barmaid as she danced her way from the juke box to her place behind the bar. And I watched her face as she laughingly responded to something someone said to her, still keeping time to the music. When she smiled one saw the little girl, one sensed the doomed, still-struggled woman beneath the battered face of the semi-whore.

"I never *give* Sonny nothing," the boy said finally, "but a long time ago I come to school high and Sonny asked me how it felt." He paused, I couldn't bear to watch him, I watched the barmaid, and I listened to the music which seemed to be causing the pavement to shake. "I told him it felt great." The music stopped, the barmaid paused and watched the juke box until the music began again. "It did."

All this was carrying me some place I didn't want to go. I certainly didn't want to know how it felt. It filled everything, the people, the houses, the music, the dark, quicksilver barmaid, with menace; and this menace was their reality.

"What's going to happen to him now?" I asked again.

"They'll send him away some place and they'll try to cure him." He shook his head. "Maybe he'll even think he's kicked the habit. Then they'll let him loose"—he gestured, throwing his cigarette into the gutter. "That's all."

"What do you mean, that's *all*?"

But I knew what he meant.

"I *mean*, that's *all*." He turned his head and looked at me, pulling down the corners of his mouth. "Don't you know what I mean?" he asked, softly.

"How the hell *would* I know what you mean?" I almost whispered it, I don't know why.

"That's right," he said to the air, "how would *he* know what I mean?" He turned toward me again, patient and calm, and yet I somehow felt him shaking, shaking as though he were going to fall apart. I felt that ice in my guts again, the dread I'd felt all afternoon; and again I watched the barmaid, moving about the bar, washing glasses, and singing. "Listen. They'll let him out and then it'll just start all over again. That's what I mean."

"You mean—they'll let him out. And then he'll just start working his way back in again. You mean he'll never kick the habit. Is that what you mean?"

"That's right," he said, cheerfully. "*You* see what I mean."

"Tell me," I said it last, "why does he want to die? He must want to die, he's killing himself, why does he want to die?"

He looked at me in surprise. He licked his lips. "He don't want to die. He wants to live. Don't nobody want to die, ever."

Then I wanted to ask him—too many things. He could not have answered, or if he had, I could not have borne the answers. I started walking. "Well, I guess it's none of my business."

"It's going to be rough on old Sonny," he said. We reached the subway station. "This is your station?" he asked. I nodded. I took one step down.

"Damn!" he said, suddenly. I looked up at him. He grinned again. "Damn it if I didn't leave all my money home. You ain't got a dollar on you, have you? Just for a couple of days, is all."

All at once something inside gave and threatened to come pouring out of me. I didn't hate him any more. I felt that in another moment I'd start crying like a child.

"Sure," I said. "Don't sweat." I looked in my wallet and didn't have a dollar, I only had a five. "Here," I said. "That hold you?"

He didn't look at it—he didn't want to look at it. A terrible, closed look came over his face, as though he were keeping the number on the bill a secret from him and me. "Thanks," he said, and now he was dying to see me go. "Don't worry about Sonny. Maybe I'll write him or something."

"Sure," I said. "You do that. So long."

"Be seeing you," he said. I went on down the steps.

And I didn't write Sonny or send him anything for a long time. When I finally did, it was just after my little girl died, he wrote me back a letter which made me feel like a bastard.

Here's what he said:

> Dear brother,
>
> You don't know how much I needed to hear from you. I wanted to write you many a time but I dug how much I must have hurt you and so I didn't write. But now I feel like a man who's been trying to climb up out of some deep, real deep and funky hole and just saw the sun up there, outside. I got to get outside.
>
> I can't tell you much about how I got here. I mean I don't know how to tell you. I guess I was afraid of something or I was trying to escape from something and you know I have never been very strong in the head (smile). I'm glad Mama and Daddy are dead and can't see what's happened to their son and I swear if I'd known what I was doing I would never have hurt you so, you and a lot of other fine people who were nice to me and who believed in me.
>
> I don't want you to think it had anything to do with me being a musician. It's more than that. Or maybe less than that. I can't get anything straight in my head down here and I try not to think about what's going to happen to me when I get outside again. Sometime I think I'm going to flip and *never* get outside and sometime I think I'll come straight back. I tell you one thing, though, I'd rather blow my brains out than go through this again. But that's what they all say, so they tell me. If I tell you when I'm coming to New York and if you could meet me, I sure would appreciate it. Give my love to Isabel and the kids and I was sure sorry to hear about little Gracie.

I wish I could be like Mama and say the Lord's will be done, but I don't
know it seems to me that trouble is the one thing that never does get stopped
and I don't know what good it does to blame it on the Lord. But maybe it
does some good if you believe it.

Your brother,

Sonny

Then I kept in constant touch with him and I sent him whatever I could
and I went to meet him when he came back to New York. When I saw him
many things I thought I had forgotten came flooding back to me. This was
because I had begun, finally, to wonder about Sonny, about the life that Sonny
lived inside. This life, whatever it was, had made him older and thinner and
it had deepened the distant stillness in which he had always moved. He looked
very unlike my baby brother. Yet, when he smiled, when we shook hands, the
baby brother I'd never known looked out from the depths of his private life,
like an animal waiting to be coaxed into the light.

"How you been keeping?" he asked me.

"All right. And you?"

"Just fine." He was smiling all over his face. "It's good to see you
again."

"It's good to see you."

The seven years' difference in our ages lay between us like a chasm: I
wondered if these years would ever operate between us as a bridge. I was
remembering, and it made it hard to catch my breath, that I had been there
when he was born; and I had heard the first words he had ever spoken. When
he started to walk, he walked from our mother straight to me. I caught him
just before he fell when he took the first steps he ever took in this world.

"How's Isabel?"

"Just fine. She's dying to see you."

"And the boys?"

"They're fine, too. They're anxious to see their uncle."

"Oh, come on. You know they don't remember me."

"Are you kidding? Of course they remember you."

He grinned again. We got into a taxi. We had a lot to say to each other,
far too much to know how to begin.

As the taxi began to move, I asked, "You still want to go to India?"

He laughed. "You still remember that. Hell, no. This place is Indian
enough for me."

"It used to belong to them," I said.

And he laughed again. "They damn sure knew what they were doing
when they got rid of it."

Years ago, when he was around fourteen, he'd been all hipped on the idea of going to India. He read books about people sitting on rocks, naked, in all kinds of weather, but mostly bad, naturally, and walking barefoot through hot coals and arriving at wisdom. I used to say that it sounded to me as though they were getting away from wisdom as fast as they could. I think he sort of looked down on me for that.

"Do you mind," he asked, "if we have the driver drive alongside the park? On the west side—I haven't seen the city in so long."

"Of course not," I said. I was afraid that I might sound as though I were humoring him, but I hoped he wouldn't take it that way.

So we drove along, between the green of the park and the stony, lifeless elegance of hotels and apartment buildings, toward the vivid, killing streets of our childhood. These streets hadn't changed, though housing projects jutted up out of them now like rocks in the middle of a boiling sea. Most of the houses in which we had grown up had vanished, as had the stores from which we had stolen, the basements in which we had first tried sex, the rooftops from which we had hurled tin cans and bricks. But houses exactly like the houses of our past yet dominated the landscape, boys exactly like the boys we once had been found themselves smothering in these houses, came down into the streets for light and air and found themselves encircled by disaster. Some escaped the trap, most didn't. Those who got out always left something of themselves behind, as some animals amputate a leg and leave it in the trap. It might be said, perhaps, that I had escaped, after all, I was a school teacher; or that Sonny had, he hadn't lived in Harlem for years. Yet, as the cab moved uptown through streets which seemed, with a rush, to darken with dark people, and as I covertly studied Sonny's face, it came to me that what we both were seeking through our separate cab windows was that part of ourselves which had been left behind. It's always at the hour of trouble and confrontation that the missing member aches.

We hit 110th Street and started rolling up Lenox Avenue. And I'd known this avenue all my life, but it seemed to me again, as it had seemed on the day I'd first heard about Sonny's trouble, filled with a hidden menace which was its very breath of life.

"We almost there," said Sonny.

"Almost." We were both too nervous to say anything more.

We live in a housing project. It hasn't been up long. A few days after it was up it seemed uninhabitably new, now, of course, it's already rundown. It looks like a parody of the good, clean, faceless life—God knows the people who live in it do their best to make it a parody. The best-looking grass lying around isn't enough to make their lives green, the hedges will never hold out the streets, and they know it. The big windows fool no one, they aren't big enough to make space out of no space. They don't bother with the windows, they watch the TV screen instead. The playground is most popular with the children who don't play at jacks, or skip rope, or roller skate, or swing, and they can be found in it after dark. We moved in partly because it's not too far from where I teach, and partly for the kids; but it's really just like the houses in which Sonny and I grew up. The same things happen, they'll have the same things to remember. The moment Sonny and I started into the house I had the feeling that I was simply bringing him back into the danger he had almost died trying to escape.

Sonny has never been talkative. So I don't know why I was sure he'd be dying to talk to me when supper was over the first night. Everything went fine, the oldest boy remembered him, and the youngest boy liked him, and Sonny had remembered to bring something for each of them; and Isabel, who is really much nicer than I am, more open and giving, had gone to a lot of trouble about dinner and was genuinely glad to see him. And she's always been able to tease Sonny in a way that I haven't. It was nice to see her face so vivid again and to hear her laugh and watch her make Sonny laugh. She wasn't, or, anyway, she didn't seem to be, at all uneasy or embarrassed. She chatted as though there were no subject which had to be avoided and she got Sonny past his first, faint stiffness. And thank God she was there, for I was filled with that icy dread again. Everything I did seemed awkward to me, and everything I said sounded freighted with hidden meaning. I was trying to remember everything I'd heard about dope addiction and I couldn't help watching Sonny for signs. I wasn't doing it out of malice. I was trying to find out something about my brother. I was dying to hear him tell me he was safe.

"Safe!" my father grunted, whenever Mama suggested trying to move to a neighborhood which might be safer for children. "Safe, hell! Ain't no place safe for kids, nor nobody."

He always went on like this, but he wasn't, ever, really as bad as he sounded, not even on weekends, when he got drunk. As a matter of fact, he was always on the lookout for "something a little better," but he died before he found it. He died suddenly, during a drunken weekend in the middle of the war, when Sonny was fifteen. He and Sonny hadn't ever got on too well. And this was partly because Sonny was the apple of his father's eye. It was because he loved Sonny so much and was frightened for him, that he was always fighting with him. It doesn't do any good to fight with Sonny. Sonny just moves back, inside himself, where he can't be reached. But the principal reason that they never hit it off is that they were so much alike. Daddy was big and rough and loud-talking, just the opposite of Sonny, but they both had—that same privacy.

Mama tried to tell me something about this, just after Daddy died. I was home on leave from the army.

This was the last time I ever saw my mother alive. Just the same, this picture gets all mixed up in my mind with pictures I had of her when she was younger. The way I always see her is the way she used to be on a Sunday afternoon, say, when the old folks were talking after the big Sunday dinner. I always see her wearing pale blue. She'd be sitting on the sofa. And my father would be sitting in the easy chair, not far from her. And the living room would be full of church folks and relatives. There they sit, in chairs all around the living room, and the night is creeping up outside, but nobody knows it yet. You can see the darkness growing against the windowpanes and you hear the street noises every now and again, or maybe the jangling beat of a tambourine from one of the churches close by, but it's real quiet in the room. For a moment nobody's talking, but every face looks darkening, like the sky outside. And my mother rocks a little from the waist, and my father's eyes are closed. Everyone is looking at something a child can't see. For a minute they've forgotten the children. Maybe a kid is lying on the rug, half asleep. Maybe somebody's got a kid in his lap and is absent-mindedly stroking the kid's head. Maybe there's a kid, quiet and big-eyed, curled up in a big chair in the corner. The silence, the darkness coming, and the darkness in the faces frightens the child obscurely. He hopes that the hand which strokes his forehead will never stop—will never die. He hopes that there will never come a time when the old folks won't be sitting around the living room, talking about where they've come from, and what they've seen, and what's happened to them and their kinfolk.

But something deep and watchful in the child knows that this is bound to end, is already ending. In a moment someone will get up and turn on the light. Then the old folks will remember the children and they won't talk any more that day. And when light fills the room, the child is filled with darkness. He knows that every time this happens he's moved just a little closer to that darkness outside. The darkness outside is what the old folks have been talking about. It's what they've come from. It's what they endure. The child knows that they won't talk any more because if he knows too much about what's happened to *them,* he'll know too much too soon, about what's going to happen to *him.*

The last time I talked to my mother, I remember I was restless. I wanted to get out and see Isabel. We weren't married then and we had a lot to straighten out between us.

There Mama sat, in black, by the window. She was humming an old church song, *Lord, you brought me from a long ways off.* Sonny was out somewhere. Mama kept watching the streets.

"I don't know," she said, "if I'll ever see you again, after you go off from here. But I hope you'll remember the things I tried to teach you."

"Don't talk like that," I said, and smiled. "You'll be here a long time yet."

She smiled, too, but she said nothing. She was quiet for a long time. And I said, "Mama, don't you worry about nothing. I'll be writing all the time, and you be getting the checks. . . ."

"I want to talk to you about your brother," she said, suddenly. "If anything happens to me he ain't going to have nobody to look out for him."

"Mama," I said, "ain't nothing going to happen to you *or* Sonny. Sonny's all right. He's a good boy and he's got good sense."

"It ain't a question of his being a good boy," Mama said, "nor of his having good sense. It ain't only the bad ones, nor yet the dumb ones that gets sucked under." She stopped, looking at me. "Your Daddy once had a brother," she said, and she smiled in a way that made me feel she was in pain. "You didn't never know that, did you?"

"No," I said, "I never knew that," and I watched her face.

"Oh, yes," she said, "your Daddy had a brother." She looked out of the window again. "I know you never saw your Daddy cry. But *I* did—many a time, through all these years."

I asked her, "What happened to his brother? How come nobody's ever talked about him?"

This was the first time I ever saw my mother look old.

"His brother got killed," she said, "when he was just a little younger than you are now. I knew him. He was a fine boy. He was maybe a little full of the devil, but he didn't mean nobody no harm."

Then she stopped and the room was silent, exactly as it had sometimes been on those Sunday afternoons. Mama kept looking out into the streets.

"He used to have a job in the mill," she said, "and, like all young folks, he just liked to perform on Saturday nights. Saturday nights, him and your father would drift around to different place, go to dances and things like that, or just sit around with people they knew, and your father's brother would sing, he had a fine voice, and play along with himself on his guitar. Well, this particular Saturday night, him and your father was coming home from some place, and they were both a little drunk and there was a moon that night, it was bright like day. Your father's brother was feeling kind of good, and he was whistling to himself, and he had his guitar slung over his shoulder. They was coming down a hill and beneath them was a road that turned off from the highway. Well, your father's brother, being always kind of frisky, decided to run down this hill, and he did, with that guitar banging and clanging behind him, and he ran across the road, and he was making water behind a tree. And your father was sort of amused at him and he was still coming down the hill, kind of slow. Then he heard a car motor and that same minute his brother stepped from behind the tree, into the road, in the moonlight. And he started to cross the road. And your father started to run down the hill, he says he don't know why. This car was full of white men. They was all drunk, and when they seen your father's brother they let out a great whoop and holler and they aimed the car straight at him. They was having fun, they just wanted to scare him, the way they do sometimes, you know. But they was drunk. And I guess the boy, being drunk, too, and scared, kind of lost his head. By the time he jumped it was too late. Your father says he heard his brother scream when the car rolled over him, and he heard the wood of that guitar when it give, and he heard them strings go flying, and he heard them white men shouting, and the car kept on a-going and it ain't stopped till this day. And, time your father got down the hill, his brother weren't nothing but blood and pulp."

Tears were gleaming on my mother's face. There wasn't anything I could say.

"He never mentioned it," she said, "because I never let him mention it before you children. Your Daddy was like a crazy man that night and for many a night thereafter. He says he never in his life seen anything as dark as that road after the lights of that car had gone away. Weren't nothing, weren't nobody on that road, just your Daddy and his brother and that busted guitar. Oh, yes. Your Daddy never did really get right again. Till the day he died he weren't sure but that every white man he saw was the man that killed his brother."

She stopped and took out her handkerchief and dried her eyes and looked at me.

"I ain't telling you all this," she said, "to make you scared or bitter or to make you hate nobody. I'm telling you this because you got a brother. And the world ain't changed."

I guess I didn't want to believe this. I guess she saw this in my face. She turned away from me, toward the window again, searching those streets.

"But I praise my Redeemer," she said at last, "that He called your Daddy home before me. I ain't saying it to throw no flowers at myself, but, I declare, it keeps me from feeling too cast down to know I helped your father get safely through this world. Your father always acted like he was the roughest, strongest man on earth. And everybody took him to be like that. But if he hadn't had *me* there—to see his tears!"

She was crying again. Still, I couldn't move. I said, "Lord, Lord, Mama, I didn't know it was like that."

"Oh, honey," she said, "there's a lot that you don't know. But you are going to find it out." She stood up from the window and came over to me. "You got to hold on to your brother," she said, "and don't let him fall, no matter what it looks like is happening to him and no matter how evil you gets with him. You going to be evil with him many a time. But don't you forget what I told you, you hear?''

"I won't forget," I said. "Don't you worry, I won't forget. I won't let nothing happen to Sonny."

My mother smiled as though she were amused at something she saw in my face. Then, "You may not be able to stop nothing from happening. But you got to let him know you's *there.*"

Two days later I was married, and then I was gone. And I had a lot of things on my mind and I pretty well forgot my promise to Mama until I got shipped home on a special furlough for her funeral.

And, after the funeral, with just Sonny and me alone in the empty kitchen, I tried to find out something about him.

"What do you want to do?" I asked him.

"I'm going to be a musician," he said.

For he had graduated, in the time I had been away, from dancing to the juke box to finding out who was playing what, and what they were doing with it, and he had bought himself a set of drums.

"You mean, you want to be a drummer?" I somehow had the feeling that being a drummer might be all right for other people but not for my brother Sonny.

"I don't think," he said, looking at me very gravely, "that I'll ever be a good drummer. But I think I can play a piano."

I frowned. I'd never played the role of the older brother quite so seriously before, had scarcely ever, in fact, *asked* Sonny a damn thing. I sensed myself in the presence of something I didn't really know how to handle, didn't understand. So I made my frown a little deeper as I asked: "What kind of musician do you want to be?"

He grinned. "How many kinds do you think there are?"

"Be *serious,*" I said.

He laughed, throwing his head back, and then looked at me. "I *am* serious."

"Well, then, for Christ's sake, stop kidding around and answer a serious question. I mean, do you want to be a concert pianist, you want to play classical music and all that, or—or what?" Long before I finished he was laughing again. "For Christ's *sake,* Sonny!"

He sobered, but with difficulty. "I'm sorry. But you sound so—*scared!*" and he was off again.

"Well, you may think it's funny now, baby, but it's not going to be so funny when you have to make your living at it, let me tell you *that.*" I was furious because I knew he was laughing at me and I didn't know why.

"No," he said, very sober now, and afraid, perhaps, that he'd hurt me, "I don't want to be a classical pianist. That isn't what interests me. I mean"—he paused, looking hard at me, as though his eyes would help me to understand, and then gestured helplessly, as though perhaps his hand would help—"I mean, I'll have a lot of studying to do, and I'll have to study *everything,* but, I mean, I want to play *with*—jazz musicians." He stopped. "I want to play jazz," he said.

Well, the word had never before sounded as heavy, as real, as it sounded that afternoon in Sonny's mouth. I just looked at him and I was probably frowning a real frown by this time. I simply couldn't see why on earth he'd want to spend his time hanging around nightclubs, clowning around on band-stands, while people pushed each other around a dance floor. It seemed—beneath him, somehow. I had never thought about it before, had never been forced to, but I suppose I had always put jazz musicians in a class with what Daddy called "good-time people."

"Are you *serious*?"

"Hell, *yes,* I'm serious."

He looked more helpless than ever, and annoyed, and deeply hurt.

I suggested, helpfully: "You mean—like Louis Armstrong?"

His face closed as though I'd struck him. "No. I'm not talking about none of that old-time, down home crap."

"Well, look, Sonny, I'm sorry, don't get mad. I just don't altogether get it, that's all. Name somebody—you know, a jazz musician you admire."

"Bird."

"Who?"

"Bird! Charlie Parker! Don't they teach you nothing in the goddamn army?"

I lit a cigarette. I was surprised and then a little amused to discover that I was trembling. "I've been out of touch," I said. "You'll have to be patient with me. Now. Who's this Parker character?"

"He's just one of the greatest jazz musicians alive," said Sonny, sullenly, his hands in his pockets, his back to me. "Maybe *the* greatest," he added, bitterly, "that's probably why *you* never heard of him."

"All right," I said, "I'm ignorant. I'm sorry. I'll go out and buy all the cat's records right away, all right?"

"It don't," said Sonny, with dignity, "make any difference to me. I don't care what you listen to. Don't do me no favors."

I was beginning to realize that I'd never seen him so upset before. With another part of my mind I was thinking that this would probably turn out to be one of those things kids go through and that I shouldn't make it seem important by pushing it too hard. Still, I didn't think it would do any harm to ask: "Doesn't all this take a lot of time? Can you make a living at it?"

He turned back to me and half leaned, half sat, on the kitchen table. "Everything takes time," he said, "and—well, yes, sure. I can make a living at it. But what I don't seem to be able to make you understand is that it's the only thing I want to do—"

"Well, Sonny," I said, gently, "you know people can't always do exactly what they *want* to do:"

"*No,* I don't know that," said Sonny, surprising me. "I think people *ought* to do what they want to do, what else are they alive for?"

"You getting to be a big boy," I said desperately, "it's time you started thinking about your future."

"I'm thinking about my future," said Sonny, grimly. "I think about it all the time."

I gave up. I decided, if he didn't change his mind, that we could always talk about it later. "In the meantime," I said, "you got to finish school." We had already decided that he'd have to move in with Isabel and her folks. I knew this wasn't the ideal arrangement because Isabel's folks are inclined to be dicey and they hadn't especially wanted Isabel to marry me. But I didn't know what else to do. "And we have to get you fixed up at Isabel's."

There was a long silence. He moved from the kitchen table to the window. "That's a terrible idea. You know it yourself."

"Do you have a *better* idea?"

He just walked up and down the kitchen for a minute. He was as tall as I was. He had started to shave. I suddenly had the feeling that I didn't know him at all.

He stopped at the kitchen table and picked up my cigarettes. Looking at me with a kind of mocking, amused defiance, he put one between his lips. "You mind?"

"You smoking already?"

He lit the cigarette and nodded, watching me through the smoke. "I just wanted to see if I'd have the courage to smoke in front of you." He grinned and blew a great cloud of smoke to the ceiling. "It was easy." He looked at my face. "Come on, now, I bet you was smoking at my age, tell the truth."

I didn't say anything but the truth was on my face, and he laughed. But now there was something very strained in his laugh. "Sure. And I bet that ain't all you was doing."

He was frightening me a little. "Cut the crap," I said. "We already decided that you was going to go and live at Isabel's. Now what's got into you all of a sudden?"

"You decided it," he pointed out. "I didn't decide nothing." He stopped in front of me, leaning against the stove, arms loosely folded. "Look, brother. I don't want to stay in Harlem no more, I really don't." He was very earnest.

He looked at me, then over toward the kitchen window. There was something in his eyes I'd never seen before, some thoughtfulness, some worry all his own. He rubbed the muscle of one arm. "It's time I was getting out of here."

"Where do you want to *go*, Sonny?"

"I want to join the army. Or the navy, I don't care. If I say I'm old enough, they'll believe me."

Then I got mad. It was because I was so scared. "You must be crazy. You goddamn fool, what the hell do you want to go and join the *army* for?"

"I just told you. To get out of Harlem."

"Sonny, you haven't even finished *school*. And if you really want to be a musician, how do you expect to study if you're in the *army?*"

He looked at me, trapped, and in anguish. "There's ways. I might be able to work out some kind of deal. Anyway, I'll have the G.I. Bill when I come out."

"*If* you come out." We stared at each other. "Sonny, please. Be reasonable. I know the setup is far from perfect. But we got to do the best we can."

"I ain't learning nothing in school," he said. "Even when I go." He turned away from me and opened the window and threw his cigarette out into the narrow alley. I watched his back. "At least, I ain't learning nothing you'd want me to learn." He slammed the window so hard I thought the glass would fly out, and turned back to me. "And I'm sick of the stink of these garbage cans!"

"Sonny," I said, "I know how you feel. But if you don't finish school now, you're going to be sorry later that you didn't." I grabbed him by the shoulders. "And you only got another year. It ain't so bad. And I'll come back and I swear I'll help you do *whatever* you want to do. Just try to put up with it till I come back. Will you please do that? For me?"

He didn't answer and he wouldn't look at me.

"Sonny. You hear me?"

He pulled away. "I hear you. But you never hear anything *I* say."

I didn't know what to say to that. He looked out of the window and then back at me. "OK," he said, and sighed. "I'll try."

Then I said, trying to cheer him up a little, "They got a piano at Isabel's. You can practice on it."

And as a matter of fact, it did cheer him up for a minute. "That's right," he said to himself. "I forgot that." His face relaxed a little. But the worry, the thoughtfulness, played on it still, the way shadows play on a face which is staring into the fire.

But I thought I'd never hear the end of that piano. At first, Isabel would write me, saying how nice it was that Sonny was so serious about his music and how, as soon as he came in from school, or wherever he had been when he was supposed to be at school, he went straight to that piano and stayed there until suppertime. And, after supper, he went back to that piano and stayed there until everybody went to bed. He was at the piano all day Saturday and all day Sunday. Then he bought a record player and started playing records. He'd play one record over and over again, all day long sometimes, and he'd improvise along with it on the piano. Or he'd play one section of the record, one chord, one change, one progression, then he'd do it on the piano. Then back to the record. Then back to the piano.

Well, I really don't know how they stood it. Isabel finally confessed that it wasn't like living with a person at all, it was like living with sound. And the sound didn't make any sense to her, didn't make any sense to any of them—naturally. They began, in a way, to be afflicted by this presence that was living in their home. It was as though Sonny were some sort of god, or monster. He moved in an atmosphere which wasn't like theirs at all. They fed him and he ate, he washed himself, he walked in and out of their door; he certainly wasn't nasty or unpleasant or rude, Sonny isn't any of those things; but it was as though he were all wrapped up in some cloud, some fire, some vision all his own; and there wasn't any way to reach him.

At the same time, he wasn't really a man yet, he was still a child, and they had to watch out for him in all kinds of ways. They certainly couldn't throw him out. Neither did they dare to make a great scene about that piano because even they dimly sensed, as I sensed, from so many thousands of miles away, that Sonny was at that piano playing for his life.

But he hadn't been going to school. One day a letter came from the school board and Isabel's mother got it—there had, apparently, been other letters but Sonny had torn them up. This day, when Sonny came in, Isabel's mother showed him the letter and asked where he'd been spending his time. And she finally got it out of him that he'd been down in Greenwich Village, with musicians and other characters, in a white girl's apartment. And this scared her and she started to scream at him and what came up, once she began—though she denies it to this day—was what sacrifices they were making to give Sonny a decent home and how little he appreciated it.

Sonny didn't play the piano that day. By evening, Isabel's mother had calmed down but then there was the old man to deal with, and Isabel herself. Isabel says she did her best to be calm but she broke down and started crying. She says she just watched Sonny's face. She could tell, by watching him, what was happening with him. And what was happening was that they penetrated his cloud, they had reached him. Even if their fingers had been a thousand times more gentle than human fingers ever are, he could hardly help feeling that they had stripped him naked and were spitting on that nakedness. For he also had to see that his presence, that music, which was life or death to him, had been torture for them and that they had endured it, not at all for his sake, but only for mine. And Sonny couldn't take that. He can take it a little better today than he could then but he's still not very good at it and, frankly, I don't know anybody who is.

The silence of the next few days must have been louder than the sound of all the music ever played since time began. One morning, before she went to work, Isabel was in his room for something and she suddenly realized that all of his records were gone. And she knew for certain that he was gone. And he was. He went as far as the navy would carry him. He finally sent me a postcard from some place in Greece and that was the first I knew that Sonny was still alive. I didn't see him any more until we were both back in New York and the war had long been over.

He was a man by then, of course, but I wasn't willing to see it. He came by the house from time to time, but we fought almost every time we met. I didn't like the way he carried himself, loose and dreamlike all the time, and I didn't like his friends, and his music seemed to be merely an excuse for the life he led. It sounded just that weird and disordered.

Then we had a fight, a pretty awful fight, and I didn't see him for months. By and by I looked him up, where he was living, in a furnished room in the Village, and I tried to make it up. But there were lots of other people in the room and Sonny just lay on his bed, and he wouldn't come downstairs with me, and he treated these other people as though they were his family and I weren't. So I got mad and then he got mad, and then I told him that he might just as well be dead as live the way he was living. Then he stood up and he told me not to worry about him any more in life, that he *was* dead as far as I was concerned. Then he pushed me to the door and the other people looked on as though nothing were happening, and he slammed the door behind me. I stood in the hallway, staring at the door. I heard somebody laugh in the room and then the tears came to my eyes. I started down the steps, whistling to keep from crying, I kept whistling to myself, *You going to need me, baby, one of these cold, rainy days.*

I read about Sonny's trouble in the spring. Little Grace died in the fall. She was a beautiful little girl. But she only lived a little over two years. She died of polio and she suffered. She had a slight fever for a couple of days, but it didn't seem like anything and we just kept her in bed. And we would certainly have called the doctor, but the fever dropped, she seemed to be all right. So we thought it had just been a cold. Then, one day, she was up, playing, Isabel was in the kitchen fixing lunch for the two boys when they'd come in from school, and she heard Grace fall down in the living room. When you have a lot of children you don't always start running when one of them falls, unless they start screaming or something. And, this time, Grace was quiet. Yet, Isabel says that when she heard that *thump* and then that silence, something happened in her to make her afraid. And she ran to the living room and there was little Grace on the floor, all twisted up, and the reason she hadn't screamed was that she couldn't get her breath. And when she did scream, it was the worst sound, Isabel says, that she'd ever heard in all her life, and she still hears it sometimes in her dreams. Isabel will sometimes wake me up with a low moaning, strangled sound and I have to be quick to awaken her and hold her to me and where Isabel is weeping against me seems a mortal wound.

I think I may have written Sonny the very day that little Grace was buried. I was sitting in the living room in the dark, by myself, and I suddenly thought of Sonny. My trouble made his real.

One Saturday afternoon, when Sonny had been living with us, or, anyway, been in our house, for nearly two weeks, I found myself wandering aimlessly about the living room, drinking from a can of beer, and trying to work up the courage to search Sonny's room. He was out, he was usually out whenever I was home, and Isabel had taken the children to see their grandparents. Suddenly I was standing still in front of the living room window, watching Seventh Avenue. The idea of searching Sonny's room made me still. I scarcely dared to admit to myself what I'd be searching for. I didn't know what I'd do if I found it. Or if I didn't.

On the sidewalk across from me, near the entrance to a barbecue joint, some people were holding an old-fashioned revival meeting. The barbecue cook, wearing a dirty white apron, his conked hair reddish and metallic in the pale sun, and a cigarette between his lips, stood in the doorway, watching them. Kids and older people paused in their errands and stood there, along with some older men and a couple of very tough-looking women who watched everything that happened on the avenue, as though they owned it, or were maybe owned by it. Well, they were watching this, too. The revival was being carried on by three sisters in black, and a brother. All they had were their voices and their Bibles and a tambourine. The brother was testifying and while he testified two of the sisters stood together, seeming to say, amen, and the third sister walked around with the tambourine outstretched and a couple of people dropped coins into it. Then the brother's testimony ended and the sister who had been taking up the collection dumped the coins into her palm and transferred them to the pocket of her long black robe. Then she raised both hands, striking the tambourine against the air, and then against one hand, and she started to sing. And the two other sisters and the brother joined in.

It was strange, suddenly, to watch, though I had been seeing these street meetings all my life. So, of course, had everybody else down there. Yet, they paused and watched and listened and I stood still at the window. "*Tis the old ship of Zion,*" they sang, and the sister with the tambourine kept a steady, jangling beat, "*it has rescued many a thousand!*" Not a soul under the sound of their voices was hearing this song for the first time, not one of them had been rescued. Nor had they seen much in the way of rescue work being done around them. Neither did they especially believe in the holiness of the three sisters and the brother, they knew too much about them, knew where they lived, and how. The woman with the tambourine, whose voice dominated the air, whose face was bright with joy, was divided by very little from the woman who stood watching her, a cigarette between her heavy, chapped lips, her hair a cuckoo's nest, her face scarred and swollen from many beatings, and her black eyes glittering like coal. Perhaps they both knew this, which was why, when, as rarely, they addressed each other, they addressed each other as Sister. As the singing filled the air the watching, listening faces underwent a change, the eyes focusing on something within; the music seemed to soothe a poison out of them; and time seemed, nearly, to fall away from the sullen, belligerent, battered faces, as though they were fleeing back to their first condition, while dreaming of their last. The barbecue cook half shook his head and smiled, and dropped his cigarette and disappeared into his joint. A man fumbled in his pockets for change and stood holding it in his hand impatiently, as though he had just remembered a pressing appointment further up the avenue. He looked furious. Then I saw Sonny, standing on the edge of the crowd. He was carrying a wide, flat notebook with a green cover, and it made him look, from where I was standing, almost like a schoolboy. The coppery sun brought out the copper in his skin, he was very faintly smiling, standing very still. Then the singing stopped, the tambourine turned into a collection plate again. The furious man dropped in his coins and vanished, so did a couple of the women, and Sonny dropped some change in the plate, looking directly at the woman with a little smile. He started across the avenue, toward the house. He has a slow, loping walk, something like the way Harlem hipsters walk, only he's imposed on this his own half-beat. I had never really noticed it before.

I stayed at the window, both relieved and apprehensive. As Sonny disappeared from my sight, they began singing again. And they were still singing when his key turned in the lock.

"Hey," he said.

"Hey, yourself. You want some beer?"

"No. Well, maybe." But he came up to the window and stood beside me, looking out. "What a warm voice," he said.

They were singing *If I could only hear my mother pray again!*

"Yes," I said, "and she can sure beat that tambourine."

"But what a terrible song," he said, and laughed. He dropped his notebook on the sofa and disappeared into the kitchen. "Where's Isabel and the kids?"

"I think they went to see their grandparents. You hungry?"

"No." He came back into the living room with his can of beer. "You want to come some place with me tonight?"

I sensed, I don't know how, that I couldn't possibly say no. "Sure. Where?"

He sat down on the sofa and picked up his notebook and started leafing through it. "I'm going to sit in with some fellows in a joint in the Village."

"You mean, you're going to play, tonight?"

"That's right." He took a swallow of his beer and moved back to the window. He gave me a sidelong look. "If you can stand it."

"I'll try," I said.

He smiled to himself and we both watched as the meeting across the way broke up. The three sisters and the brother, heads bowed, were singing *God be with you till we meet again.* The faces around them were very quiet. Then the song ended. The small crowd dispersed. We watched the three women and the lone man walk slowly up the avenue.

"When she was singing before," said Sonny, abruptly, "her voice reminded me for a minute of what heroin feels like sometimes—when it's in your veins. It makes you feel sort of warm and cool at the same time. And distant. And—and sure." He sipped his beer, very deliberately not looking at me. I watched his face. "It makes you feel—in control. Sometimes you've got to have that feeling."

"Do you?" I sat down slowly in the easy chair.

"Sometimes." He went to the sofa and picked up his notebook again. "Some people do."

"In order," I asked, "to play?" And my voice was very ugly, full of contempt and anger.

"Well"—he looked at me with great, troubled eyes, as though, in fact, he hoped his eyes would tell me things he could never otherwise say—"they *think* so. And *if* they think so—!"

"And what do *you* think?" I asked.

He sat on the sofa and put his can of beer on the floor. "I don't know," he said, and I couldn't be sure if he were answering my question or pursuing his thoughts. His face didn't tell me. "It's not so much to *play.* It's to *stand* it, to be able to make it at all. On any level." He frowned and smiled: "In order to keep from shaking to pieces."

"But these friends of yours," I said, "they seem to shake themselves to pieces pretty goddamn fast."

"Maybe." He played with the notebook. And something told me that I should curb my tongue, that Sonny was doing his best to talk, that I should listen. "But of course you only know the ones that've gone to pieces. Some

don't—or at least they haven't *yet* and that's just about all *any* of us can say."
He paused. "And then there are some who just live, really, in hell, and they
know it and they see what's happening and they go right on. I don't know."
He sighed, dropped the notebook, folded his arms. "Some guys, you can tell
from the way they play, they on something *all* the time. And you can see that,
well, it makes something real for them. But of course," he picked up his beer
from the floor and sipped it and put the can down again, "they *want* to, too,
you've got to see that. Even some of them that say they don't—*some,* not all."

"And what about you?" I asked—I couldn't help it. "What about you?
Do *you* want to?"

He stood up and walked to the window and remained silent for a long
time. Then he sighed. "Me," he said. Then: "While I was downstairs before,
on my way here, listening to that woman sing, it struck me all of a sudden how
much suffering she must have had to go through—to sing like that. It's *repulsive*
to think you have to suffer that much."

I said: "But there's no way not to suffer—is there, Sonny?"

"I believe not," he said and smiled, "but that's never stopped anyone
from trying." He looked at me. "Has it?" I realized, with this mocking look,
that there stood between us, forever, beyond the power of time or forgiveness,
the fact that I had held silence—so long!—when he had needed human speech
to help him. He turned back to the window. "No, there's no way not to suffer.
But you try all kinds of ways to keep from drowning in it, to keep on top of
it, and to make it seem—well, like *you.* Like you did something, all right, and
now you're suffering for it. You know?" I said nothing. "Well you know,"
he said, impatiently, "why *do* people suffer? Maybe it's better to do something
to give it a reason, *any* reason."

"But we just agreed," I said, "that there's no way not to suffer. Isn't it
better, then, just to—take it?"

"But nobody just takes it," Sonny cried, "that's what I'm tellin you!
Everybody tries not to. You're just hung up on the *way* some people try—it's
not *your* way!"

The hair on my face began to itch, my face felt wet. "That's not true,"
I said, "that's not true. I don't give a damn what other people do, I don't even
care how they suffer. I just care how *you* suffer." And he looked at me.
"Please believe me," I said, "I don't want to see you—die—trying not to
suffer."

"I won't," he said, flatly, "die trying not to suffer. At least, not any
faster than anybody else."

"But there's no need," I said, trying to laugh, "is there? in killing
yourself."

I wanted to say more, but I couldn't. I wanted to talk about will power and how life could be—well, beautiful. I wanted to say that it was all within; but was it? or, rather, wasn't that exactly the trouble? And I wanted to promise that I would never fail him again. But it would all have sounded—empty words and lies.

So I made the promise to myself and prayed that I would keep it.

"It's terrible sometimes, inside," he said, "that's what's the trouble. You walk these streets, black and funky and cold, and there's not really a living ass to talk to, and there's nothing shaking, and there's no way of getting it out—that storm inside. You can't talk it and you can't make love with it, and when you finally try to get with it and play it, you realize *nobody's* listening. So *you've* got to listen. You got to find a way to listen."

And then he walked away from the window and sat on the sofa again, as though all the wind had suddenly been knocked out of him. "Sometimes you'll do *anything* to play, even cut your mother's throat." He laughed and looked at me. "Or your brother's." Then he sobered. "Or your own." Then: "Don't worry. I'm all right now and I think I'll *be* all right. But I can't forget—where I've been. I don't mean just the physical place I've been, I mean where *I've* been. And *what* I've been."

"What have you been, Sonny?" I asked.

He smiled—but sat sideways on the sofa, his elbow resting on the back, his fingers playing with his mouth and chin, not looking at me. "I've been something I didn't recognize, didn't know I could be. Didn't know anybody could be." He stopped, looking inward, looking helplessly young, looking old. "I'm not talking about it now because I feel *guilty* or anything like that— maybe it would be better if I did, I don't know. Anyway, I can't really talk about it. Not to you, not to anybody," and now he turned and faced me. "Sometimes, you know, and it was actually when I was most *out* of the world, I felt that I was in it, that I was *with* it, really, and I could play or I didn't really have to *play,* it just came out of me, it was there. And I don't know how I played, thinking about it now, but I know I did awful things, those times, sometimes, to people. Or it wasn't that I *did* anything to them—it was that they weren't real." He picked up the beer can; it was empty; he rolled it between his palms: "And other times—well, I needed a fix, I needed to find a place to lean, I needed to clear a space to *listen*—and I couldn't find it, and I—went crazy, I did terrible things to *me,* I was terrible *for* me." He began pressing the beer can between his hands, I watched the metal begin to give. It glittered, as he played with it, like a knife, and I was afraid he would cut himself, but I said nothing. "Oh well, I can never tell you. I was all by myself at the bottom of something, stinking and sweating and crying and shaking, and I smelled it, you know? *my* stink, and I thought I'd die if I couldn't get away from it and yet, all the same, I knew that everything I was doing was just locking me in with it. And I didn't know," he paused, still flattening the beer can, "I didn't know, I still *don't* know, something kept telling me that maybe it was good to smell your own stink, but I didn't think that *that* was what I'd been trying to do—and—who can stand it?" and he abruptly dropped the ruined beer can, looking at me with a small, still smile, and then rose, walking to the window as though it were the lodestone rock. I watched his face, he watched the avenue. "I couldn't tell you when Mama died—but the reason I wanted to leave Harlem so bad was to get away from drugs. And then, when I ran away, that's what I was running from—really. When I came back, nothing had changed, *I* hadn't changed, I was just—older." And he stopped, drumming with his fingers on the windowpane. The sun had vanished, soon darkness would fall. I watched his face. "It can come again," he said, almost as though speaking to himself. Then he turned to me. "It can come again," he repeated. "I just want you to know that."

"All right," I said at last. "So it can come again. All right."

He smiled, but the smile was sorrowful. "I had to try to tell you" he said.

"Yes," I said. "I understand that."

"You're my brother," he said, looking straight at me, and not smiling at all.

"Yes," I repeated, "yes. I understand that."

He turned back to the window, looking out. "All that hatred down there," he said, "all that hatred and misery and love. It's a wonder it doesn't blow the avenue apart."

We went to the only nightclub on a short, dark street, downtown. We squeezed through the narrow, chattering, jampacked bar to the entrance of the big room, where the bandstand was. And we stood there for a moment, for the lights were very dim in this room and we couldn't see. Then, "Hello, boy," said a voice and an enormous black man, much older than Sonny or myself erupted out of all that atmospheric lighting and put an arm around Sonny's shoulder. "I been sitting right here," he said, "waiting for you."

He had a big voice, too, and heads in the darkness turned toward us.

Sonny grinned and pulled a little away, and said, "Creole, this is my brother. I told you about him."

Creole shook my hand. "I'm glad to meet you, son," he said, and it was clear that he was glad to meet me *there*, for Sonny's sake. And he smiled, "You got a real musician in *your* family," and he took his arm from Sonny's shoulder and slapped him, lightly, affectionately, with the back of his hand.

"Well. Now I've heard it all," said a voice behind us. This was another musician, and a friend of Sonny's, a coal-black, cheerful-looking man, built close to the ground. He immediately began confiding to me, at the top of his lungs, the most terrible things about Sonny, his teeth gleaming like a lighthouse and his laugh coming up out of him like the beginning of an earthquake. And it turned out that everyone at the bar knew Sonny, or almost everyone; some were musicians, working there, or nearby, or not working, some were simply hangers-on, and some were there to hear Sonny play. I was introduced to all of them and they were all very polite to me. Yet, it was clear that, for them, I was only Sonny's brother. Here, I was in Sonny's world. Or, rather: his kingdom. Here, it was not even a question that his veins bore royal blood.

They were going to play soon and Creole installed me, by myself, at a table in a dark corner. Then I watched them, Creole, and the little black man, and Sonny, and the others, while they horsed around, standing just below the bandstand. The light from the bandstand spilled just a little short of them and, watching them laughing and gesturing and moving about, I had the feeling that they, nevertheless, were being most careful not to step into that circle of light too suddenly: that if they moved into the light too suddenly, without thinking, they would perish in flame. Then, while I watched, one of them, the small, black man, moved into the light and crossed the bandstand and started fooling around with his drums. Then—being funny and being, also, extremely ceremonious—Creole took Sonny by the arm and led him to the piano. A woman's voice called Sonny's name and a few hands started clapping. And Sonny, also being funny and being ceremonious, and so touched, I think, that he could have cried, but neither hiding it nor showing it, riding it like a man, grinned, and put both hands to his heart and bowed from the waist.

Creole then went to the bass fiddle and a lean, very bright-skinned brown man jumped up on the bandstand and picked up his horn. So there they were, and the atmosphere on the bandstand and in the room began to change and tighten. Someone stepped up to the microphone and announced them. Then there were all kinds of murmurs. Some people at the bar shushed others. The waitress ran around, frantically getting in the last orders, guys and chicks got closer to each other, and the lights on the bandstand, on the quartet, turned to a kind of indigo. Then they all looked different there. Creole looked about him for the last time, as though he were making certain that all his chickens were in the coop, and then he—jumped and struck the fiddle. And there they were.

All I know about music is that not many people ever really hear it. And even then, on the rare occasions when something opens within, and the music enters, what we mainly hear, or hear corroborated, are personal, private, vanishing evocations. But the man who creates the music is hearing something else, is dealing with the roar rising from the void and imposing order on it as it hits the air. What is evoked in him, then, is of another order, more terrible because it has no words, and triumphant, too, for that same reason. And his triumph, when he triumphs, is ours. I just watched Sonny's face. His face was troubled, he was working hard, but he wasn't with it. And I had the feeling that, in a way, everyone on the bandstand was waiting for him, both waiting for him and pushing him along. But as I began to watch Creole, I realized that it was Creole who held them all back. He had them on a short rein. Up there, keeping the beat with his whole body, wailing on the fiddle, with his eyes half closed, he was listening to everything, but he was listening to Sonny. He was having a dialogue with Sonny. He wanted Sonny to leave the shoreline and strike out for the deep water. He was Sonny's witness that deep water and drowning were not the same thing—he had been there, and he knew. And he wanted Sonny to know. He was waiting for Sonny to do the things on the keys which would let Creole know that Sonny was in the water.

And, while Creole listened, Sonny moved, deep within, exactly like someone in torment. I had never before thought of how awful the relationship must be between the musician and his instrument. He has to fill it, this instrument, with the breath of life, his own. He has to make it do what he wants it to do. And a piano is just a piano. It's made out of so much wood and wires and little hammers and big ones, and ivory. While there's only so much you can do with it, the only way to find this out is to try; to try and make it do everything.

And Sonny hadn't been near a piano for over a year. And he wasn't on much better terms with his life, not the life that stretched before him now. He and the piano stammered, started one way, got scared, stopped; started another way, panicked, marked time, started again; then seemed to have found a direction, panicked again, got stuck. And the face I saw on Sonny I'd never seen before. Everything had been burned out of it, and, at the same time, things usually hidden were being burned in, by the fire and fury of the battle which was occurring in him up there.

Yet, watching Creole's face as they neared the end of the first set, I had the feeling that something had happened, something I hadn't heard. Then they finished, there was scattered applause, and then, without an instant's warning, Creole started into something else, it was almost sardonic, it was *Am I Blue*. And, as though he commanded, Sonny began to play. Something began to happen. And Creole let out the reins. The dry, low, black man said something awful on the drums, Creole answered, and the drums talked back. Then the horn insisted, sweet and high, slightly detached perhaps, and Creole listened, commenting now and then, dry, and driving, beautiful and calm and old. Then they all came together again, and Sonny was part of the family again. I could tell this from his face. He seemed to have found, right there beneath his fingers, a damn brand-new piano. It seemed that he couldn't get over it. Then, for awhile, just being happy with Sonny, they seemed to be agreeing with him that brand-new pianos certainly were a gas.

Then Creole stepped forward to remind them that what they were playing was the blues. He hit something in all of them, he hit something in me, myself, and the music tightened and deepened, apprehension began to beat the air. Creole began to tell us what the blues were all about. They were not about anything very new. He and his boys up there were keeping it new, at the risk of ruin, destruction, madness, and death, in order to find new ways to make us listen. For, while the tale of how we suffer, and how we are delighted, and how we may triumph is never new, it always must be heard. There isn't any other tale to tell, it's the only light we've got in all this darkness.

And this tale, according to that face, that body, those strong hands on those strings, has another aspect in every country, and a new depth in every generation. Listen, Creole seemed to be saying, listen. Now these are Sonny's blues. He made the little black man on the drums know it, and the bright, brown man of the horn. Creole wasn't trying any longer to get Sonny in the water. He was wishing him Godspeed. Then he stepped back, very slowly, filling the air with the immense suggestion that Sonny speak for himself.

Then they all gathered around Sonny and Sonny played. Every now and again one of them seemed to say, amen. Sonny's fingers filled the air with life, his life. But that life contained so many others. And Sonny went all the way back, he really began with the spare, flat statement of the opening phrase of the song. Then he began to make it his. It was very beautiful because it wasn't hurried and it was no longer a lament. I seemed to hear with what burning he had made it his, with what burning we had yet to make it ours, how we could cease lamenting. Freedom lurked around us and I understood, at last, that he could help us to be free if we would listen, that he would never be free until we did. Yet, there was no battle in his face now. I heard what he had gone through, and would continue to go through until he came to rest in earth. He had made it his: that long line, of which we knew only Mama and Daddy. And he was giving it back, as everything must be given back, so that, passing through death, it can live forever. I saw my mother's face again, and felt, for the first time, how the stones of the road she had walked on must have bruised her feet. I saw the moonlit road where my father's brother died. And it brought something else back to me, and carried me past it, I saw my little girl again and felt Isabel's tears again, and I felt my own tears begin to rise. And I was yet aware that this was only a moment, that the world waited outside, as hungry as a tiger, and that trouble stretched above us, longer than the sky.

Then it was over. Creole and Sonny let out their breath, both soaking wet, and grinning. There was a lot of applause and some of it was real. In the dark, the girl came by and I asked her to take drinks to the bandstand. There was a long pause, while they talked up there in the indigo light and after awhile I saw the girl put a Scotch and milk on top of the piano for Sonny. He didn't seem to notice it, but just before they started playing again, he sipped from it and looked toward me, and nodded. Then he put it back on top of the piano. For me, then, as they began to play again, it glowed and shook above my brother's head like the very cup of trembling.

Thinking About the Story

1. What is the relationship between Sonny and his brother?

2. Sonny maintains that there is no one to talk to when one wishes to let go of the "storm inside." Do you agree or disagree with this statement? Support your belief with examples from the story or from your personal experience.

3. What do you think Sonny's attitude is about the use of drugs?

Reading/Writing Connections

1. Baldwin writes that there is nothing very new about the **blues,** which are expressed through suffering, delight, and triumph. He also writes, ". . . there isn't any other tale to tell, it's the only light we've got in all this darkness." In your journal, describe the blues and the darkness in this story. You may want to research the tradition of the blues as a form of expression in African American music.

2. Write an essay in which you describe those things that are unique in Sonny's life as he plays the blues.

3. Sonny apparently wanted to escape the horrors of the drug culture in his community. Write a poem or a song describing his feelings about his condition.

William Melvin Kelley   (b. 1937) was born in New York City,

where he attended a private preparatory school before entering Harvard University. Kelley has received awards from the John Hay Whitney and the Rosenthal Foundations of the National Institute of Arts and Letters for his first novel, *A Different Drummer* (1962), in which the author explores how this exodus of blacks affects both whites and blacks who still live in the Southern community. Kelley's fiction is characterized by his use of stylistic variety. His thematic probing into race relations and the African American experience recurs throughout his writings. He has taught at the New School for Social Research and the State University of New York at Geneseo, and has lived in Europe and in the West Indies.

Kelley is the author of *Dancers on the Shore* (1964), a collection of sixteen short stories, and *A Drop of Patience* (1965), a novel that presents a portrait of a blind musician. The story begins when the protagonist is six years old and continues into adulthood, showing his search for identity through his music, his love affair with a white girl, her rejection of him, and his subsequent madness. Kelley portrays the blind experience through the senses of touching and hearing. His novel *dem* (1967) is a satire on white family life in relation to black people.

The Only Man on Liberty Street

WILLIAM MELVIN KELLEY

She was squatting in the front yard, digging with an old brass spoon in the dirt which was an ocean to the islands of short yellow grass. She wore a red and white checkered dress, which hung loosely from her shoulders, and obscured her legs. It was early spring and she was barefoot. Her toes stuck from under the skirt. She could not see the man yet, riding down Liberty Street, his shoulders square, the duster he wore spread back over the horse's rump, a carpetbag tied with a leather strap to his saddle horn and knocking against his leg. She could not see him until he had dismounted and tied his horse to a small, black, iron Negro jockey and unstrapped the bag. She watched now as he opened the wooden gate, came into the yard, and stood, looking down at her, his face stern, almost gray beneath the brim of his wide hat.

She knew him. Her mother called him Mister Herder and had told Jennie that he was Jennie's father. He was one of the men who came riding down Liberty Street in their fine black suits and starched shirts and large, dark ties. Each of these men had a house to go to, into which, in the evening usually, he would disappear. Only women and children lived on Liberty Street. All of them were Negroes. Some of the women were quite dark, but most were coffee-color. They were all very beautiful. Her mother was light. She was tall, had black eyes, and black hair so long she could sit on it.

The man standing over her was the one who came to her house once or twice a week. He was never there in the morning when Jennie got up. He was tall, and thin, and blond. He had a short beard that looked as coarse as the grass beneath her feet. His eyes were blue, like Jennie's. He did not speak English very well. Jennie's mother had told her he came from across the sea and Jennie often wondered if he went there between visits to their house.

"Jennie? Your mother tells me that you ask why I do not stay at night. Is so?"

She looked up at him. "Yes, Mister Herder." The hair under his jaw was darker than the hair on his cheeks.

He nodded. "I stay now. Go bring your mother."

She left the spoon in the dirt, and ran into the house, down the long hall, dark now because she had been sitting in the sun. She found her mother standing

121

over the stove, a great black lid in her left hand, a wooden spoon in her right. There were beads of sweat on her forehead. She wore a full black skirt and a white blouse. Her one waist-length braid hung straight between her shoulder blades. She turned to Jennie's running steps.

"Mama? That man? My father? He in the yard. He brung a carpetbag."

First her mother smiled, then frowned, then looked puzzled. "A carpetbag, darling?"

"Yes, Mama."

She followed her mother through the house, pausing with her at the hall mirror where the woman ran her hand up the back of her neck to smooth stray black hair. Then they went onto the porch, where the man was now seated, surveying the tiny yard and the dark green hedge that enclosed it. The carpetbag rested beside his chair.

Her mother stood with her hands beneath her apron, staring at the bag. "Mister Herder?"

He turned to them. "I will not go back this time. No matter what. Why should I live in that house when I must come here to know what home is?" He nodded sharply as if in answer to a question. "So! I stay. I give her that house. I will send her money, but I stay here."

Her mother stood silently for an instant, then turned to the door. "Dinner'll be on the table in a half hour." She opened the screen door. The spring whined and cracked. "Oh." She let go the door, and picked up the carpetbag. "I'll take this on up." She went inside. As she passed, Jennie could see she was smiling again.

After that, Jennie's mother became a celebrity on Liberty Street. The other women would stop her to ask about the man. "And he staying for good, Josie?"

"Yes."

"You have any trouble yet?"

"Not yet."

"Well, child, you make him put that there house in your name. You don't want to be no Sissie Markham. That white woman come down the same day he died and moved Sissie and her children right into the gutter. You get that house put in your name. You hear?"

"Yes."

"How is it? It different?"

Her mother would look dazed. "Yes, it different. He told me to call him Maynard."

The other women were always very surprised.

At first, Jennie too was surprised. The man was always there in the morning and sometimes even woke her up. Her mother no longer called him

Mister Herder, and at odd times, though still quite seldom, said, No. She had never before heard her mother say No to anything the man ever said. It was not long before Jennie was convinced that he actually was her father. She began to call him Papa.

Daily now a white woman had been driving by their house. Jennie did not know who she was or what she wanted, but playing in the yard, would see the white woman's gray buggy turn the corner and come slowly down the block, pulled by a speckled horse that trudged in the dry dust. A Negro driver sat erect in his black uniform, a whip in his fist. The white woman would peer at the house as if looking for an address or something special. She would look at the curtained windows, looking for someone, and sometimes even at Jennie. The look was not kind or tender, but hard and angry as if she knew something bad about the child.

Then one day the buggy stopped, the Negro pulling gently on the reins. The white woman leaned forward, spoke to the driver and handed him a small pink envelope. He jumped down, opened the gate, and without looking at Jennie, his face dark and shining, advanced on the porch, up the three steps, which knocked hollow beneath his boots, opened the screen door and twisted the polished brass bell key in the center of the open, winter door.

Her mother came drying her hands. The Negro reached out the envelope and her mother took it, looking beyond him for an instant at the buggy and the white woman who returned her look coldly. As the Negro turned, her mother opened the letter, and read it, moving her lips slightly. Then Jennie could see the twinkling at the corners of her eyes. Her mother stood framed in the black square of doorway, tall, fair, the black hair swept to hide her ears, her eyes glistening.

Jennie turned back to the white woman now and saw her lean deeper into her seat. Then she pulled forward. "Do you understand what I will have them do?" She was shouting shrilly and spoke like Jennie's father. "You tell him he has got one wife! You are something different!" She leaned back again, waved her gloved hand and the buggy lurched down the street, gained speed, and jangled out of sight around the corner.

Jennie was on her feet and pounding up the stairs. "Mama?"

"Go play, Jennie. Go on now, *play*!" Still her mother stared straight ahead, as if the buggy and the white woman remained in front of the house. She still held the letter as if to read it. The corners of her eyes were wet. Then she turned and went into the house. The screen door clacked behind her.

At nights now Jennie waited by the gate in the yard for her father to turn the corner, walking. In the beginning she had been waiting too for the one day he would not turn the corner. But each night he came, that day seemed less likely to come. Even so, she was always surprised to see him. When she did, she would wave, timidly, raising her hand only to her shoulder, wiggling only her fingers, as if to wave too wildly would somehow cause the entire picture of his advancing to collapse as only a slight wind would be enough to disarrange a design of feathers.

That night too she waved and saw him raise his hand high over his head, greeting her. She backed away when he reached the gate so he might open it, her head thrown way back, looking up at him.

"Well, my Jennie, what kind of day did you have?"

She only smiled, then remembered the white woman. "A woman come to visit Mama. She come in a buggy and give her a letter too. She made Mama cry."

His smile fled. He sucked his tongue, angry now. "We go see what is wrong. Come." He reached for her hand.

Her mother was in the kitchen. She looked as if she did not really care what she was doing or how, walking from pump to stove, stove to cupboard in a deep trance. The pink envelope was on the table.

She turned to them. Her eyes were red. Several strands of hair stuck to her temples. She cleared her nose and pointed to the letter. "She come today."

Her father let go Jennie's hand, picked up the letter and read it. When he was finished he took it to the stove and dropped it into the flame. There was a puff of smoke before he replaced the lid. He shook his head. "She cannot make me go back, Josephine."

Her mother fell heavily into a wooden chair, beginning to cry again. "But she's white, Maynard."

He raised his eyebrows like a priest or a displeased school teacher. "Your skin is whiter."

"My mother was a slave."

He threw up his hands, making fists. "Your mother did not ask to be a slave!" Then he went to her, crouched on his haunches before her, speaking quietly. "No one can make me go back."

"But she can get them to do what she say." She turned her gaze on Jennie, but looked away quickly. "You wasn't here after the war. But I seen things. I seen things happen to field niggers that . . . I was up in the house; they didn't bother me. My own father, General Dewey Willson, he stood on a platform in the center of town and promised to keep the niggers down. I was close by." She took his face in her hands. "Maynard, maybe you better go back, leastways—"

"I go back—dead! You hear! Dead. These children, these cowardly children in their masks will not move me! I go back dead. That is all. We do not discuss it." And he was gone. Jennie heard him thundering down the hall, knocking against the table near the stairs, going up to the second floor.

Her mother was looking at her now, her eyes even more red than before, her lips trembling, her hands active in her lap. "Jennie?"

"Yes, Mama." She took a step toward her, staring into the woman's eyes.

"Jennie, I want you to promise me something and not forget it."

"Yes, Mama." She was between her mother's knees, felt the woman's hands clutching her shoulders.

"Jennie, you'll be right pretty when you get grown. Did you know that? Promise me you'll go up North. Promise me if I'm not here when you get eighteen, you'll go north and get married. You understand?"

Jennie was not sure she did. She could not picture the North, except that she had heard once it was cold and white things fell from the sky. She could not picture being eighteen and her mother not being there. But she knew her mother wanted her to understand and she lied. "Yes, Mama."

"Repeat what I just said."

She did. Her mother kissed her mouth, the first time ever.

From the kitchen below came their voices. Her father's voice sound hard, cut short; Jennie knew he had made a decision and was sticking to it. Her mother was pleading, trying to change his mind. It was July the Fourth, the day of the shooting match.

She dressed in her Sunday clothes and coming downstairs, heard her mother: "Maynard, please don't take her." She was frantic now. "I'm begging you. Don't take that child with you today."

"I take her. We do not discuss it. I take her. Those sneaking cowards in their masks . . ." Jennie knew now what they were talking about. Her father had promised to take her to the shooting match. For some reason, her mother feared there would be trouble if Jennie went downtown. She did not know why her mother felt that way, except it might have something to do with the white woman, who continued to ride by their house each morning, after her father had left for the day. Perhaps her mother did not want to be alone in the house when the white woman drove by in her gray buggy, even though she had not stopped the buggy since the day two months ago, when the Negro had given her mother the pink envelope.

But other strange things had happened after that. In the beginning she and her mother, as always before, had gone downtown to the market, to stop amid the bright stalls brimming with green and yellow vegetables and brick-red meats, tended by dark, country Negroes in shabby clothes and large straw hats. It would get very quiet when they passed, and Jennie would see the Negroes look away, fear in their eyes, and knots of white men watching, sometimes giggling. But the white women in fine clothes were the most frightening; sitting on the verandas or passing in carriages, some even coming to their windows, they would stare angrily as if her mother had done something terrible to each one personally, as if all these white women could be the one who drove by each morning. Her mother would walk through it all, her back straight, very like her father's, the bun into which she wove her waist-length braid on market days, gleaming dark.

In the beginning they had gone to the suddenly quiet market. But now her mother hardly set foot from the house, and the food was brought to them in a carton by a crippled Negro boy, who was coming just as Jennie and her father left the house that morning.

Balancing the carton on his left arm, he removed his ragged hat and smiled. "Morning, Mister Herder. Good luck at the shooting match, sir." His left leg was short and he seemed to tilt.

Her father nodded. "Thank you, Felix. I do my best."

"Then you a sure thing, Mister Herder." He replaced his hat and went on around the house.

Walking, her hand in her father's, Jennie could see some of the women of Liberty Street peering out at them through their curtains.

Downtown was not the same. Flags and banners draped the verandas; people wore their best clothes. The Square had been roped off, a platform set up to one side, and New Marsails Avenue, which ran into the Square, had been cleared for two blocks. Far away down the Avenue stood a row of cotton bales onto which had been pinned oilcloth targets. From where they stood, the bull's-eyes looked no bigger than red jawbreakers.

Many men slapped her father on the back, and furtively, looked at her with a kind of clinical interest. But mostly they ignored her. The celebrity of the day was her father, and unlike her mother, he was very popular. Everyone felt sure he would win the match; he was the best shot in the state.

After everyone shot, the judge came running down from the targets, waving his arms. "Maynard Herder. Six shots, and you can cover them all with a good gob of spit!" He grabbed her father's elbow and pulled him toward the platform, where an old man with white hair and beard, wearing a gray uniform trimmed with yellow, waited. She followed them to the platform steps, but was afraid to go any farther because now some women had begun to look at her as they had at her mother.

The old man made a short speech, his voice deep, but coarse, grainy-sounding, and gave her father a silver medal in a blue velvet box. Her father turned and smiled at her. She started up the steps toward him, but just then the old man put his hand on her father's shoulder.

People had begun to walk away down the streets leading out of the Square. There was less noise now but she could not hear the first words the old man said to her father.

Her father's face tightened into the same look she had seen the day the letter came, the same as this morning in the kitchen. She went halfway up the stairs, stopped.

The old man went on: "You know I'm no meddler. Everybody knows about Liberty Street. I had a woman down there myself . . . before the war."

"I know that." The words came out of her father's face, though his lips did not move.

The old man nodded. "But Maynard, what you're doing is different."

"She's your own daughter."

"Maybe that's why . . . ." The old man looked down the street, toward the cotton bales and the targets. "But she's a nigger. And now the talking is taking an ugly turn and the folks talking are the ones I can't hold."

Her father spoke in an angry whisper. "You see what I do to that target? You tell those children in their masks I do that to the forehead of any man . . . or woman that comes near her or my house. You tell them."

"Maynard, that wouldn't do any real good *after* they'd done something to her." He stopped, looked at Jennie, and smiled. "That's my only granddaughter, you know." His eyes clicked off her. "You're a man who knows firearms. You're a gunsmith. I know firearms too. Pistols and rifles can do lots of things, but they don't make very good doctors. Nobody's asking you to give her up. Just go back home. That's all. Go back to your wife."

Her father turned away, walking fast, came down the stairs and grabbed her hand. His face was red as blood between the white of his collar and the straw yellow of his hair.

They slowed after a block, paused in a small park with green trees shading several benches and a statue of a stern-faced young man in uniform, carrying pack and rifle. "We will sit."

She squirmed up onto the bench beside him. The warm wind smelled of salt from the Gulf of Mexico. The leaves were a dull, low tambourine. Her father was quiet for a long while.

Jennie watched birds bobbing for worms in the grass near them, then looked at the young, stone soldier. Far off, but from where she viewed it, just over the soldier's hat, a gliding sea gull dived suddenly behind the rooftops. That was when she saw the white man, standing across the street from the park, smiling at her. There were other white men with him, some looking at her, others at the man, all laughing. He waved to her. She smiled at him though he was the kind of man her mother told her always to stay away from. He was dressed as poorly as any Negro. From behind his back, he produced a brown rag doll, looked at her again, then grabbed the doll by its legs, and tore it part way up the middle. . . . The other men laughed uproariously.

Jennie pulled her father's sleeve. "Papa? What he doing?"

"Who?" Her father turned. The man repeated the show and her father bolted to his feet, yelling: "I will kill you! You hear? I will kill you for that!"

The men only snickered and ambled away.

Her father was red again. He had clenched his fists; now his hands were white like the bottoms of fishes. He sighed, shook his head and sat down. "I cannot kill everybody." He shook his head again, then leaned forward to get up. But first he thrust the blue velvet medal box into her hand. It was warm from his hand, wet and prickly. "When you grow up, you go to the North like your mother tells you. And you take this with you. It is yours. Always remember I gave it to you." He stood. "Now you must go home alone. Tell your mother I come later."

That night, Jennie tried to stay awake until he came home, until he was there to kiss her good night, his whiskers scratching her cheek. But all at once there was sun at her window and the sound of carts and wagons grating outside in the dirt street. Her mother was quiet while the two of them ate. After breakfast, Jennie went into the yard to wait for the gray buggy to turn the corner, but for the first morning in many months, the white woman did not jounce by, peering at the house, searching for someone or something special.

Thinking About the Story

1. How would you describe the relationship between Josie and Mister Herder?

2. Why do you think that Josie became a celebrity on Liberty Street?

3. What **irony,** if any, do you see in the title *The Only Man on Liberty Street?*

Reading/Writing Connections

1. Assume you are Maynard (Mister Herder) and write a letter to your daughter, Jennie, telling her of your decision not to return to live with her and her mother.

2. Assume you are Jennie and write a letter to your father in answer to his letter telling you why he did not return. What would you say to him?

3. In the form of an essay, a poem, or story, write about interracial relationships and how people have handled them in the past and today.

Ernest J. Gaines   (b. 1933) was born on a Louisiana plantation. His parents moved the family to Vallejo, Ca., when he was fifteen years old. He was drafted into the army in 1953 and served for two years. Upon leaving the army in 1955, he resumed his studies at California State University, San Francisco. In 1958 he received a Wallace Stegner Creative Writing Fellowship to study at Stanford University, and in 1959 he received the Joseph Henry Jackson Literary Award. At the present, Gaines lives in California.

Gaines' first novel, *Catherine Carmier*, was published in 1964, and was followed in 1967 by *Of Love and Dust*. His most famous book, *The Autobiography of Miss Jane Pittman*, was published in 1971. The novel tells the story of an African American woman who was born a slave and lives to see the beginning of the Civil Rights Movement in the 1960s. The Commonwealth Club of Northern California awarded the novel a gold medal. In 1983 Gaines was presented another medal for *A Gathering of Old Men*. The novel deals with changes taking place in the South, with the passing of old values and customs. Most of Gaines' works center around the will to survive with dignity in the face of tremendous odds. The following is an excerpt from his novel *In My Father's House*, published in 1977.

In My Father's House

ERNEST J. GAINES

Elijah had put away his tray of cups and glasses, and now he stood in the center of the room, clapping his hands for silence. The people were making too much noise to hear him, and he clapped again and stamped his foot. When everyone had quieted down, he told them that Reverend Martin wished to say a few words to them. The people turned to Phillip, who was already surrounded by a small crowd.

Phillip Martin wore a black pin-striped suit, a light gray shirt, and a red polka-dot tie. He was sixty years old, just over six feet tall, and he weighed around two hundred pounds. His thick black hair and thick well-trimmed mustache were just beginning to show some gray. Phillip was a very handsome dark-brown-skinned man, admired by women, black and white. The black women spoke openly of their admiration for him, the white women said it around people they could trust. There were rumors that he was involved with women other than his wife, but whether these rumors were true or not, he was very much respected by most of the people who knew him. And no one ever questioned his position as leader of the civil rights movement in the parish.

The people had begun to applaud Phillip, and he raised his hands for silence. Shepherd, who stood next to Virginia's new tenant in the back of the room, could see the two big rings on his fingers, and the gold watchband around his wrist. The people would not stop applauding him, and Shepherd could see how the gold watchband sparkled in the light as Phillip shook his hands for silence.

Phillip told his audience that he didn't have a speech to give, that he only wanted to remind them about next Friday when the committee would meet with Albert Chenal.

"It took us years to get Mr. Chenal to hire black people in the first place," he said. "Now, after he hires them he don't want to pay them nothing. When we go up there Friday we go'n make it clear. Either he pay the black workers the same he pay the white, or we march before the door. Now, we spend more money in that store than white people do—the white people go to Baton Rouge and New Orleans—some of them even go up North and 'way to Europe. Poor black people don't have that kind of money to do all that traveling; we spend ours here in St. Adrienne. Therefore, we want our black workers to get the same pay, the same treatment, or we close down shop. We'll see how long he can last if no blacks go in his store. Mr. Chenal—"

Elijah, standing in the center of the room, led the applause. He clapped his hands over his head and turned completely around so others would see him and join him. Phillip waited until he had quiet again.

"But Mr. Chenal will challenge us," he went on. "Sure as I'm standing here talking to you, Mr. Chenal will challenge us. First, he'll offer us pennies. When we turn that down, he'll make it nickels. Turn that down, then dimes. When we turn all of this down, he go'n tell us to get out. See how long we can take the cold. You may recall he did the same thing before—not when it was cold, when it was hot. He beat us when it was hot. Yes, when it was hot. And you know how much black people love hot weather—we thrive on hot weather."

The people started laughing, and Phillip held up his hands.

"Just why d'you think so many our people leaving the North and coming back home?" he asked them. "Our good old Southern hot weather, that's why. Still, we let Mr. Chenal beat us on the hottest day. Took the crumbs he offered us and said thanks. So what will he do now, knowing how much black people hate cold weather? He go'n offer us crumbs again, and when we turn it down, he go'n tell us to get out his store. In the back his mind he go'n be thinking, They can't take cold weather. Ten minutes out there with Mr. Jack Frost, they go'n run home and drink hot toddy. He-he-he. Well, Mr. Chenal is wrong, deadly wrong, we can take cold weather." Phillip looked across the room. "What you say, Mills?"

Tall, gray-headed Howard Mills standing against the wall raised one big fist up in the air.

"Got my overcoat cleaned this week," he said. "And got me some new rubber boots to hit that rain."

The people laughed at Howard Mills.

"Jonathan, ain't you ready?" Phillip asked.

Jonathan, who stood next to Mills, raised both fists high up over his head.

"I'm ready to walk till next year this time," he said. "And I hope every last person in here is ready to do the same."

The people applauded Jonathan. Phillip waited for silence.

"Poor Albert Chenal," he said. "Poor, poor Albert Chenal. I don't hate Albert Chenal. I don't want you to hate Albert Chenal. I want you to pray for Albert Chenal. Tomorrow in church pray for Albert Chenal. Before you go to bed tonight, pray for Albert Chenal. Remember, love they neighbor as thyself."

One of the two white women in the room applauded quietly. But when no one else joined her in support of praying for Albert Chenal, she brought her applause to an abrupt end.

Phillip went on. "Love is the only thing. Understanding, the only thing. Persistence, the only thing. Getting up tomorrow, trying again, the only thing. Keep on pushing, the only thing. You got some out there screaming Black Power. I say, what is Black Power but what we already doing and what we been trying to do all these years? Then you have that other crowd sitting in the bars—they even worse than the Black Power screamers—they saying, 'What's the use? Nothing will ever change. Hey, Mr. Wrigley, pour me another drink.' I'll call on Brother Mills again. What you say, Mills? You seen any changes around here?''

Mills nodded his gray head. "I'm a witness to it," he said.

"Jonathan?" Phillip said. "You been there, too. Well?"

"I've seen progress," Jonathan said. "But we have a long way to go, a long way to go."

"Amen," Phillip said.

But Jonathan was not through. He raised both fists over his head and looked around at the people in the room. "We need more people," he said. "More young people. More old people. We need the ones in the bars. We need the schoolteachers. We need them who go to work for the white people every day of their lives. We need them all. All, all, all. No reason to stay back, no reason at all. The wall is crumbling—let's finish tearing it down."

"Amen, amen," Phillip said, as the people applauded Jonathan.

Jonathan wanted to say more, but Phillip didn't give him a chance to go on.

"I'll call on a sister now," Phillip said. "Remember our sisters was out there first. Miss Daisy Bates, Miss Autherine Lucy, and countless more. And there's Sister Claiborne standing over there with her fine foxy self—you seen any changes, Sister Claiborne?

A small gray-haired woman dressed entirely in black nodded to Phillip.

"Sister Jackson?" Phillip said. "Don't that bus run back of town now? And don't we even have a little bench there for you to sit on when you tired?"

Sister Jackson, who was about the same age as Sister Claiborne, also wearing black, and a red bouquet, nodded as Sister Claiborne had done.

"If you want to know about changes, talk to a couple of these sisters around here." Phillip went on. "Sister Aaron, can't you vote today for the mayor of St. Adrienne, the governor of Louisiana, the President of the United States?"

"Yes," Sister Aaron said. "And I'm go'n vote for the first black congressman from Louisiana, too, who will be no one other than our own Reverend Phillip J. Martin."

The people started to applaud, and Phillip raised his hands for silence. But the people would not be silent. Anthony McVay, the white attorney, standing on one side of Phillip, and Octave Bacheron, a white pharmacist, standing on the other side of him, each took one of his hands and held them high up in the air. And the applause was deafening.

After things had quieted down some, Howard Mills put on his overcoat and left the house. About a dozen other people left at the same time. But still the big living room remained noisy and crowded. Half the people were gathered around Phillip on one side of the room; the rest were in smaller groups throughout the house. Virginia's new tenant had moved. Now he was standing near the door that led out of the living room down the hall. But even when he moved, he never took his eyes off Phillip Martin. Whenever someone got between them he would move again, never getting any closer, but always keeping Phillip in sight. Yet he did it so discreetly that no one, not even Shepherd, who stood next to him most of the time, was suspicious of anything. Beverly had joined them, and both Shepherd and she moved about the room with Virginia's tenant. They were never aware that he was doing this on purpose. They felt that it was the crowd pushing them into different places.

For the past few minutes Joyce Anne, Phillip's ten-year-old daughter, had been playing the piano. But there was so much noise in the room that no one paid any attention to her until Crystal McVay, the wife of the attorney, moved away from the crowd around Phillip and turned to the girl at the piano. Others in the room soon joined her. Elijah, who was Joyce Anne's teacher, stood behind the crowd with his tray of cups and glasses. Each time she played a difficult piece well he would shut his eyes and shake his head from side to side. But when she came to a part that might give her some trouble, he would catch his breath and wait. Then when it was over, when she had done it in good form, he would sigh deeply (loud enough for others to hear), nod, and continue on through the crowd with his tray.

But not everyone near the piano was listening to the music. Phillip Martin was not. Neither to the music nor to the people around him. For the past couple of minutes he had been looking across the room where Shepherd, Beverly, and Virginia's tenant were standing. Shepherd, who had noticed it, didn't think Phillip was looking at them in particular. They were at opposite ends of the room, there were at least three dozen people between them, so he could have been looking at anyone in that direction. Still, he looked nowhere else. And even when someone would speak to him or touch him on the arm, he would give that person his attention only a moment, then look back across the room again. He looked puzzled, confused; a deep furrow came into his forehead, and he raised his hand up to his temple as if he were in pain. Shepherd continued to watch him watching them. Suddenly he became very jealous. He knew of the minister's past reputation with women, so maybe he was eyeing Beverly now. Shepherd was angry for a moment, then he thought better of it, and he grinned at Phillip to let him know that he knew what was going on in his mind. But if Phillip saw him grin, he showed no sign that he did. Yet he looked only in that direction. When someone got between him and them, he craned his neck to see them better. Shepherd told Beverly what was going on.

"He's a handsome man, isn't he?" she said.

"Yes," Shepherd said. "And if I ever catch you anywhere near him, somebody's getting hurt."

"Really?" she teased him.

"Really," he told her.

Phillip was not aware that they were talking about him, he was not aware that they were even looking at him; yet he continued to stare at them, the expression on his face still showing confusion.

Joyce Anne was bringing her third song to an end now, and the people were applauding her performance. But Phillip Martin was not hearing a thing. He pushed his way out of the crowd and started across the room. He had taken only two or three steps when he suddenly staggered and fell heavily to the floor.

The pharmacist, Octave Bacheron, was the first to reach him and told everyone else to stay back. But the people did not get back, they pressed in closer. Sister Aaron, whom Phillip had called on during his short speech, cried out that he had been poisoned, and soon the word was all over the house that he had been drugged. The little wife of Octave Bacheron, who was hard of hearing, kept asking who had fallen. The other white woman, the attorney's wife, told her that it was Phillip.

"Phillip drunk?" Phoebe Bacheron asked. "Phillip drunk?" She was a very small woman, and she had to lean her head back to look up at the people around her. "Phillip drunk?" she asked. "Phillip drunk?"

No one answered her. They moved in to look at Phillip on the floor. Virginia's new tenant was there with all the others. His reddish eyes narrowed, his face trembled as he stared down at him. It seemed for a moment that he might say something, maybe even scream, but he jerked away from the crowd and went out. He was the only one who left, but there was so much confusion in the room that no one paid him any attention.

Alma, who had rushed to Phillip when he fell, now knelt beside him holding his head up off the floor in her lap. He had lost consciousness only a moment, as a fighter might who has been hit hard on the jaw, but now he began recognizing people around him again, and he tried quickly, desperately, to push himself up. Octave Bacheron, who knelt on the other side of him, put his small white hand on Phillip's chest and told him to lie still a moment."

"I'm all right," he said to Octave Bacheron. "I'm all right," he said to Alma. He looked up at all the people standing over him. "I'm all right, I'm all right," he said to them.

"No," Octave Bacheron said, pressing his small white hand on his chest. "Be quiet a moment. Listen to me. Can you hear me, Phillip? Be quiet. Lie still a moment.

"I'm all right," Phillip said. The people who stood over him canopylike could see tears in his eyes. "I'm all right. Please let me up. I have to get up. Don't let me deny him again."

No one knew what he was talking about. No one asked him what he was talking about.

"You don't feel well, Phillip," Octave Bacheron said. "Listen, you don't feel well."

"Alma?" Phillip said. "Alma, please," he begged her. "I'm on the floor. I'm on the floor."

Octave Bacheron nodded to Anthony to help him get Phillip to his feet. Jonathan, who was closer to Phillip, took his arm, but Anthony pushed him roughly aside.

"What do you think you doing?" Jonathan asked him.

"Helping your pastor," Anthony said.

"Ain't y'all done enough helping for one day?" Jonathan said. "That's why he's on his back now."

"Watch it, boy," Anthony said. "Watch your tongue there, now."

"Boy?" Jonathan said. "Boy?" He turned to the others in the room. "Y'all hear that, don't you? It's boy now. It's boy all over again."

"Please Jonathan," Alma said. "Please. Phillip's on his back. Please."

Jonathan and Anthony glared at each other a moment, then Anthony turned to Phillip. Phillip told them again that he was all right and he could stand on his own. But the two white men insisted on helping him to his feet, and they made him lean on them as they followed Alma down the hall to the bedroom. Elijah, Joyce Anne, and another woman followed after them.

Everyone had deserted the two white women now. The smaller one, Phoebe, was crying and asking why was Phillip drunk. Why did he drink? Didn't he know drinking was no good? The other white woman did not try to explain but took Phoebe in her arms and patted her shoulders. The rest of the people watched the door and waited for some kind of news from the bedroom.

After about ten minutes Octave Bacheron came back into the front. He told the people he believed that Phillip had fallen from exhaustion, but he was calling the doctor to be sure. He told them that both he and Alma would appreciate it if they did not take the rumor out of here that Phillip had been poisoned. Now, he wished that they would all get their coats and leave quietly, because their pastor needed rest more than anything else.

The doctor, a small clean-shaven bald man wearing a trench coat over a brown tweed suit, came to the house a half hour later. He was in the bedroom only a couple of minutes, then he wrote out a prescription for two bottles of pills. Elijah followed the pharmacist uptown and brought back the medicine.

Now that everyone else had gone, the house was deadly quiet. The doctor, repeating exactly what the pharmacist had said earlier, told Alma that what Phillip needed most was rest—quiet and rest. Alma, Elijah, and Joyce Anne sat in the living room talking so softly among themselves that they could hardly hear each other.

But things were quiet and peaceful only a short while, then the telephone started ringing. Elijah, who sat nearest the telephone, would try to reach it before it rang a second time. Everyone wanted to know what the doctor had said about Phillip. "He's tired and needs rest," Elijah told them. "Other than that he's fine. Fine. Fine. He just needs his rest." Elijah would hang up the telephone, but no sooner had he sat down than it would ring again. Several people had heard that Phillip had been poisoned. "It's nothing like that," Elijah assured them. "Nothing like that. That's the kind of rumor we don't want out." Virginia Colar called from the boardinghouse. "You sure he's just tired?" she asked. "You sure he wasn't poisoned? You know how these white folks are. Remember President Kennedy, don't you? They ain't straightened that mess out yet—putting it all on poor Oswald. Remember King, don't you? Remember Long, don't you?"

"I remember all of them," Elijah told her. "But Reverend Martin is just tired. Everybody ate the same food. Everybody drank out the same pot of eggnog, which I made myself. Mr. Octave drank out the same cup Reverend Martin drank from. Nothing happened to him."

"And how you know it was the same cup?" Virginia asked. "You got to watch white folks. They sharp, them. Can switch a cup right 'fore your eyes and you'll never see it."

"It was the same cup," Elijah said. "Reverend Martin's little blue-and-white china cup from Maison Blanche. I know that little cup like I know my name. He drinks out the same cup every day."

"That's the trouble right there," Virginia said. "He drinks out the same little blue-and-white cup, and everybody knows it. Can't they go to Maison Blanche and buy another little blue-and-white cup just like his?"

"Listen, Virginia, now listen," Elijah said. "It was his little blue-and-white cup. His. Now, good night. I'll see you in church tomorrow."

Elijah sat up answering the telephone long after Alma and Joyce Anne had gone to bed. Then around midnight he went down the hall to his own room. He had been lying in bed wide-awake for about an hour when he heard Alma and Phillip arguing out in the hall. Phillip had gotten out of bed and gone into his office, and Alma was trying to get him out of there. Elijah could hear her saying that she was going into the kitchen to warm up a glass of milk, because those pills weren't doing any good. He heard her passing by his room on her way into the kitchen, and a few minutes later he heard her going back up the hall again. It was quiet another hour, then more footsteps. Elijah listened for Alma's voice but didn't hear it. Now he called her, calling quietly: "Alma? Alma?" When she didn't answer, he got up and went to Phillip's office and knocked. It was quiet in the office, and Elijah pushed the door open and went in. Phillip sat behind his desk in the dark, facing the curtains over the window.

"Something the matter?" Elijah asked him.

"Thinking about service tomorrow," Phillip said without looking around.

"You ought to be in bed," Elijah said. "Let Jonathan conduct service tomorrow."

"I'm all right," Phillip said, still facing the curtains.

"The doctor want you to stay in bed," Elijah said.

Phillip didn't answer him.

"Reverend Martin, sir?"

"Leave me alone, will you?" Phillip said, looking back over his shoulder. "I just want to sit here and think a while."

Elijah went back to his room and lay on top of the covers, but a few minutes later he was knocking on the office door again.

"Reverend Martin? Reverend Martin, sir?"

"All right," Phillip said, coming out. "Good night, Elijah."

Phillip Martin went back to bed, but he couldn't sleep. He lay wide-awake for hours, listening to his wife snorting quietly beside him. He was trying not to think about the boy. He didn't want to think about him in here because he couldn't think clearly enough in here. The only place where he could think at all was in his office, but they came and got him out each time he went in there. He lay wide-awake, hoping for tomorrow to hurry up and get here. Alma, Elijah, and Joyce Anne would go to church, and he would have the entire house to himself.

Phillip lay on his side facing the wall. He wondered about the boy. But, no, how could it be? If anyone had known who the boy was, they would have brought it up yesterday.

Again in his mind's eye he saw the boy's thin, bearded face watching him from across the room. At first he paid it little attention, but after noticing it each time he looked in that direction, he began to ask himself why. Who was he? How did he get in here? Who invited him? He was sure he had never seen him anywhere before. He would look away a moment to answer someone's question, but when he looked back across the room he would find the boy still watching him as if no time whatever had passed. Why? he asked himself. Why? Who is he?

Then he remembered having heard about a stranger in St. Adrienne. The stranger had sat behind his church door the first night that he was here. Several people had seen him passing by the house. One or two had even seen him standing out in the street watching the house. Yes, and now that he remembered, Elijah had said something about inviting him to the party. But why was he standing there watching him? Why?

Then he knew. Even when he told himself no, it couldn't be so, he knew definitely that it was. The dream that he had a night or two before the boy got here was more than a dream; it was a vision, an omen, a warning.

Phillip pressed his face down against the sheet and tried not to think about it anymore. Let him think about anything else but not about this. Think about Chenal. Chenal wasn't going to be easy. Chenal knew the people needed work. Even if he paid them less than minimum they still had to work for him, because there weren't any other jobs. Phillip wondered what he would do if Chenal said no to their demands. Demonstrate against the store? Yes. What else? But suppose Chenal fired the people working for him, then what? They could eventually close down Chenal if the people demonstrated long enough against the store, but where would they work during that time?

Phillip started thinking about the boy again. Why? he asked himself. Why after all these years—why? And how did he know where to find me? Did she send him here? And if she did, why this game? Why sit behind the church door? Why for a week walk the street and watch the house? Come into the house, watch me, but say nothing—why? What's he want? What's he up to? He's got to be up to something. What?

Phillip Martin felt tired and confused. He looked at the two little bottles of pills and the glass of water on the small lamp table by the bed. He picked up one of the bottles and started to unscrew the cap, then threw it back. He wanted to knock everything on the floor, but he knew Alma would hear the noise and come into the room.

Thinking About the Story

1. Who do you believe is the mysterious "boy" in the story? Give information from the story to support your belief.

2. What is or is not significant about the title of the story?

3. Do you agree or disagree with the statement made by Rev. Phillip Martin that black people hate cold weather? Why or why not? Is he dealing in stereotyping? Give specific examples to support your answer.

Reading/Writing Connections

1. Assume the boy and Rev. Martin have never met before. Pretend you are the boy in the story and write a dialogue between yourself and the Rev. Martin.

2. Reflect on Phillip's statement "He beat us when it was hot. Yes, when it was hot. And you know how much black people love hot weather—we thrive on hot weather." Examine the stereotypical assumptions the speaker is deriding; write an essay on stereotypes and the negative effects they have.

Malcolm X (Malcolm Little)   (1925–1965) was born in

Omaha, Neb. In his teens he moved to Boston and then to Harlem where he became involved in a series of crimes that led to a ten-year prison term. While he was in prison, he became a Black Muslim. He was devoted to the movement and built his congregation to be the largest in America. He became an outstanding spokesperson for the Muslim movement, headed by the Honorable Elijah Muhammed. He denounced his Christian surname—his "slavename"—and took the name X. Malcolm X visited Mecca, the holiest city in the Muslim religion—located in Saudi Arabia, in 1964; upon his return to America, he broke with Elijah Muhammed and formed his own congregation—the Organization of Afro-American Unity—in order to concentrate on political rights for African Americans. He no longer accepted the doctrine that all white men were evil. His life story, *The Autobiography of Malcolm X*, was completed with the assistance of Alex Haley, author of *Roots*.

On February 21, 1965, during a meeting of his organization in New York, Malcolm X was assassinated. He left a legacy of speeches, one of which is "To Mississippi Youth." This speech was given to a group of black teenagers from McComb, Mississippi, two months before his death.

To Mississippi Youth

MALCOLM X

One of the first things I think young people, especially nowadays, should learn is how to see for yourself and listen for yourself and think for yourself. Then you can come to an intelligent decision for yourself. If you form the habit of going by what you hear others say about someone, or going by what others think about someone, instead of searching that thing out for yourself and seeing for yourself, you will be walking west when you think you're going east, and you will be walking east when you think you're going west. This generation, especially of our people, has a burden, more so than any other time in history. The most important thing that we can learn to do today is think for ourselves.

It's good to keep wide-open ears and listen to what everybody else has to say, but when you come to make a decision, you have to weigh all of what you've heard on its own, and place it where it belongs, and come to a decision for yourself; you'll never regret it. But if you form the habit of taking what someone else says about a thing without checking it out for yourself, you'll find that other people will have you hating your friends and loving your enemies. This is one of the things that our people are beginning to learn today— that it is very important to think out a situation for yourself. If you don't do it, you'll always be maneuvered into a situation where you are never fighting your actual enemies, where you will find yourself fighting your own self.

I think our people in this country are the best examples of that. Many of us want to be nonviolent and we talk very loudly, you know, about being nonviolent. Here in Harlem, where there are probably more black people concentrated than any place in the world, some talk about nonviolent talk too. But we find that they aren't nonviolent with each other. You can go out to Harlem Hospital, where there are more black patients than any hospital in the world, and see them going in there all cut up and shot up and busted up where they got violent with each other.

My experience has been that in many instances where you find Negroes talking about nonviolence, they are not nonviolent with each other, and they're not loving with each other, or forgiving with each other. Usually when they say they're nonviolent, they mean they're nonviolent with somebody else. I think you understand what I mean. They are nonviolent with the enemy. A person can come to your home, and if he's white and wants to heap some kind of brutality on you, you're nonviolent; or he can come to take your father and put a rope around his neck, and you're nonviolent. But if another Negro just stomps his foot, you'll rumble with him in a minute. Which shows you that there's an inconsistency there.

I myself would go for nonviolence if it was consistent, if everybody was going to be nonviolent all the time. I'd say, okay, let's get with it, we'll all be nonviolent. But I don't go along with any kind of nonviolence unless everybody's going to be nonviolent. If they make the Ku Klux Klan nonviolent, I'll be nonviolent. If they make the White Citizens Council nonviolent, I'll be nonviolent. But as long as you've got somebody else not being nonviolent, I don't want anybody coming to me talking any nonviolent talk. I don't think it is fair to tell our people to be nonviolent unless someone is out there making the Klan and the Citizens Council and these other groups also be nonviolent.

Now, I'm not criticizing those here who are nonviolent. I think everybody should do it the way they feel is best, and I congratulate anybody who can be nonviolent in the face of all that kind of action in that part of the world. I don't think that in 1965 you will find the upcoming generation of our people, especially those who have been doing some thinking, who will go along with any form of nonviolence unless nonviolence is going to be practiced all the way around.

If the leaders of the nonviolent movement can go into the white community and teach nonviolence, good. I'd go along with that. But as long as I see them teaching nonviolence only in the black community, we can't go along with that. We believe in equality, and equality means that you have to put the same thing over here that you put over there. And if black people alone are going to be the ones who are nonviolent, then it's not fair. We throw ourselves off guard. In fact, we disarm ourselves and make ourselves defenseless. . . .

The Organization of Afro-American Unity is a nonreligious group of black people who believe that the problems confronting our people in this country need to be re-analyzed and a new approach devised toward trying to get a solution. Studying the problem, we recall that prior to 1939 all of our people, in the North, South, East, and West, no matter how much education we had, were segregated. We were segregated in the North just as much as we were segregated in the South. Even now there's as much segregation in the North as there is in the South. There's some worse segregation right here in New York City than there is in McComb, Mississippi; but up here they're subtle and tricky and deceitful, and they make you think you've got it made when you haven't even begun to make it yet.

Prior to 1939, our people were in a very menial position or condition. Most of us were waiters and porters and bellhops and janitors and waitresses and things of that sort. It was not until war was declared with Germany, and America became involved in a manpower shortage in regards to her factories plus her army, that the black man in this country was permitted to make a few strides forward. It was never out of some kind of moral enlightenment or moral awareness on the part of Uncle Sam. Uncle Sam only let the black man take a step forward when he himself had his back to the wall.

In Michigan, where I was brought up at that time, I recall that the best jobs in the city for blacks were waiters out at the country club. In those days if you had a job waiting tables in the country club, you had it made. Or if you had a job at the State House. Having a job at the State House didn't mean that you were a clerk or something of that sort; you had a shoeshine stand at the State House. Just by being there you could be around all those big-shot politicians—that made you a big-shot Negro. You were shining shoes, but you were a big-shot Negro because you were around big-shot white people and you could bend their ear and get up next to them. And ofttimes you were chosen by them to be the voice of the Negro community.

Around that time, 1939 or '40 or '41, they weren't drafting Negroes in the army or navy. A Negro couldn't join the navy in 1940 or '41. They wouldn't take a black man in the navy except to make him a cook. He couldn't just go and join the navy, and I don't think he could just go and join the army. They weren't drafting him when the war first started. This is what they thought of you and me in those days. For one thing, they didn't trust us; they feared that if they put us in the army and trained us in how to use rifles and other things, we might shoot at some targets that they hadn't picked out. And we would have. Any thinking man knows what target to shoot at. If a man has to have someone else to choose his target, then he isn't thinking for himself—they're doing the thinking for him.

The Negro leaders in those days were the same type we have today. When the Negro leaders saw all the white fellows being drafted and taken into the army and dying on the battlefield, and no Negroes were dying because they weren't being drafted, the Negro leaders came up and said, "We've got to die too. We want to be drafted too, and we demand that you take us in there and let us die for our country too." That was what the Negro leaders said back in 1940. I remember. A. Philip Randolph was one of the leading Negroes in those days who said it, and he's one of the Big Six right now; and this is why he's one of the Big Six.

So they started drafting Negro soldiers then, and started letting Negroes get into the navy. But not until Hitler and Tojo and the foreign powers were strong enough to put pressure on this country, so that it had its back to the wall and needed us, [did] they let us work in factories. Up until that time we couldn't work in the factories; I'm talking about the North as well as the South. And when they let us work in the factories, at first they let us in only as janitors. After a year or so passed by, they let us work on machines. We became machinists, got a little more skill. If we got a little more skill, we made a little more money, which enabled us to live in a little better neighborhood. When we lived in a little better neighborhood, we went to a little better school, got a little better education and could come out and get a little better job. So the cycle was broken somewhat.

But the cycle was not broken out of some kind of sense of moral responsibility on the part of the government. No, the only time that cycle was broken even to a degree was when world pressure was brought to bear on the United States government. They didn't look at us as human beings—they just put us into their system and let us advance a little bit father because it served their interests. They never let us advance a little bit farther because they were interested in us as human beings. Any of you who have a knowledge of history, sociology, or political science, or the economic development of this country and its race relations—go back and do some research on it and you'll have to admit that this is true.

It was during the time that Hitler and Tojo made war with this country and put pressure on it [that] Negroes in this country advanced a little bit. At the end of the war with Germany and Japan, then Joe Stalin and Communist Russia were a threat. During that period we made a little more headway. Now the point that I'm making is this: Never at any time in the history of our people in this country have we made advances or progress in any way based upon the internal good will of this country. We have made advancement in this country only when this country was under pressure from forces above and beyond its control. The internal moral consciousness of this country is bankrupt. It hasn't existed since they first brought us over here and made slaves out of us. They make it appear they have our good interests at heart, but when you study it, every time, no matter how many steps they take us forward, it's like we're standing on a—what do you call that thing?—a treadmill. The treadmill is moving backwards faster than we're able to go forward in this direction. We're not even standing still—we're going backwards.

In studying the process of this so-called progress during the past twenty years, we of the Organization of Afro-American Unity realized that the only time the black man in this country is given any kind of recognition, or even listened to, is when America is afraid of outside pressure, or when she's afraid of her image abroad. So we saw that it was necessary to expand the problem and the struggle of the black man in this country until it went above and beyond the jurisdiction of the United States. . . .

I was fortunate enough to be able to take a tour of the African continent during the summer. I went to Egypt, then to Arabia, Kuwait, Lebanon, Sudan, Ethiopia, Kenya, Tanganyika, Zanzibar, Nigeria, Ghana, Guinea, Liberia, and Algeria. I found, while I was traveling on the African continent, I had already detected it in May, that someone had very shrewdly planted the seed of division on this continent to make the Africans not show genuine concern with our problem, just as they plant seeds in your and my minds so that we won't show concern with the African problem. . . .

I also found that in many of these African countries the head of state is genuinely concerned with the problem of the black man in this country; but many of them thought if they opened their mouths and voiced their concern that they would be insulted by the American Negro leaders. Because one head of state in Asia voiced his support of the civil-rights struggle [in 1963] and a couple of the Big Six had the audacity to slap his face and say they weren't interested in that kind of help—which in my opinion is asinine. So the African leaders only had to be convinced that if they took an open stand at the governmental level and showed interest in the problem of black people in this country, they wouldn't be rebuffed.

And today you'll find in the United Nations, and it's not an accident, that every time the Congo question or anything on the African continent is being debated, they couple it with what is going on, or what is happening to you and me, in Mississippi and Alabama and these other places. In my opinion, the greatest accomplishment that was made in the struggle of the black man in America in 1964 toward some kind of real progress was the successful linking together of our problem with the African problem, or making our problem a world problem. Because now, whenever anything happens to you in Mississippi, it's not just a case of somebody in Alabama getting indignant, or somebody in New York getting indignant. The same repercussions that you see all over the world when an imperialist or foreign power interferes in some section of Africa—you see repercussions, you see the embassies being bombed and burned and overturned—nowadays, when something happens to black people in Mississippi, you'll see the same repercussions all over the world.

I wanted to point this out to you because it is important for you to know that when you're in Mississippi, you're not alone. As long as you think you're alone, then you take a stand as if you're a minority or as if you're outnumbered, and that kind of stand will never enable you to win a battle. You've got to know that you've got as much power on your side as that Ku Klux Klan has on its side. And when you know that you've got as much power on your side as the Klan has on its side, you'll talk the same kind of language with that Klan as the Klan is talking with you. . . .

I think in 1965, whether you like it, or I like it, or they like it, or not, you will see that there is a generation of black people becoming mature to the point where they feel that they have no more business being asked to take a peaceful approach than anybody else takes, unless everybody's going to take a peaceful approach.

So we here in the Organization of Afro-American Unity are with the struggle in Mississippi one thousand percent. We're with the efforts to register our people in Mississippi to vote one thousand percent. But we do not go along with anybody telling us to help nonviolently. We think that if the government says that Negroes have a right to vote, and then some Negroes come out to vote, and some kind of Ku Klux Klan is going to put them in the river, and the government doesn't do anything about it, it's time for us to organize and band together and equip ourselves and qualify ourselves to protect ourselves. And once you can protect yourself, you don't have to worry about being hurt. . . .

I hope you don't think I'm trying to incite you. Just look here: Look at yourselves. Some of you are teenagers, students. How do you think I feel—and I belong to a generation ahead of you—how do you think I feel to have to tell you, "We, my generation, sat around like a knot on a wall while the whole world was fighting for its human rights—and you've got to be born into a society where you still have the same fight." What did we do, who preceded you? I'll tell you what we did: Nothing. And don't you make the same mistake we made. . . .

Thinking About the Speech

1. Malcolm X says that young people should look, listen, and think for themselves before taking action. Is this valuable advice? Give specific examples to support your answer.

2. Nonviolence, according to Malcolm X, is not the best way for African Americans to achieve their human and civil rights. Do you agree or disagree with this philosophy? Give specific examples from history, from your reading, or from your personal experience.

3. Malcolm X says that he does not criticize anyone who is nonviolent. About whom do you think he is speaking?

Reading/Writing Connections

1. Malcolm X says "We [African Americans] have made advancement in this country only when this country was under pressure from forces above and beyond its control." Write an essay in which you agree or disagree with this statement. Cite specific examples from literature, from history, or from your personal experience.

2. Assume you are a member of Malcolm X's generation. Write a speech in which you explain what is meant by the statement "We, my generation, sat around like a knot on a wall while the whole world was fighting for its human rights. . . ."

3. Imagine it is 1965 and that you were in the audience and have just returned to your home in McComb from New York City. Write Malcolm X a letter of appreciation for the advice he gave and how his speech changed (or did not change) your life.

Langston Hughes   (1902–1967) In his work, Langston Hughes, acknowledged as the best-known and most versatile writer produced by the Harlem Renaissance, consistently wrote of ordinary people—people who, like the mother in the following poem, struggle to survive. Note Hughes' choice of simple words and realistic speech, as well as how he used punctuation for its greatest effect. (For biographical information on Langston Hughes, see page 32.)

Mother to Son

LANGSTON HUGHES

Well, son, I'll tell you:
Life for me ain't been no crystal stair.
It's had tacks in it,
And splinters,
And boards torn up   5
And places with no carpet on the floor—
Bare.
But all the time
I'se been a-climbin' on,
And reachin' landin's,   10
And turnin' corners
And sometimes goin' in the dark
Where there ain't been no light.
So boy, don't you turn back.
Don't you set down on the steps,   15
'Cause you finds it's kinder hard.
Don't you fall now—
For I'se still goin', honey,
I'se still climbin',
And life for me ain't been no crystal stair.   20

Thinking About the Poem

1. The persona in this poem—the mother—speaks in contrasts throughout the poem. What different things and ideas is she contrasting?

2. What can you infer from this poem about the mother's life? Support your statements with evidence from the poem.

3. Is there any indication of a sustaining dream in "Mother to Son"? Find evidence in the poem to back up your answer.

Reading/Writing Connections

1. Assume that you are the parent of a son. What advice would you give him today? Write a letter to your son in which you specifically state that advice.

2. Would advice given a son be different from that given a daughter? In your writing journal, explain your answer. Use specific examples.

3. Throughout "Mother to Son" the poet uses the metaphor "crystal stair." Write an essay in which you explain the meaning of this metaphor.

"Woman," 1965, by Romare Bearden. Medium: Collage, crayon and ink on masonite. Size: 36 × 23 ⁷/₈ in. Reprinted courtesy of Sid Deutsch Gallery, New York.

5

ON BEING A WOMAN

African American women have struggled for a place in society since they were brought to this country as slaves. They performed strenuous labor and gave birth to children who often were taken away from them. After slavery and well into the twentieth century, it was women who were able to find jobs (most often as housekeepers, cooks, and maids), which allowed the African American family to survive financially. At the same time, African American women have been viewed as intellectually inferior to men.

When confronted by negative stereotypes from society as a whole or even from the African American community itself, African American women have not given in to defeat. They have continued to rise and to demand their rightful place in society. As individuals, mothers, daughters, sisters, aunts, and grandmothers, they have worked within their families, in their jobs, and in their communities to search for and create a sense of themselves as African Americans and as women.

African American women writers have created women characters who pass on their knowledge of life and survival through their culture and history from one generation to the next. These characters are neither perfect nor flawed. They are all trying to survive in an imperfect world that judges them because of the color of their skin and their gender. This knowledge enables the next generation of African American women to rise above the conditions in which they live and to reach a new level of understanding about life and about what it means to be an African American woman.

Ntozake Shange (b. 1948) was born Paulette Williams in Trenton, N.J., to Paul T. Williams, a surgeon, and Eloise Williams, a psychiatric social worker and educator. In 1971 she took her African name, Ntozake (ĕn-tō-zä′ ke) meaning "she comes with her own things" and Shange (shän′gä) meaning "who walks like a lion." At a young age, Shange met such notable African American musicians and singers as Charlie Parker, Miles Davis, and Josephine Baker, who were friends of her parents. One particular friend, W. E. B. Du Bois, an African American scholar and intellectual, made a great impression on Shange. Shange received a bachelor's degree with honors in American studies from Barnard College in 1970 and a master's degree in American studies from the University of Southern California at Los Angeles in 1973. It was not until the 1976 Broadway production of *For Colored Girls Who Have Considered Suicide / When the Rainbow Is Enuf*, a choreopoem—a work combining poetry, music, dance, and drama—that Shange became well known as a writer. *For Colored Girls* won several awards, including an Obie in 1977. Shange has taught at several universities and colleges, including Sonoma State College, Mills College, and the University of California Extension.

Shange's writing has been influenced by the diverse facets of her experience. She is an educator, dancer, writer, actress, and lecturer. Her writing focuses on the strength of African American women and she often expresses this strength in her poetry, fiction, and drama through the use of dance and music. Her works include *Nappy Edges* (1978), *Sassafrass, Cypress and Indigo* (1982), and *See No Evil: Prefaces, Essays and Accounts, 1976–1983* (1984). The following poem is from Shange's work *For Colored Girls*; this poem is spoken by the character "lady in blue."

one thing i dont need

NTOZAKE SHANGE

one thing i dont need
is any more apologies
i got sorry greetin me at my front door
you can keep yrs
i dont know what to do wit em   5
they dont open doors
or bring the sun back
they dont make me happy
or get a mornin paper
didnt nobody stop usin my tears to wash cars   10
cuz a sorry

i am simply tired
of collectin
      i didnt know
      i was so important toyou'   15
i'm gonna haveta throw some away
i cant get to the clothes in my closet
for alla the sorries
i'm gonna tack a sign to my door
leave a message by the phone   20
      'if you called
      to say yr sorry
      call somebody
      else
      i dont use em anymore'   25
i let sorry/didnt meanta/& how cd i know abt that
take a walk down a dark & musty street in brooklyn
i'm gonna do exactly what i want to
& i wont be sorry for none of it
letta sorry soothe yr soul/i'm gonna soothe mine   30

you were always inconsistent
doin somethin & then bein sorry

beatin my heart to death
talkin bout you sorry
well   35
i will not call
i'm not goin to be nice
i will raise my voice
& scream & holler
& break things & race the engine   40
& tell all yr secrets bout yrself to yr face
& i will list in detail everyone of my wonderful lovers
& their ways
i will play oliver lake
loud   45
& i wont be sorry for none of it

i loved you on purpose
i was open on purpose
i still crave vulnerability & close talk
& i'm not even sorry bout you bein sorry   50
you can carry all the guilt & grime ya wanna
just dont give it to me
i cant use another sorry
next time
you should admit   55
you're mean/low-down/triflin/& no count straight out
steada bein sorry alla the time
enjoy bein yrself

---

44. *oliver lake*: a jazz saxophonist.

Thinking About the Poem

1. How does Shange's use of all lower case letters and lack of formal punctuation affect the way in which you read the poem? How does Shange's spelling style add to or detract from the way in which you read the poem?

2. Use specific examples from the poem to illustrate how "sorry" has filled the speaker's life.

3. In lines 14–15 and 21–25, who is speaking? What function do these indented lines serve?

4. Compare the speaker's tone at the beginning of the poem to that at the end of the poem. Are there similarities? Differences? What do you think these tones reveal about the speaker's attitude changes?

Reading/Writing Connections

1. In your journal write about a time when someone apologized for something, but you could tell the person was not sincere. How did you feel? Did the person's apology make you feel better or worse about the situation?

2. In the last lines of the poem, the lady in blue says "steada bein sorry alla the time / enjoy bein yrself." As a journal entry, explain what she means when she says "enjoy bein yrself."

3. Write an apology to a person you should have apologized to but never did. Do not use the word *sorry* in your apology. After you write, examine how you feel. How difficult was it to apologize without using the word *sorry*?

Paule Marshall   (b. 1929) was born in Brooklyn, N.Y., to Samuel and Ada Burke, who emigrated from Barbados after World War I. The mixture of Caribbean and American cultures provided Marshall with a sense of ritual, a sense of the importance of history. This background later became the foundation for her fiction. In 1953 Marshall received her B.A. degree, Phi Beta Kappa, from Brooklyn College. While she wrote her first novel, *Brown Girl, Brownstone* (1959), she worked as a writer for *Our World*, an African American magazine. Marshall left the magazine in 1956 and since 1959 has maintained her career as a fiction writer.

Despite the fact that Marshall's novels did not do well commercially in the 1960s, she has continued to write about topics of importance to her: African American women and the culture within which they exist. Her other works include *Soul Clap Hands and Sing* (1961), a collection of short stories, and *The Chosen Place, the Timeless People* (1969). Beginning in the 1980s, Marshall began to enjoy commercial success as well as critical acclaim with the publication of *Praisesong for the Widow* (1984) and *Daughters* (1991).

To Da-duh,
In Memoriam

PAULE MARSHALL

" . . . Oh Nana! all of you is not involved in this evil business
Death,
Nor all of us in life."
> —From "At My Grandmother's Grave," by Lebert Bethune

I did not see her at first I remember. For not only was it dark inside the crowded disembarkation shed in spite of the daylight flooding in from outside, but standing there waiting for her with my mother and sister I was still somewhat blinded from the sheen of tropical sunlight on the water of the bay which we had just crossed in the landing boat, leaving behind us the ship that had brought us from New York lying in the offing. Besides, being only nine years of age at the time and knowing nothing of islands I was busy attending to the alien sights and sounds of Barbados, the unfamiliar smells.

I did not see her, but I was alerted to her approach by my mother's hand which suddenly tightened around mine, and looking up I traced her gaze through the gloom in the shed until I finally made out the small, purposeful, painfully erect figure of the old woman headed our way.

Her face was drowned in the shadow of an ugly rolled-brim brown felt hat, but the details of her slight body and of the struggle taking place within it were clear enough—an intense, unrelenting struggle between her back which was beginning to bend ever so slightly under the weight of her eighty-odd years and the rest of her which sought to deny those years and hold that back straight, keep it in line. Moving swiftly toward us (so swiftly it seemed she did not intend stopping when she reached us but would sweep past us out the doorway which opened onto the sea and like Christ walk upon the water!), she was caught between the sunlight at her end of the building and the darkness inside— and for a moment she appeared to contain them both: the light in the long severe old-fashioned white dress she wore which brought the sense of a past that was still alive into our bustling present and in the snatch of white at her eye; the darkness in her black high-top shoes and in her face which was visible now that she was closer.

It was as stark and fleshless as a death mask, that face. The maggots might have already done their work, leaving only the framework of bone beneath the ruined skin and deep wells at the temple and jaw. But her eyes were alive, unnervingly so for one so old, with a sharp light that flicked out of the dim clouded depths like a lizard's tongue to snap up all in her view. Those eyes betrayed a child's curiosity about the world, and I wondered vaguely seeing them, and seeing the way the bodice of her ancient dress had collapsed in on her flat chest (what had happened to her breasts?), whether she might not be some kind of child at the same time that she was a woman, with fourteen children, my mother included to prove it. Perhaps she was both, both child and woman, darkness and light, past and present, life and death—all the opposites contained and reconciled in her.

"My Da-duh," my mother said formally and stepped forward. The name sounded like thunder fading softly in the distance.

"Child," Da-duh said, and her tone, her quick scrutiny of my mother, the brief embrace in which they appeared to shy from each other rather than touch, wiped out the fifteen years my mother had been away and restored the old relationship. My mother, who was such a formidable figure in my eyes, had suddenly with a word been reduced to my status.

"Yes, God is good," Da-duh said with a nod that was like a tic. "He has spared me to see my child again."

We were led forward then, apologetically because not only did Da-duh prefer boys but she also liked her grandchildren to be "white," that is, fair-skinned, and we had, I was to discover, a number of cousins, the outside children of white estate managers and the like, who qualified. We, though, were as black as she.

My sister being the oldest was presented first. "This one takes after the father," my mother said and waited to be reproved.

Frowning, Da-duh tilted my sister's face toward the light. But her frown soon gave way to a grudging smile, for my sister with her large mild eyes and little broad winged nose, with our father's high-cheeked Barbadian cast to her face, was pretty.

"She's goin' be lucky," Da-duh said and patted her once on the cheek. "Any girl child that takes after the father does be lucky."

She turned then to me. But oddly enough she did not touch me. Instead learning close, she peered hard at me, and then quickly drew back. I thought I saw her hand start up as though to shield her eyes. It was almost as if she saw not only me, a thin truculent child who it was said took after no one but myself, but something in me which for some reason she found disturbing, even threatening. We looked silently at each other for a long time in the noisy shed, our gaze locked. She was the first to look away.

"But Adry," she said to my mother and her laugh was cracked, thin, apprehensive. "Where did you get this one here with this fierce look?"

"We don't know where she came out of, my Da-duh," my mother said, laughing also. Even I smiled to myself. After all I had won the encounter. Da-duh had recognized my small strength—and this was all I ever asked of the adults in my life then.

"Come, soul," Da-duh said and took my hand. "You must be one of those New York terrors you hear so much about."

She led us, me at her side and my sister and mother behind, out of the shed into the sunlight that was like a bright driving summer rain and over to a group of people clustered beside a decrepit lorry.[1] They were our relatives, most of them from St. Andrews although Da-duh herself lived in St. Thomas, the women wearing bright print dresses, the colors vivid against their darkness, the men rusty black suits that encased them like straightjackets. Da-duh, holding fast to my hand, became my anchor as they circled round us like a nervous sea, exclaiming, touching us with their calloused hands, embracing us shyly. They laughed in awed bursts, "But look Adry got big-big children!" /"And see the nice things they wearing, wrist watch and all!" / "I tell you, Adry has done all right for sheself in New York. . . ."

Da-duh, ashamed at their wonder, embarrassed for them, admonished them the while. "But oh Christ," she said, "why you all got to get on like you never saw people from 'Away' before? You would think New York is the only place in the world to hear wunna. That's why I don't like to go anyplace with you St. Andrews people, you know. You all ain't been colonized."[2]

We were in the back of the lorry finally, packed in among the barrels of ham, flour, cornmeal, and rice and the trunks of clothes that my mother had brought as gifts. We made our way slowly through Bridgetown's clogged streets, part of a funeral procession of cars and open-sided buses, bicycles and donkey carts. The dim little limestone shops and offices along the way marched with us, at the same mournful pace, toward the same grave ceremony—as did the people, the women balancing huge baskets on top their heads as if they were no more than hats they wore to shade them from the sun. Looking over the edge of the lorry I watched as their feet slurred the dust. I listened, and their voices, raw and loud and dissonant in the heat, seemed to be grappling with each other high overhead.

---

[1]*lorry*: a large motor vehicle, a bus.
[2]*"You all ain't been colonized"*: a satirical comment referring to the British Empire's colonial influence in Barbados.

Da-duh sat on a trunk in our midst, a monarch amid her court. She still held my hand, but it was different now. I had suddenly become her anchor, for I felt her fear of the lorry with its asthmatic motor (a fear and distrust, I later learned, she held of all machines) beating like a pulse in her rough palm.

As soon as we left Bridgetown behind though, she relaxed, and while the others around us talked she gazed at the canes standing tall on either side of the winding marl road. "C'dear," she said softly to herself after a time. "The canes this side are pretty enough."

They were too much for me. I thought of them as giant weeds that had overrun the island, leaving scarcely any room for the small tottering houses of sunbleached pine we passed or the people, dark streaks as our lorry hurtled by. I suddenly feared that we were journeying, unaware that we were, toward some dangerous place where the canes, grown as high and thick as a forest, would close in on us and run us through with their stiletto blades. I longed then for the familiar; for the street in Brooklyn where I lived, for my father who had refused to accompany us ("Blowing out good money on foolishness," he had said of the trip), for a game of tag with my friends under the chestnut tree outside our aging brownstone house.

"Yes, but wait till you see St. Thomas canes," Da-duh was saying to me. "They's canes father,[3] bo," she gave a proud arrogant nod. "Tomorrow, God willing, I goin' take you out in the ground and show them to you."

True to her word, Da-duh took me with her the following day out into the ground. It was a fairly large plot adjoining her weathered board and shingle house and consisting of a small orchard, a good-sized canepiece and behind the canes, where the land sloped abruptly down, a gully. She had purchased it with Panama money sent her by her eldest son, my uncle Joseph, who had died working on the canal. We entered the ground along a trail no wider than her body and as devious and complex as her reasons for showing me her land. Da-duh strode briskly ahead, her slight form filled out this morning by the layers of sacking petticoats she wore under her working dress to protect her against the damp. A fresh white cloth, elaborately arranged around her head, added to her height, and lent her a vain, almost roguish air.

Her pace slowed once we reached the orchard, and glancing back at me occasionally over her shoulder, she pointed out the various trees.

"This here is a breadfruit," she said. "That one yonder is a papaw. Here's a guava. This is a mango. I know you don't have anything like these in New York. Here's a sugar apple." (The fruit looked more like artichokes than apples to me.) "This one bears limes. . . ." She went on for some time, intoning the names of the trees as though they were those of her gods. Finally,

---

[3] *"They's canes father"*: meaning the St. Thomas variety of sugar canes were larger.

turning to me, she said, "I know you don't have anything this nice where you come from." Then, as I hesitated: "I said I know you don't have anything this nice where you come from. . . ."

"No," I said and my world did seem suddenly lacking.

Da-duh nodded and passed on. The orchard ended and we were on the narrow cart road that led through the canepiece, the canes clashing like swords above my cowering head. Again she turned and her thin muscular arms spread wide, her dim gaze embracing the small field of canes, she said—and her voice almost broke under the weight of her pride, "Tell me, have you got anything like these in that place where you were born?"

"No."

"I din' think so. I bet you don't even know that these canes here and the sugar you eat is one and the same thing. That they does throw the canes into some damn machine at the factory and squeeze out all the little life in them to make sugar for you all so in New York to eat. I bet you don't know that."

"I've got two cavities and I'm not allowed to eat a lot of sugar."

But Da-duh didn't hear me. She had turned with an inexplicably angry motion and was making her way rapidly out of the canes and down the slope at the edge of the field which led to the gully below. Following her apprehensively down the incline amid a stand of banana plants whose leaves flapped like elephants ears in the wind, I found myself in the middle of a small tropical wood—a place dense and damp and gloomy and tremulous with the fitful play of light and shadow as the leaves high above moved against the sun that was almost hidden from view. It was a violent place, the tangled foliage fighting each other for a chance at the sunlight, the branches of the trees locked in what seemed an immemorial struggle, one both necessary and inevitable. But despite the violence, it was pleasant, almost peaceful in the gully, and beneath the thick undergrowth the earth smelled like spring.

This time Da-duh didn't even bother to ask her usual question, but simply turned and waited for me to speak.

"No," I said, my head bowed. "We don't have anything like this in New York."

"Ah," she cried, her triumph complete. " I din' think so. Why, I've heard that's a place where you can walk till you drop and never see a tree."

"We've got a chestnut tree in front of our house," I said.

"Does it bear?" She waited. "I ask you, does it bear?"

"Not anymore," I muttered. "It used to, but not anymore."

She gave the nod that was like a nervous twitch. "You see," she said. "Nothing can bear there." Then, secure behind her scorn, she added, "But tell me, what's this snow like that you hear so much about?"

Looking up, I studied her closely, sensing my chance, and then I told her, describing at length and with as much drama as I could summon not only what snow in the city was like, but what it would be like here, in her perennial summer kingdom.

"... And you see all these trees you got here," I said. "Well, they'd be bare. No leaves, no fruit, nothing. They'd be covered in snow. You see your canes. They'd be buried under tons of snow. The snow would be higher than your head, higher than your house, and you wouldn't be able to come down into this here gully because it would be snowed under. ..."

She searched my face for the lie, still scornful but intrigued. "What a thing, huh?" she said finally, whispering it softly to herself.

"And when it snows you couldn't dress like you are now," I said. "Oh no, you'd freeze to death. You'd have to wear a hat and gloves and galoshes and ear muffs so your ears wouldn't freeze and drop off, and a heavy coat. I've got a Shirley Temple coat with fur on the collar. I can dance. You wanna see?"

Before she could answer I began, with a dance called the Truck which was popular back then in the 1930's. My right forefinger waving, I trucked around the nearby trees and around Da-duh's awed and rigid form. After the Truck I did the Suzy-Q, my lean hips swishing, my sneakers sidling zigzag over the ground "I can sing," I said and did so, starting with "I'm Gonna Sit Right Down and Write Myself a Letter," then without pausing, "Tea for Two," and ending with "I Found a Million Dollar Baby in a Five and Ten Cent Store."

For long moments afterwards Da-duh stared at me as if I were a creature from Mars, an emissary from some world she did not know but which intrigued her and whose power she both felt and feared. Yet something about my performance must have pleased her, because bending down she slowly lifted her long skirt and then, one by one, the layers of petticoats until she came to a drawstring purse dangling at the end of a long strip of cloth tied round her waist. Opening the purse she handed me a penny. "Here," she said half-smiling against her will. "Take this to buy yourself a sweet at the shop up the road. There's nothing to be done with you, soul."

From then on, whenever I wasn't taken to visit relatives, I accompanied Da-duh out into the ground, and alone with her amid the canes or down in the gully I told her about New York. It always began with some slighting remark on her part: "I know they don't have anything this nice where you come from," or "Tell me, I hear those foolish people in New York does do such and such. . . ." But as I answered, recreating my towering world of steel and concrete and machines for her, building the city out of words, I would feel her give way. I came to know the signs of her surrender: the total stillness that would come over her little hard dry form, the probing gaze that like a surgeon's knife sought to cut through my skull to get at the images there, to see if I were lying, above all, her fear, a fear nameless and profound, the same one I had felt beating in the palm of her hand that day in the lorry.

Over the weeks I told her about refrigerators, radios, gas stoves, elevators, trolley cars, wringer washing machines, movies, airplanes, the cyclone at Coney Island, subways, toasters, electric lights: "At night, see, all you have to do is flip this little switch on the wall and all the lights in the house go on just like that. Like magic. It's like turning on the sun at night."

"But tell me," she said to me once with a faint mocking smile, "do the white people have all these things too or it's only the people looking like us?"

I laughed. "What d'ya mean," I said. "The white people have even better." Then: "I beat up a white girl in my class last term."

"Beating up white people!" Her tone was incredulous.

"How you mean!" I said, using an expression of hers. "She called me a name."

For some reason Da-duh could not quite get over this and repeated in the same hushed, shocked voice, "Beating up white people now! Oh, the lord, the world's changing up so I can scarce recognize it anymore."

One morning toward the end of our stay, Da-duh led me into a part of the gully that we had never visited before, an area darker and more thickly overgrown than the rest, almost impenetrable. There in a small clearing amid the dense bush, she stopped before an incredibly tall royal palm which rose cleanly out of the ground, and drawing the eye up with it, soared high above the trees around it into the sky. It appeared to be touching the blue dome of sky, to be flaunting its dark crown of fronds right in the blinding white face of the late morning sun.

Da-duh watched me a long time before she spoke, and then she said very quietly, "All right, now, tell me if you've got anything this tall in that place you're from."

I almost wished, seeing her face, that I could have said no. "Yes," I said. "We've got buildings hundreds of times this tall in New York. There's one called the Empire State Building that's the tallest in the world. My class visited it last year and I went all the way to the top. It's got over a hundred floors. I can't describe how tall it is. Wait a minute. What's the name of that hill I went to visit the other day, where they have the police station?"

"You mean Bissex?"

"Yes, Bissex. Well, the Empire State Building is way taller than that."

"You're lying now!" she shouted, trembling with rage. Her hand lifted to strike me.

"No, I'm not," I said. "It really is, if you don't believe me I'll send you a picture postcard of it as soon as I get back home so you can see for yourself. But it's way taller than Bissex."

All the fight went out of her at that. The hand poised to strike me fell limp to her side, and as she stared at me, seeing not me but the building that was taller than the highest hill she knew, the small stubborn light in her eyes (it was the same amber as the flame in the kerosene lamp she lit at dusk) began to fail. Finally, with a vague gesture that even in the midst of her defeat still tried to dismiss me and my world, she turned and started back through the gully, walking slowly, her steps groping and uncertain, as if she were suddenly no longer sure of the way, while I followed triumphant yet strangely saddened behind.

The next morning I found her dressed for our morning walk but stretched out on the Berbice[4] chair in the tiny drawing room where she sometimes napped during the afternoon heat, her face turned to the window beside her. She appeared thinner and suddenly indescribably old.

"My Da-duh," I said.

"Yes, nuh," she said. Her voice was listless and the face she slowly turned my way was, now that I think back on it, like a Benin[5] mask, the features drawn and almost distorted by an ancient abstract sorrow.

"Don't you feel well?" I asked.

"Girl, I don't know."

"My Da-duh, I goin' boil you some bush tea," my aunt, Da-duh's youngest child, who lived with her, called from the shed roof kitchen.

"Who tell you I need bush tea?" she cried, her voice assuming for a moment its old authority. "You can't even rest nowadays without some malicious person looking for you to be dead. Come girl," she motioned to me to a place beside her on the old-fashioned lounge chair, "give us a tune."

I sang for her until breakfast at eleven, all my brash irreverent Tin Pan Alley[6] songs, and then just before noon we went out into the ground. But it was a short, dispirited walk. Da-duh didn't even notice that the mangoes were beginning to ripen and would have to be picked before the village boys got to them. And when she paused occasionally and looked out across the canes or up at her trees it wasn't as if she were seeing them but something else. Some huge, monolithic shape had imposed itself, it seemed, between her and the land, obstructing her vision. Returning to the house she slept the entire afternoon on the Berbice chair.

She remained like this until we left, languishing away the mornings on the chair at the window gazing out at the land as if it were already doomed; then, at noon, taking the brief stroll with me through the ground during which

---

[4]*Berbice*: in reference to a type of lounge chair. (Berbice is the name of a river in South America.)
[5]*Benin*: a West African country, famous for its fine metalwork.
[6]*Tin Pan Alley*: a term that originated in New York City in the early 1900s, Tin Pan Alley refers to a district that is the center for composers and publishers of popular music.

she seldom spoke, and afterwards returning home to sleep till almost dusk sometimes.

On the day of our departure she put on the austere, ankle-length white dress, the black shoes and brown felt hat (her town clothes she called them), but she did not go with us to town. She saw us off on the road outside her house and in the midst of my mother's tearful protracted farewell, she leaned down and whispered in my ear, ''Girl, you're not to forget now to send me the picture of that building, you hear.''

By the time I mailed her the large colored picture postcard of the Empire State Building she was dead. She died during the famous '37 strike which began shortly after we left. On the day of her death England sent planes flying low over the island in a show of force—so low, according to my aunt's letter, that the downdraft from them shook the ripened mangoes from the trees in Da-duh's orchard. Frightened, everyone in the village fled into the canes. Except Da-duh. She remained in the house at the window so my aunt said, watching as the planes came swooping and screaming like monstrous birds down over the village, over her house, rattling her trees and flattening the young canes in her field. It must have seemed to her lying there that they did not intend pulling out of their dive, but like the hardback beetles which hurled themselves with suicidal force against the walls of the house at night, those menacing silver shapes would hurl themselves in an ecstasy of self-immolation[7] on the land, destroying it utterly.

When the planes finally left and the villagers returned they found her dead on the Berbice chair at the window.

She died and I lived, but always, to this day even, within the shadow of her death. For a brief period after I was grown I went to live alone, like one doing penance, in a loft above a noisy factory in downtown New York and there painted seas of sugarcane and huge swirling Van Gogh suns and palm trees striding like brightly-plumed Tutsi[8] warriors across a tropical landscape, while the thunderous tread of the machines downstairs jarred the floor beneath my easel, mocking my efforts.

---

[7]*self-immolation*: suicide, usually by burning oneself in public—deliberate self-sacrifice.
[8]*Tutsi*: a tribe of Burundi, an east central African country; also known as the Watusi.

Thinking About the Story

1. Why does Da-duh fear her granddaughter when she meets her for the first time?

2. Da-duh shows her granddaughter the lushness and beauty of her homeland and she ends her descriptions by saying, "I know you don't have anything this nice where you come from." How does this make her granddaughter feel? How does the granddaughter handle her feelings?

3. Compare and contrast Da-duh's personality and the granddaughter's personality. In what ways are they similar? What do these similarities and differences say about them?

4. Da-duh becomes ill after her granddaughter tells her that the Empire State Building is taller than the tallest hill on the island. Why does this information disturb the grandmother?

5. Is the granddaughter really responsible for Da-duh's death? Why does she consider her painting of tropical landscapes penance, or atonement for a sin?

Reading/Writing Connections

1. After the granddaughter tells Da-duh that the Empire State Building is taller than the largest hill on the island, she says she wishes that she could have told her grandmother that it was not so. Imagine that you are the granddaughter. After you return to New York, write a postcard to Da-duh in which you downplay the size of the Empire State Building.

2. In your writing journal, discuss a time in your life when you paid attention to a story that an older relative told you. Since you heard that story, has anything about it had an impact on the way you think or act?

3. Write an essay in which you explain to a younger person the importance of listening to older relatives.

Rita Dove   (b. 1952) was born in Akron, Ohio, to Ray Dove, a chemist, and Elvira Dove. In 1970 Rita Dove was invited to the White House as a Presidential Scholar, one of the best high-school graduates in the United States. In 1973 she received her B.A. degree, summa cum laude, from Miami University in Oxford, Ohio. During 1974 and 1975 she attended the University of Tübingen, West Germany, on a Fulbright scholarship. Dove married Fred Viebahn, a writer, in 1979. She received her M.F.A. degree from the University of Iowa in 1977. Dove had already received national acclaim for her work in anthologies and magazines when her first book of poetry, *The Yellow House on the Corner*, was published in 1980. In 1987 Dove received the Pulitzer Prize for another book of poetry, *Thomas and Beulah* (1986), a collection of poems based on stories she knew about her grandfather and grandmother. Dove has received numerous awards for her poetry and has served on numerous panels and committees. She taught at Arizona State University and is now a professor of English at the University of Virginia.

Dove's poetry and fiction are insightful and poignant. She has published several books of poetry, including *Museum* (1983) and *Grace Notes* (1989). In addition, she has published fiction—*Fifth Sunday* (1985) and *Through the Ivory Gate* (1992)—and a full-length verse drama entitled *The Darker Face of Earth* (1993).

Magic

R I T A   D O V E

Practice makes perfect, the old folks said.
So she rehearsed deception
until ice cubes
dangled willingly
from a plain white string   5
and she could change
an egg into her last nickel.
Sent to the yard to sharpen,

she bent so long over
the wheel the knives   10
grew thin. When she stood up,
her brow shorn clean
as a wheatfield and
stippled with blood,
she felt nothing, even   15
when Mama screamed.

She fed sauerkraut to the apple tree;
the apples bloomed tarter
every year. Like all art
useless and beautiful,   20
like sailing in air,
things happened
to her. One night she awoke
and on the lawn blazed
a scaffolding strung in lights.   25
Next morning the Sunday paper
showed the Eiffel Tower
soaring through clouds.
It was a sign
she would make it to Paris one day.   30

Thinking About the Poem

1. How does the girl in the poem feel about her life? Describe the emotional connection between the girl and the world in which she lives. Use words and phrases from the poem to support your description.

2. The poem states "So she rehearsed deception. . . ." Why does the girl practice deception? Who or what is she deceiving? What purpose does the deception serve?

3. Why is the picture in the Sunday paper of the Eiffel Tower a sign? Why is it important to the girl to "make it to Paris one day"?

4. How realistic is the young girl's dream of going to Paris? Based on evidence found in the poem, what might keep her from obtaining her dream?

Reading/Writing Connections

1. In your writing journal, discuss how you separate yourself from the world around you.

2. Write an essay appropriate for a magazine like *Time* or *Newsweek* in which you discuss how social and economic restraints can keep some African American women from reaching their dreams.

3. Today, are African American women able to achieve any dream that they have for themselves? Support your response with examples from recent news or other material you have read or from situations you have experienced in your life.

Georgia Douglas Johnson (1886–1966) was born in Atlanta, Ga., to George and Laura Jackson Camp. She attended public schools in Atlanta and briefly attended Atlanta University. She then attended Howard University in Washington, D.C., and Oberlin Conservatory of Music in Ohio. She married Henry Lincoln Johnson, a Washington lawyer and politician. Johnson's Washington, D.C., home was the meeting place of such Harlem Renaissance writers as Langston Hughes, Countee Cullen, Jessie Fauset, and Alain Locke. Throughout her career as a writer, Johnson was committed to the concerns of women and minorities.

Johnson was one of the first modern African American woman poets to gain recognition. Over two hundred of her poems were published in four volumes: *The Heart of a Woman and Other Poems* (1918), *Bronze: A Book of Verse* (1922), *An Autumn Love Cycle* (1928), and *Share My World* (1962). In the late 1920s, she began to write drama, producing *Plumes: A Play in One Act* (1927), *Blue Blood* (1927), and *Frederick Douglass Leaves for Freedom* (1940).

Plumes

GEORGIA DOUGLAS JOHNSON

CHARACTERS

CHARITY BROWN,	the mother
EMMERLINE BROWN,	the daughter
TILDY,	the friend
DOCTOR SCOTT,	physician

Scene: A poor cottage in the South.
Time: Contemporary.

SCENE: *The kitchen of a two-room cottage. A window overlooking the street. A door leading to street, one leading to the backyard and one to the inner room. A stove, a table with shelf over it, a washtub. A rocking-chair, a cane-bottom chair. Needle, thread, scissors, etc., on table.*

Scene opens with CHARITY BROWN *heating a poultice over the stove. A groaning is heard from the inner room.*

CHARITY. Yes, honey, mamma is fixing somethin' to do you good. Yes, my baby, jus' you wait—I'm a-coming.

(Knock is heard at door. It is gently pushed open and TILDY *comes in cautiously.)*

TILDY. *(Whispering)* How is she?

CHARITY. Poorly, poorly. Didn't rest last night none hardly. Move that dress and set in th' rocker. I been trying to snatch a minute to finish it but don't seem like I can. She won't have nothing to wear if she—she—

TILDY. I understands. How near done is it?

CHARITY. Ain't so much more to do.

TILDY. *(Takes up dress from chair, looks at it)* I'll do some on it.

CHARITY. Thank you, sister Tildy. Whip that torshon[1] on and turn down the hem in the skirt.

TILDY. *(Measuring dress against herself)* How deep?

CHARITY. Let me see, now *(Studies a minute with finger against lip)* I tell you— jus' baste it, 'cause you see—she wears 'em short, but—it might be—*(Stops.)*

TILDY. *(Bowing her head comprehendingly)* Huh-uh, I see exzackly. *(Sighs)* You'd want it long—over her feet—then.

---

[1] *torshon:* decorative trim.

CHARITY. That's it, sister Tildy. (*Listening*) She's some easy now! (*Stirring poultice*) Jest can't get this poltis' hot enough somehow this morning.

TILDY. Put some red pepper in it. Got any?

CHARITY. Yes. There ought to be some in one of them boxes on the shelf there. (*Points.*)

TILDY. (*Goes to shelf, looks about and gets the pepper*) Here, put a-plenty of this in.

CHARITY. (*Groans are heard from the next room*) Good Lord, them pains got her again. She suffers so, when she's 'wake.

TILDY. Poor little thing. How old is she now, sister Charity?

CHARITY. Turning fourteen this coming July.

TILDY. (*Shaking her head dubiously*) I sho' hope she'll be mended by then.

CHARITY. It don't look much like it, but I trusts so—(*Looking worried*) That doctor's mighty late this morning.

TILDY. I expects he'll be 'long in no time. Doctors is mighty onconcerned here lately.

CHARITY. (*Going toward inner room with poultice*) They surely is and I don't have too much confidence in none of 'em. (*You can hear her soothing the child.*)

TILDY. (*Listening*) Want me to help you put it on, sister Charity?

CHARITY. (*From inner room*) No, I can fix it. (*Coming back from sickroom shaking her head rather dejectedly.*)

TILDY. How is she, sister Charity?

CHARITY. Mighty feeble. Gone back to sleep now. My poor little baby. (*Bracing herself*) I'm going to put on some coffee now.

TILDY. I'm sho' glad. I feel kinder low-spirited.

CHARITY. It's me that low-sperited. The doctor said last time he was here he might have to oparate—said, she mought have a chance then. But I tell you the truth, I've got no faith a-tall in 'em. They takes all your money for nothing.

TILDY. They sho' do and don't leave a cent for putting you away decent.

CHARITY. That's jest it. They takes all you got and then you dies jest the same. It ain't like they was sure.

TILDY. No, they ain't sure. That's it exzackly. But they takes your money jest the same, and leaves you flat.

CHARITY. I been thinking 'bout Zeke these last few days—how he was put away—

TILDY. I wouldn't worry 'bout him now. He's out of his troubles.

CHARITY. I know. But it worries me when I think about how he was put away . . . that ugly pine coffin, jest one shabby old hack[2] and nothing else to show—to show—what we thought about him.

---

[2]*hack*: horse carriage for hire.

TILDY. Hush, sister! Don't you worry over him. He's happy now, anyhow.

CHARITY. I can't help it! Then little Bessie. We all jest scrooged in one hack and took her little coffin in our lap all the way out to the graveyard. (*Breaks out crying.*)

TILDY. Do hush, sister Charity. You done the best you could. Poor folks got to make the best of it. The Lord understands—

CHARITY. I know that—but I made up my mind the time Bessie went that the next one of us what died would have a shore nuff funeral, everything grand,—with plumes[3]!—I saved and saved and now—this yah doctor—

TILDY. All they think about is cuttin' and killing and taking your money. I got nothin' to put 'em doing.

CHARITY. (*Goes over to washtub and rubs on clothes*) Me neither. These clothes got to get out somehow, I needs every cent.

TILDY. How much that washing bring you?

CHARITY. Dollar and a half. It's worth a whole lot more. But what can you do?

TILDY. You can't do nothing—Look there, sister Charity, ain't that coffee boiling?

CHARITY. (*Wipes hands on apron and goes to stove*) Yes it's boiling good fashioned. Come on, drink some.

TILDY. There ain't nothing I'd rather have than a good strong cup of coffee. (*Charity pours Tildy's cup.*) (*Sweetening and stirring hers*) Pour you some. (*Charity pours her own cup*) I'd been dead, too, long ago if it hadn't a been for my coffee.

CHARITY. I love it, but it don't love me—gives me the shortness of breath.

TILDY. (*Finishing her cup, taking up sugar with spoon*) Don't hurt me. I could drink a barrel.

CHARITY. (*Drinking more slowly—reaching for coffeepot*) Here, drink another cup.

TILDY. I shore will, that cup done me a lot of good.

CHARITY. (*Looking into her empty cup thoughtfully*) I wish Dinah Morris would drop in now. I'd ask her what these grounds mean.

TILDY. I can read em a little myself.

CHARITY. You can? Well, for the Lord's sake, look here and tell me what this cup says! (*Offers cup to Tildy. Tildy wards it off.*)

TILDY. You got to turn it 'round in your saucer three times first.

CHARITY. Yes, that's right, I forgot. (*Turns cup 'round, counting*) One, two, three. (*Starts to pick it up.*)

TILDY. Huhudh. (*Meaning no*) Let it set a minute. It might be watery. (*After a minute, while she finishes her own cup*) Now let me see. (*Takes cup and examines it very scrutinizingly.*)

---

[3]*plumes*: ornate, fluffy feathers that decorate horses pulling a funeral hearse.

CHARITY. What you see?

TILDY. (*Hesitatingly*) I ain't seen a cup like this one for many a year. Not since—not since—

CHARITY. When?

TILDY. Not since jest before ma died. I looked in the cup then and saw things and—I stopped looking . . .

CHARITY. Tell me what you see, I want to know.

TILDY. I don't like to tell no bad news—

CHARITY. Go on. I can stan' anything after all I been thru'.

TILDY. Since you're bound to know I'll tell you. (*Charity draws nearer*) I sees a big gethering!

CHARITY. Gethering, you say?

TILDY. Yes, a big gethering. People all crowded together. Then I see 'em going one by one and two by two. Long line stretching out and out and out!

CHARITY. (*In a whisper*) What you think it is?

TILDY. (*Awed like*) Looks like (*Hesitates*) a possession!

CHARITY. (*Shouting*) You sure!

TILDY. I know it is. (*Just then the toll of a church bell is heard and then the steady and slow tramp, tramp of horses' hoofs. Both women look at each other.*)

TILDY. (*In a hushed voice.*) That must be Bell Gibson's funeral coming 'way from Mt. Zion. (*Gets up and goes to window*) Yes, it sho' is.

CHARITY. (*Looking out of the window also*) Poor Bell suffered many a year; she's out of her pain now.

TILDY. Look, here comes the hearse now!

CHARITY. My Lord! ain't it grand! Look at them horses—look at their heads—plumes—how they shake 'em! Land o' mighty! It's a fine sight, sister Tildy.

TILDY. That must be Jer'miah in that first carriage, bending over like; he shorely is putting her away grand.

CHARITY. No mistake about it. That's Pickett's best funeral turnout he's got.

TILDY. I'll bet it cost a lot.

CHARITY. Fifty dollars, so Matilda Jenkins told me. She had it for Bud. The plumes is what cost.

TILDY. Look at the hacks—(*Counts*) I believe to my soul there's eight.

CHARITY. Got somebody in all of 'em too—and flowers—She shore got a lot of 'em. (*Both women's eyes follow the tail end of the procession, horses' hoofs die away as they turn away from window. The two women look at each other significantly.*)

TILDY. (*Significantly*) Well!— (*They look at each other without speaking for a minute. Charity goes to the washtub*) Want these cups washed up?

CHARITY. No don't mind 'em. I'd rather you get that dress done. I got to get these clothes out.

TILDY. (*Picking up dress*) Shore, there ain't so much more to do on it now. (*Knock is heard on the door. Charity answers knock and admits* DR. SCOTT.)

DR. SCOTT. Good morning. How's the patient today?

CHARITY. Not so good, doctor. When she ain't 'sleep she suffers so; but she sleeps mostly.

DR. SCOTT. Well, let's see, let's see. Just hand me a pan of warm water and I'll soon find out just what's what.

CHARITY. All right, doctor. I'll bring it to you right away. (*Bustles about fixing water—looking toward dress Tildy is working on*) Poor little Emmerline's been wanting a white dress trimmed with torshon a long time—now she's got it and it looks like—well—(*Hesitates*) t'warn't made to wear.

TILDY. Don't take on so, sister Charity—The Lord giveth and the Lord taketh.

CHARITY. I know—but it's hard—hard—(*Goes into inner room with water. You can hear her talking with the doctor after a minute and the doctor expostulating with her—in a minute she appears at the door, being led from the room by the doctor.*)

DR. SCOTT. No, my dear Mrs. Brown. It will be much better for you to remain outside.

CHARITY. But, doctor—

DR. SCOTT. NO. You stay outside and get your mind on something else. You can't possibly be of any service. Now be calm, will you?

CHARITY. I'll try, doctor.

TILDY. The doctor's right. You can't do no good in there.

CHARITY. I knows, but I thought I could hold the pan or somethin'. (*Lowering her voice*) Says he got to see if her heart is all right or somethin'. I tell you—nowadays—

TILDY. I know.

CHARITY. (*Softly to Tildy*) Hope he won't come out here saying he got to operate. (*Goes to washtub.*)

TILDY. I hope so, too. Won't it cost a lot?

CHARITY. That's jest it. It would take all I got saved up.

TILDY. Of course, if he's goin' to get her up—but I don't believe in 'em. I don't believe in 'em.

CHARITY. He didn't promise tho'—even if he did, he said maybe it wouldn't do no good.

TILDY. I'd think a long time before I'd let him operate on my chile. Taking all yuh money, promising nothing and ten to one killing her to boot.

CHARITY. This is a hard world.

TILDY. Don't you trus' him. Coffee grounds don't lie!

CHARITY. I don't trust him. I jest want to do what's right by her. I ought to put these clothes on the line while you're settin' in here, but I jes hate to go outdoors while he's in there.

TILDY. (*Getting up*) I'll hang 'em out. You stay here. Where your clothespins at?

CHARITY. Hanging right there by the back door in the bag. They ought to dry before dark and then I can iron tonight.

TILDY. (*Picking up tub*) They ought to blow dry in no time. (*Goes toward back door.*)

CHARITY. Then I can shore rub 'em over tonight. Say, sister Tildy, hist 'em up with that long saplin' prop leaning in the fence corner.

TILDY. (*Going out*) All right.

CHARITY. (*Standing by the table beating nervously on it with her fingers— listens—and then starts to bustling about the kitchen*) (*Enter Doctor from inner room.*)

DR. SCOTT. Well, Mrs. Brown, I've decided I'll have to operate.

CHARITY. MY Lord! Doctor—don't say that!

DR. SCOTT. It's the only chance.

CHARITY. You mean she'll get well if you do?

DR. SCOTT. No, I can't say that—It's just a chance—a last chance. And I'll do just what I said, cut the price of the operation down to fifty dollars. I'm willing to do that for you. (*Charity throws up her hands in dismay.*)

CHARITY. Doctor, I was so in hopes you wouldn't operate—I—I—And yo' say you ain't a bit sure she'll get well—even then?

DR. SCOTT. No. I can't be sure. We'll just have to take the chance. But I'm sure you want to do everything—

CHARITY. Sure, doctor, I do want to—do—everything I can do to—to—Doctor, look at this cup. (*Picks up fortune cup and shows the doctor*) My fortune's jes' been told this morning—look at these grounds—they says—(*Softly*) it ain't no use, no use a-tall.

DR. SCOTT. Why, my good woman, don't you believe in such senseless things! That cup of grounds can't show you anything. Wash them out and forget it.

CHARITY. I can't forget it. I feel like it ain't no use; I'd just be spendin' the money that I needs—for nothing—nothing.

DR. SCOTT. But you won't though—You'll have a clear conscience. You'd know that you did everything you could.

CHARITY. I know that, doctor. But there's things you don't know 'bout— there's other things I got to think about. If she goes—if she must go . . . I had plans—I been getting ready—now—Oh, doctor, I jest can't see how I can have this operation—you say you can't promise—nothing?

DR. SCOTT. I didn't think you'd hesitate about it—I imagined your love for your child—

CHARITY. (*Breaking in*) I do love my child. My God, I do love my child. You don't understand . . . but . . . but—can't I have a little time to think about it, doctor? It means so much—to her—and—me!

DR. SCOTT. I tell you. I'll go on over to the office. I'd have to get my (*Hesitates*) my things, anyhow. And as soon as you make up your mind, get one of the neighbors to run over and tell me. I'll come right back. But don't waste any time now, Mrs. Brown, every minute counts.

CHARITY. Thank you, doctor, thank you. I'll shore send you word as soon as I can. I'm so upset and worried I'm half crazy.

DR. SCOTT. I know you are . . . but don't take too long to make up your mind. . . . It ought to be done today. Remember—it may save her. (*Exits.*)

CHARITY. (*Goes to door of sickroom—looks inside for a few minutes, then starts walking up and down the little kitchen, first holding a hand up to her head and then wringing them. Enter Tildy from yard with tub under her arm.*)

TILDY. Well, they're all out, sister Charity—(*Stops*) Why, what's the matter?

CHARITY. The doctor wants to operate.

TILDY. (*Softly*) Where he—gone?

CHARITY. Yes—he's gone, but he's coming back—if I send for him.

TILDY. You going to? (*Puts down tub and picks up white dress and begins sewing.*)

CHARITY. I dunno—I got to think.

TILDY. I can't see what's the use myself. He can't save her with no operation— Coffee grounds don't lie.

CHARITY. It would take all the money I got for the operation and then what about puttin' her away? He can't save her—don't even promise ter. I know he can't—I feel it . . . I feel it. . . .

TILDY. It's in the air. . . . (*Both women sit tense in the silence. Tildy has commenced sewing again. Just then a strange, strangling noise comes from the inner room.*)

TILDY. What's that?

CHARITY. (*Running toward and into inner room*) Oh, my God! (*From inside*) Sister Tildy—Come here—No,—Some water, quick.

(*Tildy with dress in hand starts towards inner room. Stops at door, sighs and then goes hurriedly back for the water pitcher. Charity is heard moaning softly in the next room, then she appears at doorway and leans against jamb of door*) Rip the hem out, sister Tildy.

CURTAIN

Thinking About the Play

1. The play *Plumes* takes place in "a poor cottage in the South" in "contemporary times." Explain how the **setting** of the play influences the action. Use specific examples from the play to support your response.

2. In a play, an actor's facial expressions and body language convey as much information to the audience as the lines the actor speaks. Examine the stage directions for Charity. Describe her characteristics using specific examples from the stage directions to support your response.

3. Why is it so important to Charity that her daughter, Emmerline, have a nice "putting away"? What do the "plumes" represent to Charity?

4. Charity states that she loves Emmerline, but when the doctor offers to operate on Emmerline for fifty dollars, Charity hesitates because of what Tildy read in the coffee grounds. Why do you think Charity would place more trust in the "reading" of coffee grounds than in the white doctor's attempt at saving her daughter's life?

5. The play ends with Charity saying "Rip the hem out, sister Tildy." What do you think is the significance of this line?

Reading/Writing Connections

1. Rewrite the ending of the play so that Charity agrees to let the doctor operate. However, Emmerline dies after the operation and Charity gives the doctor the fifty dollars she has saved. How will Charity bury her daughter? What can she do to ensure that Emmerline has a nice "putting away"?

2. In your journal, state your opinion on the decision Charity has to make between believing the coffee grounds and relying on medical science. Support your responses with evidence from the play, from other readings, or both.

3. In many rural communities, people cannot afford routine health-care costs. Write an essay in which you argue for the establishment of community health-care centers in poor rural communities.

Paulette Childress White   (b. 1948) was born in Hamtramck, Mich., to Norris Childress, a welder, and Effie Childress. She attended high school in Ecorse, Mich., and married Bennie White, Jr., a postal employee and artist. Since 1972 she has pursued a career as a writer and presently lives in Detroit.

White's work examines the survival of African American women in the urban environment. Her fiction gives substance to everyday occurrences in African American women's lives. She is the author of *Love Poem to a Black Junkie* (1975) and *The Watermelon Dress* (1983). Her work is represented in anthologies such as *Sturdy Black Bridges* (1979) and *Midnight Birds* (1980) and has appeared in *Essence, Redbook,* and *Callaloo* magazines.

Getting the Facts of Life

PAULETTE CHILDRESS WHITE

The August morning was ripening into a day that promised to be a burner. By the time we'd walked three blocks, dark patches were showing beneath Momma's arms, and inside tennis shoes thick with white polish, my feet were wet against the cushions. I was beginning to regret how quickly I'd volunteered to go.

"Dog. My feet are getting mushy," I complained.

"You should've wore socks," Momma said, without looking my way or slowing down.

I frowned. In 1961, nobody wore socks with tennis shoes. It was bare legs, Bermuda shorts and a sleeveless blouse. Period.

Momma was chubby but she could really walk. She walked the same way she washed clothes—up-and-down, up-and-down until she was done. She didn't believe in taking breaks.

This was my first time going to the welfare office with Momma. After breakfast, before we'd had time to scatter, she corralled everyone old enough to consider and announced in her serious-business voice that someone was going to the welfare office with her this morning. Cries went up.

Junior had his papers to do. Stella was going swimming at the high school. Dennis was already pulling the *Free Press* wagon across town every first Wednesday to get the surplus food—like that.

"You want clothes for school, don't you?" That landed. School opened in two weeks.

"I'll go," I said.

"Who's going to baby-sit if Minerva goes?" Momma asked.

Stella smiled and lifted her golden nose. "I will," she said. "I'd rather baby-sit than do *that*."

That should have warned me. Anything that would make Stella offer to baby-sit had to be bad.

A small cheer probably went up among my younger brothers in the back rooms where I was not too secretly known as "The Witch" because of the criminal licks I'd learned to give on my rise to power. I was twelve, third oldest under Junior and Stella, but I had long established myself as first in command among the kids. I was chief baby-sitter, biscuit-maker and broom-wielder. Unlike Stella, who'd begun her development at ten, I still had my girl's body and wasn't anxious to have that changed. What would it mean but a loss of power? I liked things just the way they were. My interest in bras was even less than my interest in boys, and that was limited to keeping my brothers—who seemed destined for wildness—from taking over completely.

Even before we left, Stella had Little Stevie Wonder turned up on the radio in the living room, and suspicious jumping-bumping sounds were beginning in the back. They'll tear the house down, I thought, following Momma out the door.

We turned at Salliotte, the street that would take us straight up to Jefferson Avenue where the welfare office was. Momma's face was pinking in the heat, and I was huffing to keep up. From here, it was seven more blocks on the colored side, the railroad tracks, five blocks on the white side and there you were. We'd be cooked.

"Is the welfare office near the Harbor Show?" I asked. I knew the answer, I just wanted some talk.

"Across the street."

"Umm. Glad it's not way down Jefferson somewhere."

Nothing. Momma didn't talk much when she was outside. I knew that the reason she wanted one of us along when she had far to go was not for company but so she wouldn't have to walk by herself. I could understand that. To me, walking alone was like being naked or deformed—everyone seemed to look at you harder and longer. With Momma, the feeling was probably worse because you knew people were wondering if she where white, Indian maybe or really colored. Having one of us along, brown and clearly hers, probably helped define that. Still, it was like being a little parade, with Momma's pale skin and straight brown hair turning heads like the clang of cymbals. Especially on the colored side.

"Well," I said, "here we come to the bad part."

Momma gave a tiny laugh.

Most of Salliotte was a business street, with Old West–looking storefronts and some office places that never seemed to open. Ecorse, hinged onto southwest Detroit like a clothes closet, didn't seem to take itself seriously. There were lots of empty fields, some of which folks down the residential streets turned into vegetable gardens every summer. And there was this block where the Moonflower Hotel raised itself to three stories over the poolroom and Beaman's drugstore. Here, bad boys and drunks made their noise and did an occasional stabbing. Except for the cars that lined both sides of the block, only one side was busy—the other bordered a field of weeds. We walked on the safe side.

If you were a woman or a girl over twelve, walking this block—even on the safe side—could be painful. They usually hollered at you and never mind what they said. Today, because it was hot and early, we made it by with only one weak *Hey baby* from a drunk sitting in the poolroom door.

"Hey baby yourself," I said but not too loudly, pushing my flat chest out and stabbing my eyes in his direction.

"Minerva girl, you better watch your mouth with grown men like that," Momma said, her eyes catching me up in real warning though I could see that she was holding down a smile.

"Well, he can't do nothing to me when I'm with you, can he?" I asked, striving to match the rise and fall of her black pumps.

She said nothing. She just walked on, churning away under a sun that clearly meant to melt us. From here to the tracks it was mostly gardens. It felt like the Dixie Peach[1] I'd used to help water-wave my hair was sliding down with the sweat on my face, and my throat was tight with thirst. Boy, did I want a pop. I looked at the last little store before we crossed the tracks without bothering to ask.

Across the tracks, there were no stores and no gardens. It was shady, and the grass was June green. Perfect-looking houses sat in unfenced spaces far back from the street. We walked these five blocks without a word. We just looked and hurried to get through it. I was beginning to worry about the welfare office in earnest. A fool could see that in this part of Ecorse, things got serious.

We had been on welfare for almost a year. I didn't have any strong feelings about it—my life went on pretty much the same. It just meant watching the mail for a check instead of Daddy getting paid, and occasional visits from a social worker that I'd always managed to miss. For Momma and whoever went with her, it meant this walk to the office and whatever went on there that made everyone hate to go. For Daddy, it seemed to bring the most change. For him, it meant staying away from home more than when he was working and a reason not to answer the phone.

At Jefferson, we turned left and there it was, halfway down the block. The Department of Social Services. I discovered some strong feelings. That fine name meant nothing. This was the welfare. The place for poor people. People who couldn't or wouldn't take care of themselves. Now I was going to face it, and suddenly I thought what I knew the others had thought, *What if I see someone I know?* I wanted to run back all those blocks to home.

I looked at Momma for comfort, but her face was closed and her mouth looked locked.

Inside, the place was gray. There were rows of long benches like church pews facing each other across a middle aisle that led to a central desk. Beyond the benches and the desk, four hallways led off to a maze of partitioned offices.

---

[1]*Dixie Peach*: a brand of hair oil.

In opposite corners, huge fans hung from the ceiling, humming from side to side, blowing the heavy air for a breeze.

Momma walked to the desk, answered some questions, was given a number and told to take a seat. I followed her through, trying not to see the waiting people—as though that would keep them from seeing me.

Gradually, as we waited, I took them all in. There was no one there that I knew, but somehow they all looked familiar. Or maybe I only thought they did, because when your eyes connected with someone's, they didn't quickly look away and they usually smiled. They were mostly women and children, and a few low-looking men. Some of them were white, which surprised me. I hadn't expected to see them in there.

Directly in front of the bench where we sat, a little girl with blond curls was trying to handle a bottle of Coke. Now and then, she'd manage to turn herself and the bottle around and watch me with big gray eyes that seemed to know quite well how badly I wanted a pop. I thought of asking Momma for fifteen cents so I could get one from the machine in the back but I was afraid she'd still say no so I just kept planning more and more convincing ways to ask. Besides, there was a water fountain near the door if I could make myself rise and walk to it.

We waited three hours. White ladies dressed like secretaries kept coming out to call numbers, and people on the benches would get up and follow down a hall. Then more people came in to replace them. I drank water from the fountain three times and was ready to put my feet up on the bench before us— the little girl with the Coke and her momma got called—by the time we heard Momma's number.

"You wait here," Momma said as I rose with her.

I sat down with a plop.

The lady with the number looked at me. Her face reminded me of the librarian's at Bunch school. Looked like she never cracked a smile. "Let her come," she said.

"She can wait here," Momma repeated, weakly.

"It's OK. She can come in. Come on," the lady insisted at me.

I hesitated, knowing that Momma's face was telling me to sit.

"Come on," the woman said.

Momma said nothing.

I got up and followed them into the maze. We came to a small room where there was a desk and three chairs. The woman sat behind the desk and we before it.

For a while, no one spoke. The woman studied a folder open before her, brows drawn together. On the wall behind her there was a calendar with one heavy black line drawn slantwise through each day of August, up to the twenty-first. That was today.

"Mrs. Blue, I have a notation here that Mr. Blue has not reported to the department on his efforts to obtain employment since the sixteenth of June. Before that, it was the tenth of April. You understand that department regulations require that he report monthly to this office, do you not?" Eyes brown as a wren's belly came up at Momma.

"Yes," Momma answered, sounding as small as I felt.

"Can you explain his failure to do so?"

Pause. "He's been looking. He says he's been looking."

"That may be. However, his failure to report those efforts here is my only concern."

Silence.

"We cannot continue with your case as it now stands if Mr. Blue refuses to comply with departmental regulations. He is still residing with the family, is he not?"

"Yes, he is. I've been reminding him to come in . . . he said he would."

"Well, he hasn't. Regulations are that any able-bodied man, head-of-household and receiving assistance who neglects to report to this office any effort to obtain work for a period of sixty days or more is to be cut off for a minimum of three months, at which time he may reapply. As of this date, Mr. Blue is over sixty days delinquent, and officially, I am obliged to close the case and direct you to other sources of aid."

"What is that?"

"Aid to Dependent Children would be the only source available to you. Then, of course, you would not be eligible unless it was verified that Mr. Blue was no longer residing with the family."

Another silence. I stared into the gray steel front of the desk, everything stopped but my heart.

"Well, can you keep the case open until Monday? If he comes in by Monday?"

"According to my records, Mr. Blue failed to come in May and such an agreement was made then. In all, we allowed him a period of seventy days. You must understand that what happens in such cases as this is not wholly my decision." She sighed and watched Momma with hopeless eyes, tapping the soft end of her pencil on the papers before her. "Mrs. Blue, I will speak to my superiors on your behalf. I can allow you until Monday next . . . that's the"—she swung around to the calendar—"twenty-sixth of August, to get him in here."

"Thank you. He'll be in," Momma breathed. "Will I be able to get the clothing order today?"

Hands and eyes searched in the folder for an answer before she cleared her throat and tilted her face at Momma. "We'll see what we can do," she said, finally.

My back touched the chair. Without turning my head, I moved my eyes down to Momma's dusty feet and wondered if she could still feel them; my own were numb. I felt bodyless—there was only my face, which wouldn't disappear, and behind it, one word pinging against another in a buzz that made no sense. At home, we'd have the house cleaned by now, and I'd be waiting for the daily appearance of my best friend, Bernadine, so we could comb each other's hair or talk about stuck-up Evelyn and Brenda. Maybe Bernadine was already there, and Stella was teaching her to dance the bop.

Then I heard our names and ages—all eight of them—being called off like items in a grocery list.

"Clifford, Junior, age fourteen." She waited.

"Yes."

"Born? Give me the month and year."

"October 1946," Momma answered, and I could hear in her voice that she'd been through these questions before.

"Stella, age thirteen."

"Yes."

"Born?"

"November 1947."

"Minerva, age twelve." She looked at me. "This is Minerva?"

"Yes."

No. I thought, no, this is not Minerva. You can write it down if you want to, but Minerva is not here.

"Born?"

"December 1948."

The woman went on down the list, sounding more and more like Momma should be sorry or ashamed, and Momma's answers grew fainter and fainter. So this was welfare. I wondered how many times Momma had had to do this. Once before? Three times? Every time?

More questions. How many in school? Six. Who needs shoes? Everybody.

"Everybody needs shoes? The youngest two?"

"Well, they don't go to school . . . but they walk."

My head came up to look at Momma and the woman. The woman's mouth was left open. Momma didn't blink.

The brown eyes went down. "Our allowances are based on the median costs for moderately priced clothing at Sears, Roebuck." She figured on paper as she spoke. "That will mean thirty-four dollars for children over ten . . . thirty dollars for children under ten. It comes to one hundred ninety-eight dollars. I can allow eight dollars for two additional pairs of shoes."

"Thank you."

"You will present your clothing order to a salesperson at the store, who will be happy to assist you in your selections. Please be practical as further clothing requests will not be considered for a period of six months. In cases of necessity, however, requests for winter outerwear will be considered beginning November first.''

Momma said nothing.

The woman rose and left the room.

For the first time, I shifted in the chair. Momma was looking into the calendar as though she could see through the pages to November first. Everybody needed a coat.

I'm never coming here again, I thought. If I do, I'll stay out front. Not coming back in here. Ever again.

She came back and sat behind her desk. ''Mrs. Blue, I must make it clear that, regardless of my feelings, I will be forced to close your case if your husband does not report to this office by Monday, the twenty-sixth. Do you understand?''

''Yes. Thank you. He'll come. I'll see to it.''

''Very well.'' She held a paper out to Momma.

We stood. Momma reached over and took the slip of paper. I moved toward the door.

''Excuse me, Mrs. Blue, but are you pregnant?''

''What?''

''I asked if you were expecting another child.''

''Oh. No, I'm not,'' Momma answered, biting down on her lips.

''Well, I'm sure you'll want to be careful about a thing like that in your present situation.''

''Yes.''

I looked quickly to Momma's loose white blouse. We'd never known when another baby was coming until it was almost there.

''I suppose that eight children are enough for anyone,'' the woman said, and for the first time her face broke into a smile.

Momma didn't answer that. Somehow, we left the room and found our way out onto the street. We stood for a moment as though lost. My eyes followed Momma's up to where the sun was burning high. It was still there, blazing white against a cloudless blue. Slowly, Momma put the clothing order into her purse and snapped it shut. She looked around as if uncertain which way to go. I led the way to the corner. We turned. We walked the first five blocks.

I was thinking about how stupid I'd been a year ago, when Daddy lost his job. I'd been happy.

''You all better be thinking about moving to Indianapolis,'' he announced one day after work, looking like he didn't think much of it himself. He was a welder with the railroad company. He'd worked there for eleven years. But now, "Company's moving to Indianapolis," he said. "Gonna be gone by November. If I want to keep my job, we've got to move with it."

We didn't. Nobody wanted to move to Indianapolis—not even Daddy. Here, we had uncles, aunts and cousins on both sides. Friends. Everybody and everything we knew. Daddy could get another job. First came unemployment compensation. Then came welfare. Thank goodness for welfare, we said, while we waited and waited for that job that hadn't yet come.

The problem was that Daddy couldn't take it. If something got repossessed or somebody took sick or something was broken or another kid was coming, he'd carry on terribly until things got better—by which time things were always worse. He'd always been that way. So when the railroad left, he began to do everything wrong. Stayed out all hours. Drank and drank some more. When he was home, he was so grouchy we were afraid to squeak. Now when we saw him coming, we got lost. Even our friends ran for cover.

At the railroad tracks, we sped up. The tracks were as far across as a block was long. Silently, I counted the rails by the heat of the steel bars through my thin soles. On the other side, I felt something heavy rise up in my chest and I knew that I wanted to cry. I wanted to cry or run or kiss the dusty ground. The little houses with their sun scorched lawns and backyard gardens were mansions in my eyes. "Ohh, Ma . . . look at those collards!"

"Umm-hummm," she agreed, and I knew that she saw it too.

"Wonder how they grew so big?"

"Cow dung, probably. Big Poppa used to put cow dung out to fertilize the vegetable plots, and everything just grew like crazy. We used to get tomatoes this big"—she circled with her hands—"and don't talk about squash or melons."

"I bet y'all ate like rich people. Bet y'all had everything you could want."

"We sure did," she said. "We never wanted for anything when it came to food. And when the cash crops were sold, we could get whatever else that was needed. We never wanted for a thing."

"What about the time you and cousin Emma threw out the supper peas?"

"Oh! Did I tell you about that?" she asked. Then she told it all over again. I didn't listen. I watched her face and guarded her smile with a smile of my own.

We walked together, step for step. The sun was still burning, but we forgot to mind it. We talked about an Alabama girlhood in a time and place I'd never know. We talked about the wringer washer and how it could be fixed, because washing every day on a scrub-board was something Alabama could keep. We talked about how to get Daddy to the Department of Social Services.

Then we talked about having babies. She began to tell me things I'd never known, and the idea of womanhood blossomed in my mind like some kind of suffocating rose.

"Momma," I said, "I don't think I can be a woman."

"You can," she laughed. "and if you live, you will be. You gotta be some kind of woman."

"But it's hard," I said, "sometimes it must be hard."

"Umm-humm," she said, "sometimes it is hard."

When we got to the bad block, we crossed to Beaman's drugstore for two orange crushes. Then we walked right through the groups of men standing in the shadows of the poolroom and the Moonflower Hotel. Not one of them said a word to us. I supposed they could see in the way we walked that we weren't afraid. We'd been to the welfare office and back again. And the facts of life, fixed in our minds like the sun in the sky, were no burning mysteries.

Thinking About the Story

1. Why do you think Minerva has not thought about her family being on welfare, when the family had been on welfare for a year?

2. What type of relationship do Minerva and her mother have? What type of relationship do Minerva and her father have? How have Minerva's relationships with her parents influenced her development as a person?

3. How do Minerva and her mother interact in private? In public? What do you think is the importance of the two types of behavior?

4. Minerva describes herself as "chief baby-sitter, biscuit-maker and broom-wielder." How are these descriptions of herself influenced by her being one of two sisters in a family of eight children?

5. How does Minerva feel about moving from childhood into womanhood? What limitations might Minerva encounter as she becomes a woman that she might not encounter if she were a boy becoming a man?

Reading/Writing Connections

1. Minerva imagines that her body is invisible as a reaction to the conversation she hears between her mother and the caseworker at the welfare office. In your journal write about a time when you were embarrassed about a situation, but you were powerless to change the situation. How did you feel? How did you react to the situation?

2. "Getting the Facts of Life" is set in 1961. Write an essay in which you contrast the types of careers that African American women usually could have in the early 1960s with the types of careers African American women follow today.

3. In your journal discuss how the "facts of life" that Minerva learns—from her family situation, from the African American community she lives in, and from the white caseworker—prepare her for life. Use examples from the story to support your response.

Lucille Clifton   (b. 1936) was born in DePew, N.Y. She attended Howard University and graduated from Fredonia State Teachers College. An important person in Clifton's life was her great-grandmother, Caroline Donald Sale. Sale was born in the Dahomey tribe in Africa, where she was captured as a child and brought as a slave to America. When she was eight years old, Caroline Sale reportedly walked from New Orleans to Bedford County, Va. For Clifton, this accomplishment served both as an indication of the power of African American women and as an inspiration for her poetry about the strength, love, and compassion of African American women.

Clifton's poetry is powerful not only because of its realistic urban images but also because of its poetic devices. The combination of strong images and well-crafted poetic lines creates a complex message about the characters and locations in the poems. Clifton has published several volumes of poetry: *Good Times* (1969), *Good News About the Earth* (1972), *An Ordinary Woman* (1974), *Generations* (1976), *Next* (1987), and *Quilting* (1991). In addition she has published a large number of children's books, including *The Black BC's* (1970), *The Boy Who Didn't Believe in Spring* (1973), and *The Lucky Stone* (1979).

Miss Rosie

LUCILLE CLIFTON

When I watch you
wrapped up like garbage
sitting, surrounded by the smell
of too old potato peels
or   5
when I watch you
in your old man's shoes
with the little toe cut out
sitting, waiting for your mind
like next weeks grocery   10
I say
when I watch you
you wet brown bag of a woman
who used to be the best looking gal in Georgia
used to be called the Georgia Rose   15
I stand up
through your destruction
I stand up

Thinking About the Poem

1. The title of the poem names the homeless woman as Miss Rosie. What is the significance of the speaker in the poem knowing Miss Rosie's name? Of the speaker knowing that the homeless woman was once called the "Georgia Rose"?

2. When the speaker watches Miss Rosie, she sees the conditions in which Miss Rosie is living. These conditions, however, do not make the speaker lose respect for Miss Rosie. Why do you think the speaker doesn't lose respect for Miss Rosie?

3. The poem ends with the speaker saying "I stand up / through your destruction / I stand up." What do you think is meant by these statements? Why do you think the speaker feels this way about Miss Rosie's situation?

Reading/Writing Connections

1. Write an entry in your journal in which you discuss your reactions to homeless people in general. How do they make you feel? What do you think about them?

2. Imagine that you have been asked by your city council to discuss what your city should do about its homeless people. In your letter discuss Miss Rosie's situation and outline some type of action that the city should follow.

3. Compare and contrast Clifton's use of the phrase "stand up" with Angelou's use of the phrases "I keep on movin'," "I keep on followin'," and "I keep comin' " in the poem "Willie" (Chapter Two). Do the phrases of Clifton's and Angelou's poems mean the same thing? Why or why not?

"The 'Perfect' Partner" by Phoebe Beasley. Medium: Collage. Reprinted by permission of the Isobel Neal Gallery, Chicago, Illinois.

6

RELATIONSHIPS, LOVE, AND CONFLICTS

Relationships between men and women are often influenced by external forces from society. Some external forces can prevent people from having relationships. During the times of slavery, for example, African American men and women were not allowed to marry. Later, when they could marry, external forces, such as racism and poverty, could tear apart a relationship that otherwise might have survived. If people are consistently mistreated by society, sometimes they turn their frustrations against the people they love. Or if there is not enough money for the necessities of life (food, clothing, and shelter), people might separate from one another in order not to be a burden on those that they love. On the other hand, the same external forces that can tear apart a relationship can also act as a driving force to unite two people. For example, during slavery many slaves went against their owners' wishes and considered themselves married. Furthermore, many relationships have faced such negative forces as racism and poverty as common enemies that they are determined to destroy through the survival of their relationship.

In addition to external forces, internal forces, such as how men and women feel about themselves, can affect a relationship. If people do not have a strong sense of themselves as individuals, the relationship can fall apart if one person is called upon to put the other person's welfare first. On the other hand, if the people in a relationship are confident about themselves as individuals, they can use this strength to help their relationships survive.

In African American writers' stories and poems in this chapter, writers illustrate the pain that racism, poverty, and ignorance can cause in a relationship. Also, they show the joy that pride and dignity can contribute to that same relationship.

Charles Waddell Chesnutt

(1858–1932) was born in Cleveland, Ohio. When he was very young, Chesnutt and his family moved to Fayetteville, N.C., where he lived until he was twenty-five. In addition to his formal education, Chesnutt studied German, French, and Greek. At the age of fourteen, while still a student, he began teaching at the Howard School in Fayetteville. By his early twenties, Chesnutt had become principal of the State Normal School in Fayetteville, mastered stenography, continued his literary studies on his own, and begun his career as a writer of short fiction. In 1883 Chesnutt left the South and secured a job as an interviewer and reporter for a Wall Street news agency. Within six months he left this job and took a position in the accounting department of a railroad company in Cleveland. Chesnutt had published short stories, poetry, and articles before receiving national attention in 1887 when the *Atlantic Monthly* published "The Goophered Grapevine." For the rest of his life, Chesnutt lived in Cleveland where he achieved literary fame, business success, and civic recognition.

Chesnutt's works reflect a realistic and unsympathetic view of slavery and Reconstruction. Much of his fiction focuses on the problems and prejudices of those blacks who were light enough to pass for white. Heralded as the pioneer of African American fiction, Chesnutt did not publish any fiction after 1905. His published fiction includes *The Conjure Woman* (1899), *The Wife of His Youth and Other Stories of the Color Line* (1899), *The House Behind the Cedars* (1900), *The Marrow of Tradition* (1901), and *The Colonel's Dream* (1905).

The Wife of His Youth

CHARLES W. CHESNUTT

I

Mr. Ryder was going to give a ball. There were several reasons why this was an opportune time for such an event.

Mr. Ryder might aptly be called the dean of the Blue Veins. The original Blue Veins were a little society of colored persons organized in a certain Northern city shortly after the war. Its purpose was to establish and maintain correct social standards among a people whose social condition presented almost unlimited room for improvement. By accident, combined perhaps with some natural affinity, the society consisted of individuals who were, generally speaking, more white than black. Some envious outsider made the suggestion that no one was eligible for membership who was not white enough to show blue veins. The suggestion was readily adopted by those who were not of the favored few, and since that time the society, though possessing a longer and more pretentious name, had been known far and wide as the "Blue Vein Society," and its members as the "Blue Veins."

The Blue Veins did not allow that any such requirement existed for admission to their circle, but, on the contrary, declared that character and culture were the only things considered; and that if most of their members were light-colored, it was because such persons, as a rule, had had better opportunities to qualify themselves for membership. Opinions differed, too, as to the usefulness of the society. There were those who had been known to assail it violently as a glaring example of the very prejudice from which the colored race had suffered most; and later, when such critics had succeeded in getting on the inside, they had been heard to maintain with zeal and earnestness that the society was a lifeboat, an anchor, a bulwark and a shield—a pillar of cloud by day and of fire by night, to guide their people through the social wilderness. Another alleged prerequisite for Blue Vein membership was that of free birth; and while there was really no such requirement, it is doubtless true that very few of the members would have been unable to meet it if there had been. If there were one or two of the older members who had come up from the South and from slavery, their history presented enough romantic circumstances to rob their servile origin of its grosser aspects.

While there were no such tests of eligibility, it is true that the Blue Veins had their notions on these subjects, and that not all of them were equally liberal in regard to the things they collectively disclaimed. Mr. Ryder was one of the most conservative. Though he had not been among the founders of the society, but had come in some years later, his genius for social leadership was such that he had speedily become its recognized adviser and head, the custodian of its standards, and the preserver of its traditions. He shaped its social policy, was active in providing for its entertainment, and when the interest fell off, as it sometimes did, he fanned the embers until they burst again into a cheerful flame.

There were still other reasons for his popularity. While he was not as white as some of the Blue Veins, his appearance was such as to confer distinction upon them. His features were of a refined type, his hair was almost straight; he was always neatly dressed; his manners were irreproachable, and his morals above suspicion. He had come to Groveland a young man, and obtaining employment in the office of a railroad company as messenger had in time worked himself up to the position of stationery clerk, having charge of the distribution of the office supplies for the whole company. Although the lack of early training had hindered the orderly development of a naturally fine mind, it had not prevented him from doing a great deal of reading or from forming decidedly literary tastes. Poetry was his passion. He could repeat whole pages of the great English poets; and if his pronunciation was sometimes faulty, his eye, his voice, his gestures, would respond to the changing sentiment with a precision that revealed a poetic soul and disarmed criticism. He was economical, and had saved money; he owned and occupied a very comfortable house on a respectable street. His residence was handsomely furnished, containing among other things a good library, especially rich in poetry, a piano, and some choice engravings. He generally shared his house with some young couple, who looked after his wants and were company for him; for Mr. Ryder was a single man. In the early days of his connection with the Blue Veins he had been regarded as quite a catch, and young ladies and their mothers had manoeuvred with much ingenuity to capture him. Not, however, until Mrs. Molly Dixon visited Groveland had any woman ever made him wish to change his condition to that of a married man.

Mrs. Dixon had come to Groveland from Washington in the spring, and before the summer was over she had won Mr. Ryder's heart. She possessed many attractive qualities. She was much younger than he; he was old enough to have been her father, though no one knew exactly how old he was. She was whiter than he, and better educated. She had moved in the best colored society of the country, at Washington, and had taught in the schools of that city. Such a superior person had been eagerly welcomed to the Blue Vein Society, and had taken a leading part in its activities. Mr. Ryder had at first been attracted by her charms of person, for she was very good looking and not over twenty-five; then by her refined manners and the vivacity of her wit. Her husband had been a government clerk, and at his death had left a considerable life insurance. She was visiting friends in Groveland, and, finding the town and the people to her liking, had prolonged her stay indefinitely. She had not seemed displeased at Mr. Ryder's attentions, but on the contrary had given him every proper encouragement; indeed, a younger and less cautious man would long since have spoken. But he had made up his mind, and had only to determine the time when he would ask her to be his wife. He decided to give a ball in her honor, and at some time during the evening of the ball to offer her his heart and hand. He had no special fears about the outcome, but, with a little touch of romance, he wanted the surroundings to be in harmony with his own feelings when he should have received the answer he expected.

Mr. Ryder resolved that this ball should mark an epoch in the social history of Groveland. He knew, of course,—no one could know better,—the entertainments that had taken place in past years, and what must be done to surpass them. His ball must be worthy of the lady in which honor it was to be given, and must, by the quality of its guests, set an example for the future. He had observed of late a growing liberality, almost a laxity, in social matters, even among members of his own set, and had several times been forced to meet in a social way persons whose complexions and callings in life were hardly up to the standard which he considered proper for the society to maintain. He had a theory of his own.

"I have no race prejudice," he would say, "but we people of mixed blood are ground between the upper and the nether millstone. Our fate lies between absorption by the white race and extinction in the black. The one doesn't want us yet, but may take us in time. The other would welcome us, but it would be for us a backward step. 'With malice towards none, with charity for all,' we must do the best we can for ourselves and those who are to follow us. Self-presentation is the first law of nature."

His ball would serve by its exclusiveness to counteract leveling tendencies, and his marriage with Mrs. Dixon would help to further the upward process of absorption he had been wishing and waiting for.

II

The ball was to take place on Friday night. The house had been put in order, the carpets covered with canvas, the halls and stairs decorated with palms and potted plants; and in the afternoon Mr. Ryder sat on his front porch, which the shade of a vine running up over a wire netting made a cool and pleasant lounging place. He expected to respond to the toast "The Ladies" at the supper, and from a volume of Tennyson—his favorite poet—was fortifying himself with apt quotations. The volume was open at "A Dream of Fair Women." His eyes fell on these lines, and he read them aloud to judge better of their effect:—

> At length I saw a lady within call,
>   Stiller than chisell'd marble, standing there;
> A daughter of the gods, divinely tall,
>   And most divinely fair.

He marked the verse, and turning the page read the stanza beginning,—

> O sweet pale Margaret,
>   O rare pale Margaret.

He weighed the passage a moment, and decided that it would not do. Mrs. Dixon was the palest lady he expected at the ball, and she was of a rather ruddy complexion, and of lively disposition and buxom build. So he ran over the leaves until his eye rested on the description of Queen Guinevere:—

> She seem'd a part of joyous Spring:
> A gown of grass-green silk she wore,
> Buckled with golden clasps before;
> A light-green tuft of plumes she bore
> Closed in a golden ring.

> She look'd so lovely, as she sway'd
> The rein with dainty finger-tips,
> A man had given all other bliss,
> And all his worldly worth for this,
> To waste his whole heart in one kiss
> Upon her perfect lips.

As Mr. Ryder murmured these words audibly, with an appreciative thrill, he heard the latch of his gate click, and a light footfall sounding on the steps. He turned his head, and saw a woman standing before his door.

She was a little woman, not five feet tall, and proportioned to her height. Although she stood erect, and looked around her with very bright and restless eyes, she seemed quite old; for her face was crossed and recrossed with a hundred wrinkles, and around the edges of her bonnet could be seen protruding here and there a tuft of short gray wool. She wore a blue calico gown of ancient cut, a little red shawl fastened around her shoulders with an old-fashioned brass brooch, and a large bonnet profusely ornamented with faded red and yellow artificial flowers. And she was very black,—so black that her toothless gums, revealed when she opened her mouth to speak, were not red, but blue. She looked like a bit of the old plantation life, summoned up from the past by the wave of a magician's wand, as the poet's fancy had called into being the gracious shapes of which Mr. Ryder had just been reading.

He rose from his chair and came over to where she stood.

"Good-afternoon, madam," he said.

"Good-evenin', suh," she answered, ducking suddenly with a quaint curtsy. Her voice was shrill and piping, but softened somewhat by age. "Is dis yere whar Mistuh Ryduh lib, suh?" she asked, looking around her doubt-fully, and glancing into the open windows, through which some of the prepara-tions for the evening were visible.

"Yes," he replied, with an air of kindly patronage, unconsciously flat-tered by her manner, "I am Mr. Ryder. Did you want to see me?"

"Yas, suh, ef I ain't 'sturbin' of you too much."

"Not at all. Have a seat over here behind the vine, where it is cool. What can I do for you?"

"Scuse me, suh," she continued, when she had sat down on the edge of a chair, "'scuse me, suh, I's lookin' for my husban'. I heerd you wuz a big man an' had libbed heah a long time, an' I 'lowed you would n't min' ef I 'd come roun' an' ax you ef you'd ever heer of a merlatter man by de name er Sam Taylor 'quirin' roun' in de chu'ches ermongs' de people fer his wife 'Liza Jane?"

Mr. Ryder seemed to think for a moment.

"There used to be many such cases right after the war," he said, "but it has been so long that I have forgotten them. There are very few now. But tell me your story, and it may refresh my memory."

She sat back farther in her chair so as to be more comfortable, and folded her withered hands in her lap.

"My name's 'Liza," she began, "'Liza Jane. W'en I wuz young I us'ter b'long ter Marse Bob Smif, down in ole Missoura. I wuz bawn down dere. W'en I wuz a gal I wuz married ter a man named Jim. But Jim died, an' after dat I married a merlatter man named Sam Taylor. Sam wuz free-bawn, but his mammy and daddy died, an' de w'it folks 'prenticed him ter my marster fer ter work fer 'im 'tel he wuz growed up. Sam worked in de fiel', an' I wuz de cook. One day Ma'y Ann, ole miss's maid, came rushin' out ter de kitchen, an' says she, "Liza Jane, ole marse gwine sell yo' Sam down de ribber.'

"'Go way f'm yere,' says I; 'my husban' 's free!'

"'Don' make no diff'ence. I heerd ole marse tell ole miss he wuz gwine take yo' Sam 'way wid 'im ter-morrow, fer he needed money, an' he knowed whar he could git a t'ousan' dollars fer Sam an' no questions axed.'

"W'en Sam come home f'm de fiel' dat night, I tole him 'bout old marse gwine steal 'im, an' Sam run erway. His time wuz mos' up, an' he swo' dat w'en he wuz twenty-one he would come back an he'p me run erway, er else save up de money ter buy my freedom. An' I know he'd 'a' done it, fer he thought a heap er me, Sam did. But w'en he come back he did n' fin' me, fer I wuz n' dere. Ole marse had heerd dat I warned Sam, so he had me whip' an' sol' down de ribber.

"Den de wah broke out, an' w'en it wuz ober de cullud folks wuz scattered. I went back ter de ole home; but Sam wuz n' dere, an' I could n' l'arn nuffin' 'bout 'im. But I knowed he'd be'n dere to look fer me an' had n' foun' me, an' had gone erway ter hunt fer me.

"I's be'n lookin' fer 'im eber sense," she added simply, as though twenty-five years were but a couple of weeks, "an' I knows he's be'n lookin' fer me. Fer he sot a heap er sto' by me, Sam did, an' I know he's be'n huntin' fer me all dese years,—'less'n he's be'n sick er sump'n, so he could n' work, er out'n his head, so he could n' 'member his promise. I went back down de ribber, fer I 'lowed he'd gone down dere lookin' fer me. I's be'n ter Noo Orleens, an' Atlanty, an' Charleston, an' Richmon'; an' w'en I'd be'n all ober de Souf I come ter de Norf. Fer I knows I'll fin' 'im some er dese days," she added softly, "er he'll fin' me, an' den we'll bofe be as happy in freedom as we wuz in de ole days befo' de wah." A smile stole over her withered countenance as she paused a moment, and her bright eyes softened into a far-away look.

This was the substance of the old woman's story. She had wandered a little here and there. Mr. Ryder was looking at her curiously when she finished.

"How have you lived all these years?" he asked.

"Cookin', suh. I's a good cook. Does you know anybody w'at needs a good cook, suh? I's stoppin' wid a cullud fam'ly roun' de corner yonder 'tel I kin git a place."

"Do you really expect to find your husband? He may be dead long ago."

She shook her head emphatically. "Oh no, he ain' dead. De signs an' de tokens tells me. I dremp three nights runnin' on'y dis las' week dat I foun' him."

"He may have married another woman. Your slave marriage would not have prevented him, for you never lived with him after the war, and without that your marriage doesn't count."

"Would n' make no diff'ence wid Sam. He would n' marry no yuther 'ooman 'tel he foun' out 'bout me. I knows it," she added. "Sump'n's be'n tellin' me all dese years dat I's gwine fin' Sam 'fo' I dies."

"Perhaps he's outgrown you, and climbed up in the world where he wouldn't care to have you find him."

"No, indeed, suh," she replied. "Sam ain' dat kin' er man. He wuz good ter me, Sam wuz, but he wuz n' much good ter nobody e'se, fer he wuz one er de triflin'es' han's on de plantation. I 'spec's ter haf ter suppo't 'im w'en I fin' 'im, fer he nebber would work 'less'n he had ter. But den he wuz free, an' he did n' git no pay fer his work, an' I don' blame 'im much. Mebbe he's done better sence he run erway, but I ain' 'spectin' much."

"You may have passed him on the street a hundred times during the twenty-five years, and not have known him; time works great changes."

She smiled incredulously. "I'd know 'im 'mongs' a hund'ed men. Fer dey wuz n' no yuther merlatter man like my man Sam, an' I could n' be mistook. I's toted his picture roun' wid me twenty-five years."

"May I see it?" asked Mr. Ryder. "It might help me to remember whether I have seen the original."

As she drew a small parcel from her bosom he saw that it was fastened to a string that went around her neck. Removing several wrappers, she brought to light an old-fashioned daguerreotype in a black case. He looked long and intently at the portrait. It was faded with time, but the features were still distinct, and it was easy to see what manner of man it had represented.

He closed the case, and with a slow movement handed it back to her.

"I don't know of any man in town who goes by that name," he said, "nor have I heard of any one making such inquiries. But if you will leave me your address, I will give the matter some attention, and if I find out anything I will let you know."

She gave him the number of a house in the neighborhood, and went away, after thanking him warmly.

He wrote the address on the fly-leaf of the volume of Tennyson, and, when she had gone, rose to his feet and stood looking after her curiously. As she walked down the street with mincing step, he saw several persons whom she passed turn and look back at her with a smile of kindly amusement. When she had turned the corner, he went upstairs to his bedroom, and stood for a long time before the mirror of his dressing-case, gazing thoughtfully at the reflection of his own face.

III

At eight o'clock the ballroom was a blaze of light and the guests had begun to assemble; for there was a literary programme and some routine business of the society to be gone through with before the dancing. A black servant in evening dress waited at the door and directed the guests to the dressing-rooms.

The occasion was long memorable among the colored people of the city; not alone for the dress and display, but for the high average of intelligence and culture that distinguished the gathering as a whole. There were a number of schoolteachers, several young doctors, three or four lawyers, some professional singers, an editor, a lieutenant in the United States army spending his furlough in the city, and others in various polite callings; these were colored, though most of them would not have attracted even a casual glance because of any marked difference from white people. Most of the ladies were in evening costume, and dress coats and dancing pumps were the rule among the men. A band of string music, stationed in an alcove behind a row of palms, played popular airs while the guests were gathering.

The dancing began at half past nine. At eleven o'clock supper was served. Mr. Ryder had left the ballroom some little time before the intermission, but reappeared at the supper-table. The spread was worthy of the occasion, and the guests did full justice to it. When the coffee had been served, the toast-master, Mr. Solomon Sadler, rapped for order. He made a brief introductory speech, complimenting host and guests, and then presented in their order the toasts of the evening. They were responded to with a very fair display of after-dinner wit.

"The last toast," said the toast-master, when he reached the end of the list, "is one which must appeal to us all. There is no one of us of the sterner sex who is not at some time dependent upon woman,—in infancy for protection, in manhood for companionship, in old age for care and comforting. Our good host has been trying to live alone, but the fair faces I see around me to-night prove that he too is largely dependent upon the gentler sex for most that makes life worth living,—the society and love of friends,—and rumor is at fault if he does not soon yield entire subjection to one of them. Mr. Ryder will now respond to the toast,—The Ladies."

There was a pensive look in Mr. Ryder's eyes as he took the floor and adjusted his eyeglasses. He began by speaking of woman as the gift of Heaven to man, and after some general observations on the relations of the sexes he said: "But perhaps the quality which most distinguishes woman is her fidelity and devotion to those she loves. History is full of examples, but has recorded none more striking than one which only today came under my notice."

He then related, simply but effectively, the story told by his visitor of the afternoon. He gave it in the same soft dialect, which came readily to his lips, while the company listened attentively and sympathetically. For the story had awakened a responsive thrill in many hearts. There were some present who had seen, and others who had heard their fathers and grandfathers tell, the wrongs and sufferings of this past generation, and all of them still felt, in their darker moments, the shadow hanging over them. Mr. Ryder went on:—

"Such devotion and confidence are rare even among women. There are many who would have searched a year, some who would have waited five years, a few who might have hoped ten years; but for twenty-five years this woman has retained her affection for and her faith in a man she has not seen or heard of in all that time.

"She came to me today in the hope that I might be able to help her find this long-lost husband. And when she was gone I gave my fancy rein, and imagined a case I will put to you.

"Suppose that this husband, soon after his escape, had learned that his wife had been sold away, and that such inquiries as he could make brought no information of her whereabouts. Suppose that he was young, and she much older than he; that he was light, and she was black; that their marriage was a slave marriage, and legally binding only if they chose to make it so after the war. Suppose, too, that he made his way to the North, as some of us have done, and there, where he had larger opportunities, had improved them, and had in the course of all these years grown to be as different from the ignorant boy who ran away from fear of slavery as the day is from the night. Suppose, even, that he had qualified himself, by industry, by thrift, and by study, to win the friendship and be considered worthy the society of such people as these I see around me tonight, gracing my board and filling my heart with gladness; for I am old enough to remember the day when such a gathering would not have been possible in this land. Suppose, too, that, as the years went by, this man's memory of the past grew more and more indistinct, until at last it was rarely, except in his dreams, that any image of this bygone period rose before his mind. And then suppose that accident should bring to his knowledge the fact that the wife of his youth, the wife he had left behind him,—not one who had walked by his side and kept pace with him in his upward struggle, but one upon whom advancing years and a laborious life had set their mark, was alive and seeking him, but that he was absolutely safe from recognition or discovery, unless he chose to reveal himself. My friends, what would the man do? I will presume that he was one who loved honor, and tried to deal justly with all men. I will even carry the case further, and suppose that perhaps he had set his heart upon another, whom he had hoped to call his own. What would he do, or rather what ought he to do, in such a crisis of a lifetime?

"It seemed to me that he might hesitate, and I imagined that I was an old friend, a near friend, and that he had come to me for advice; and I argued the case with him. I tried to discuss it impartially. After we had looked upon the matter from every point of view, I said to him, in words that we all know:—

This above all: to thine own self be true,
and it must follow, as the night the day,
Thou canst not then be false to any man.

Then, finally, I put the question to him, 'Shall you acknowledge her?'

"And now, ladies and gentlemen, friends and companions, I ask you, what should he have done?"

There was something in Mr. Ryder's voice that stirred the hearts of those who sat around him. It suggested more than mere sympathy with an imaginary situation; it seemed rather in the nature of a personal appeal. It was observed, too, that his look rested more especially upon Mrs. Dixon, with a mingled expressed of renunciation and inquiry.

She had listened, with parted lips and streaming eyes. She was the first to speak: "He should have acknowledged her."

"Yes," they all echoed, "he should have acknowledged her."

"My friends and companions," responded Mr. Ryder, "I thank you, one and all. It is the answer I expected, for I knew your hearts."

He turned and walked toward the closed door of an adjoining room, while every eye followed him in wondering curiosity. He came back in a moment, leading by the hand his visitor of the afternoon, who stood startled and trembling at the sudden plunge into this scene of brilliant gayety. She was neatly dressed in gray, and wore the white cap of an elderly woman.

"Ladies and gentlemen," he said, "this is the woman, and I am the man, whose story I have told you. Permit me to introduce to you the wife of my youth."

Thinking About the Story

1. What are the goals and purposes of the Blue Vein Society? Do these goals and purposes work toward unity within the African American society? Why or why not?

2. Mr. Ryder is not described as fitting perfectly into the Blue Vein Society. Why do you think he is allowed to stay? What role does he play for the society?

3. 'Liza Jane tells Mr. Ryder that she has been searching for her husband, Sam, for over twenty-five years. Discuss why you think 'Liza Jane has continued to search for Sam after twenty-five years. Use specific information from the story to support your conclusions.

4. After talking with 'Liza Jane, Mr. Ryder went into his house: ". . . he went upstairs to his bedroom, and stood for a long time before the mirror of his dressing-case, gazing thoughtfully at the reflection of his own face." What do you think were some of his thoughts as he stood in front of the mirror?

5. When Mr. Ryder introduces 'Liza Jane as "the wife of [his] youth," what does he gain? What does he lose?

Reading/Writing Connections

1. At the end of telling the story, Mr. Ryder asks the people at the party for their opinion on whether the man should acknowledge the wife of his youth. Rewrite the ending of this story so that the people at the party tell Mr. Ryder that the man should not acknowledge his wife. How would the story have ended?

2. In your journal write about a time when you knew the truth about something, but you did not tell the truth because someone else would have taken something away from you. How did you feel afterwards? Do you still feel as though you made the right decision?

3. Intraracial prejudice among African Americans is what allowed the Blue Vein Society to exist. Write an essay in which you first analyze the problem of intraracial prejudice in the short story and then discuss a solution to the problem.

Ann Petry   (b. 1908) was born in Old Saybrook, Conn., to Peter C. and Bertha James. Her family lived an economically comfortable life. Her father, a pharmacist, owned his own drugstore in Old Saybrook. Her mother graduated from the New York School of Chiropody and earned her license to practice in 1915. Petry graduated from Old Saybrook High School as the only African American student in her class. In 1931 she graduated with a degree from the University of Connecticut School of Pharmacy and worked for the next seven years as a pharmacist in her family's drugstore. In 1938 she married George D. Petry and moved to New York City to pursue a career as a writer. In New York City she took a job as a reporter for the *People's Voice*. In the evenings she took creative writing classes at Columbia University. After receiving several rejections from magazine editors for her stories, she quit her job in order to commit herself to her writing full time. In 1943 *Crisis* magazine published Petry's short story "On Saturday the Siren Sounds at Noon." Her short story "Like a Winding Sheet" brought her national attention. In 1945 she won a Houghton Mifflin Literary Fellowship for a portion of her first novel, *The Street* (1946).

Petry's experiences growing up as one of only a few black families in her hometown, graduating from pharmacy school as the only African American in her class, and reporting on Harlem for the *People's Voice* provided her with a rich background for her stories. Her further novels, which often focus on the effects of environment and bigotry on an individual, include *Country Place* (1947), *The Narrows* (1954), and *The Common Ground* (1964). Her short stories are collected in *Miss Muriel and Other Stories* (1971). In addition to writing adult fiction, Petry has written fiction for children, publishing *The Drugstore Cat* (1949), *Tituba of Salem Village* (1964), and *Legends of the Saints* (1974).

Like a Winding Sheet

A N N   P E T R Y

He had planned to get up before Mae did and surprise her by fixing breakfast. Instead he went back to sleep and she got out of bed so quietly he didn't know she wasn't there beside him until he woke up and heard the queer soft gurgle of water running out of the sink in the bathroom.

He knew he ought to get up but instead he put his arms across his forehead to shut the afternoon sunlight out of his eyes, pulled his legs up close to his body, testing them to see if the ache was still in them.

Mae had finished in the bathroom. He could tell because she never closed the door when she was in there and now the sweet smell of talcum powder was drifting down the hall and into the bedroom. Then he heard her coming down the hall.

"Hi, babe," she said affectionately.

"Hum," he grunted, and moved his arms away from his head, opened one eye.

"It's a nice morning."

"Yeah," he rolled over and the sheet twisted around him, outlining his thighs, his chest. "You mean afternoon, don't ya?"

Mae looked at the twisted sheet and giggled. "Looks like a winding sheet," she said. "A shroud—."[1] Laughter tangled with her words and she had to pause for a moment before she could continue. "You look like a huckleberry—in a winding sheet—"

"That's no way to talk. Early in the day like this," he protested.

He looked at his arms silhouetted against the white of the sheets. They were inky black by contrast and he had to smile in spite of himself and he lay there smiling and savouring the sweet sound of Mae's giggling.

"Early?" She pointed a finger at the alarm clock on the table near the bed, and giggled again. "It's almost four o'clock. And if you don't spring up out of there you're going to be late again."

"What do you mean 'again'?"

"Twice last week. Three times the week before. And once the week before and—"

"I can't get used to sleeping in the daytime," he said fretfully. He pushed his legs out from under the covers experimentally. Some of the ache had gone

---

[1] *winding sheet . . . shroud:* a burial garment.

out of them but they weren't really rested yet. "It's too light for good sleeping. And all that standing beats the hell out of my legs."

"After two years you oughtta be used to it," Mae said.

He watched her as she fixed her hair, powdered her face, slipping into a pair of blue denim overalls. She moved quickly and yet she didn't seem to hurry.

"You look like you'd had plenty of sleep," he said lazily. He had to get up but he kept putting the moment off, not wanting to move, yet he didn't dare let his legs go completely limp because if he did he'd go back to sleep. It was getting later and later but the thought of putting his weight on his legs kept him lying there.

When he finally got up he had to hurry and he gulped his breakfast so fast that he wondered if his stomach could possibly use food thrown at it at such a rate of speed. He was still wondering about it as he and Mae were putting their coats on in the hall.

Mae paused to look at the calendar. "It's the thirteenth," she said. Then a faint excitement in her voice. "Why it's Friday the thirteenth." She had one arm in her coat sleeve and she held it there while she stared at the calendar. "I oughtta stay home," she said. "I shouldn't go otta the house."

"Aw don't be a fool," he said. "Today's payday. And payday is a good luck day everywhere, any way you look at it." And as she stood hesitating he said, "Aw, come on."

And he was late for work again because they spent fifteen minutes arguing before he could convince her she ought to go to work just the same. He had to talk persuasively, urging her gently and it took time. But he couldn't bring himself to talk to her roughly or threaten to strike her like a lot of men might have done. He wasn't made that way.

So when he reached the plant he was late and he had to wait to punch the time clock because the day shift workers were streaming out in long lines, in groups and bunches that impeded his progress.

Even now just starting his workday his legs ached. He had to force himself to struggle past the outgoing workers, punch the time clock, and get the little cart he pushed around all night because he kept toying with the idea of going home and getting back in bed.

He pushed the cart out on the concrete floor, thinking that if this was his plant he'd make a lot of changes in it. There were too many standing up jobs for one thing. He'd figure out some way most of 'em could be done sitting down and he'd put a lot more benches around. And this job he had—this job that forced him to walk ten hours a night, pushing this little cart, well, he'd turn it into a sittin-down job. One of those little trucks they used around railroad stations would be good for a job like this. Guys sat on a seat and the thing moved easily, taking up little room and turning in hardly any space at all, like on a dime.

He pushed the cart near the foreman. He never could remember to refer to her as the forelady even in his mind. It was funny to have a woman for a boss in a plant like this one.

She was sore about something. He could tell by the way her face was red and her eyes were half shut until they were slits. Probably been out late and didn't get enough sleep. He avoided looking at her and hurried a little, head down, as he passed her though he couldn't resist stealing a glance at her out of the corner of his eyes. He saw the edge of the light colored slacks she wore and the tip end of a big tan shoe.

"Hey, Johnson!" the woman said.

The machines had started full blast. The whirr and the grinding made the building shake, made it impossible to hear conversations. The men and women at the machines talked to each other but looking at them from just a little distance away they appeared to be simply moving their lips because you couldn't hear what they were saying. Yet the woman's voice cut across the machine sounds—harsh, angry.

He turned his head slowly. "Good Evenin', Mrs. Scott," he said and waited.

"You're late again."

"That's right. My legs were bothering me."

The woman's face grew redder, angrier looking. "Half this shift comes in late," she said. "And you're the worst one of all. You're always late. Whatsa matter with ya?"

"It's my legs," he said. "Somehow they don't ever get rested. I don't seem to get used to sleeping days. And I just can't get started."

"Excuses. You guys always got excuses," her anger grew and spread. "Every guy comes in here late always has an excuse. His wife's sick or his grandmother died or somebody in the family had to go to the hospital," she paused, drew a deep breath. "And the niggers are the worse. I don't care what's wrong with your legs. You get in here on time. I'm sick of you niggers—"

"You got the right to get mad," he interrupted softly. "You got the right to cuss me four ways to Sunday but I ain't letting nobody call me a nigger."

He stepped closer to her. His fists were doubled. His lips were drawn back in a thin narrow line. A vein in his forehead stood out swollen, thick.

And the woman backed away from him, not hurriedly but slowly—two, three steps back.

"Aw, forget it," she said. "I didn't mean nothing by it. It slipped out. It was a accident." The red of her face deepened until the small blood vessels in her cheeks were purple. "Go on and get to work," she urged. And she took three more slow backward steps.

He stood motionless for a moment and then turned away from the red lipstick on her mouth that made him remember that the foreman was a woman. And he couldn't bring himself to hit a woman. He felt a curious tingling in his fingers and he looked down at his hands. They were clenched tight, hard, ready to smash some of those purple veins in her face.

He pushed the cart ahead of him, walking slowly. When he turned his head, she was staring in his direction, mopping her forehead with a dark blue handkerchief. Their eyes met and then they both looked away.

He didn't glance in her direction again but moved past the long work benches, carefully collecting the finished parts, going slowly and steadily up and down, back and forth the length of the building and as he walked he forced himself to swallow his anger, get rid of it.

And he succeeded so that he was able to think about what had happened without getting upset about it. An hour went by but the tension stayed in his hands. They were clenched and knotted on the handles of the cart as though ready to aim a blow.

And he thought he should have hit her anyway, smacked her hard in the face, felt the soft flesh of her face give under the hardness of his hands. He tried to make his hands relax by offering them a description of what it would have been like to strike her because he had the queer feeling that his hands were not exactly a part of him any more—they had developed a separate life of their own over which he had no control. So he dwelt on the pleasure his hands would have felt—both of them cracking at her, first one and then the other. If he had done that his hands would have felt good now—relaxed, rested.

And he decided that even if he'd lost his job for it he should have let her have it and it would have been a long time, maybe the rest of her life before she called anybody else a nigger.

The only trouble was he couldn't hit a woman. A woman couldn't hit back the same way a man did. But it would have been a deeply satisfying thing to have cracked her narrow lips wide open with just one blow, beautifully timed and with all his weight in back of it. That way he would have gotten rid of all the energy and tension his anger had created in him. He kept remembering how his heart had started pumping blood so fast he had felt it tingle even in the tips of his fingers.

With the approach of night fatigue nibbled at him. The corners of his mouth dropped, the frown between his eyes deepened, his shoulders sagged; but his hands stayed tight and tense. As the hours dragged by he noticed that the women workers had started to snap and snarl at each other. He couldn't hear what they said because of the sound of machines but he could see the quick lip movements that sent words tumbling from the sides of their mouths. They gestured irritably with their hands and scowled as their mouths moved.

Their violent jerky motions told him that it was getting close on to quitting time but somehow he felt that the night still stretched ahead of him, composed of endless hours of steady walking on his aching legs. When the whistle finally blew he went on pushing the cart, unable to believe that it had sounded. The whirring of the machines died away to a murmur and he knew then that he'd really heard the whistle. He stood still for a moment filled with a relief that made him sigh.

Then he moved briskly, putting the cart in the store room, hurrying to take his place in the line forming before the paymaster. That was another thing he'd change, he thought. He'd have the pay envelopes handed to the people right at their benches so there wouldn't be ten or fifteen minutes lost waiting for the pay. He always got home about fifteen minutes late on payday. They did it better in the plant where Mae worked, brought the money right to them at their benches.

He stuck his pay envelope in his pants' pocket and followed the line of workers heading for the subway in a slow moving stream. He glanced up at the sky. It was a nice night, the sky looked packed full to running over with stars. And he thought if he and Mae would go right to bed when they got home from work they'd catch a few hours of darkness for sleeping. But they never did. They fooled around—cooking and eating and listening to the radio and he always stayed in a big chair in the living room and went almost but not quite to sleep and when they finally got to bed it was five or six in the morning and daylight was already seeping around the edges of the sky.

He walked slowly, putting off the moment when he would have to plunge into the crowd hurrying toward the subway. It was a long ride to Harlem and tonight the thought of it appalled him. He paused outside an all-night restaurant to kill time, so that some of the first rush of workers would be gone when he reached the subway.

The lights in the restaurant were brilliant, enticing. There was life and motion inside. And as he looked through the window he thought that everything within range of his eyes gleamed—the long imitation marble counter, the tall stools, the white porcelain topped tables and especially the big metal coffee urn right near the window. Steam issued from its top and a gas flame flickered under it—a lively, dancing, blue flame.

A lot of the workers from his shift—men and women—were lining up near the coffee urn. He watched them walk to the porcelain topped tables carrying steaming cups of coffee and he saw that just the smell of the coffee lessened the fatigue lines in their faces. After the first sip their faces softened, they smiled, they began to talk and laugh.

On a sudden impulse he shoved the door open and joined the line in front of the coffee urn. The line moved slowly. And as he stood there the smell of the coffee, the sound of the laughter and of the voices, helped dull the sharp ache in his legs.

He didn't pay any attention to the girl who was serving the coffee at the urn. He kept looking at the cups in the hands of the men who had been ahead of him. Each time a man stepped out of the line with one of the thick white cups the fragrant steam got in his nostrils. He saw that they walked carefully so as not to spill a single drop. There was a broth of bubbles at the top of each cup and he thought about how he would let the bubbles break against his lips before he actually took a big deep swallow.

Then it was his turn. "A cup of coffee," he said, just as he had heard the others say.

The girl looked past him, put her hands up to her head and gently lifted her hair away from the back of her neck, tossing her head back a little. "No more coffee for awhile," she said.

He wasn't certain he'd heard her correctly and he said, "What?" blankly.

"No more coffee for awhile," she repeated.

There was silence behind him and then uneasy movement. He thought someone would say something, ask why or protest, but there was only silence and then a faint shuffling sound as though the men standing behind him had simultaneously shifted their weight from one foot to the other.

He looked at her without saying anything. He felt his hands begin to tingle and the tingling went all the way down to his finger tips so that he glanced down at them. They were clenched tight, hard, into fists. Then he looked at the girl again. What he wanted to do was hit her so hard that the scarlet lipstick on her mouth would smear and spread over her nose, her chin, out toward her cheeks; so hard that she would never toss her head again and refuse a man a cup of coffee because he was black.

He estimated the distance across the counter and reached forward, balancing his weight on the balls of his feet, ready to let the blow go. And then his hands fell back down to his sides because he forced himself to lower them, to unclench them and make them dangle loose. The effort took his breath away because his hands fought against him. But he couldn't hit her. He couldn't even now bring himself to hit a woman, not even this one, who had refused him a cup of coffee with a toss of her head. He kept seeing the gesture with which she had lifted the length of her blond hair from the back of her neck as expressive of her contempt for him.

When he went out the door he didn't look back. If he had he would have seen the flickering blue flame under the shiny coffee urn being extinguished. The line of men who had stood behind him lingered a moment to watch the people drinking coffee at the tables and then they left just as he had without having had the coffee they wanted so badly. The girl behind the counter poured water in the urn and swabbed it out and as she waited for the water to run out she lifted her hair gently from the back of her neck and tossed her head before she began making a fresh lot of coffee.

But he walked away without a backward look, his head down, his hands in his pockets, raging at himself and whatever it was inside of him that had forced him to stand quiet and still when he wanted to strike out.

The subway was crowded and he had to stand. He tried grasping an overhead strap and his hands were too tense to grip it. So he moved near the train door and stood there swaying back and forth with the rocking of the train. The roar of the train beat inside his head, making it ache and throb, and the pain in his legs clawed up into his groin so that he seemed to be bursting with pain and he told himself that it was due to all that anger-born energy that had piled up in him and not been used and so it had spread through him like a poison—from his feet and legs all the way up to his head.

Mae was in the house before he was. He knew she was home before he put the key in the door of the apartment. The radio was going. She had it tuned up loud and she was singing along with it.

"Hello, Babe," she called out as soon as he opened the door.

He tried to say "hello" and it came out half a grunt and half sigh.

"You sure sound cheerful," she said.

She was in the bedroom and he went and leaned against the door jamb. The denim overalls she wore to work were carefully draped over the back of a chair by the bed. She was standing in front of the dresser, tying the sash of a yellow housecoat around her waist and chewing gum vigorously as she admired her reflection in the mirror over the dresser.

"Whatsa matter?" she said. "You get bawled out by the boss or somep'n?"

"Just tired," he said slowly. "For God's sake do you have to crack that gum like that?"

"You don't have to lissen to me," she said complacently. She patted a curl in place near the side of her head and then lifted her hair away from the back of her neck, ducking her head forward and then back.

He winced away from the gesture. "What you got to be always fooling with your hair for?" he protested.

"Say, what's the matter with you, anyway?" she turned away from the mirror to face him, put her hands on her hips. "You ain't been in the house two minutes and you're picking on me."

He didn't answer her because her eyes were angry and he didn't want to quarrel with her. They'd been married too long and got along too well and so he walked all the way into the room and sat down in the chair by the bed and stretched his legs out in front of him, putting his weight on the heels of his shoes, leaning way back in the chair, not saying anything.

"Lissen," she said sharply. "I've got to wear those overalls again tomorrow. You're going to get them all wrinkled up leaning against them like that."

He didn't move. He was too tired and his legs were throbbing now that he had sat down. Besides the overalls were already wrinkled and dirty, he thought. They couldn't help but be for she'd worn them all week. He leaned further back in the chair.

"Come on, get up," she ordered.

"Oh, what the hell," he said wearily and got up from the chair. "I'd just as soon live in a subway. There'd be just as much place to sit down."

He saw that her sense of humor was struggling with her anger. But her sense of humor won because she giggled.

"Aw, come on and eat," she said. There was a coaxing note in her voice. "You're nothing but a old hungry nigger trying to act tough and—" she paused to giggle and then continued, "You—"

He had always found her giggling pleasant and deliberately said things that might amuse her and then waited, listening for the delicate sound to emerge from her throat. This time he didn't even hear the giggle. He didn't let her finish what she was saying. She was standing close to him and that funny tingling started in his finger tips, went fast up his arms and sent his fist shooting straight for her face.

There was the smacking sound of soft flesh being struck by a hard object and it wasn't until she screamed that he realized he had hit her in the mouth— so hard that the dark red lipstick had blurred and spread over her full lips, reaching up toward the tip of her nose, down toward her chin, out toward her cheeks.

The knowledge that he had struck her seeped through him slowly and he was appalled but he couldn't drag his hands away from her face. He kept striking her and he thought with horror that something inside him was holding him, binding him to this act, wrapping and twisting about him so that he had to continue it. He had lost all control over his hands. And he groped for a phrase, a word, something to describe what this thing was like that was happening to him and he thought it was like being enmeshed in a winding sheet—that was it—like a winding sheet. And even as the thought formed in his mind his hands reached for her face again and yet again.

Thinking About the Story

1. Describe the relationship between Mae and her husband at the beginning of the story. How does this compare to their relationship at the end of the story?

2. According to the story, Mae's husband was late because "he couldn't bring himself to talk to her roughly or threaten to strike her like a lot of men might have done. He wasn't made that way." What type of man is he? In which way is he made? Use specific evidence from the story to support your conclusions.

3. The term *winding sheet* is used twice in this story, once in the beginning and once at the end. What is the purpose for using this term at the end? What new meaning of the word is established?

4. Throughout the story Mae's husband is not identified by his name. What is the significance of his not being addressed by his first name?

5. What types of pressures does Mr. Johnson, as an African American man, encounter every day? At home? On his job? In the community?

6. Why does Mae's husband continue to beat her even after he recognizes what he is doing? Why doesn't he stop?

Reading/Writing Connections

1. In your journal discuss some of the other ways Mr. Johnson could have responded to the "forelady" and the clerk in the coffee shop that might not have left him feeling angry.

2. In your journal write about your reaction to the ending of the story. Did you expect Mr. Johnson to beat his wife?

3. The physical abuse of another person is not an acceptable solution to any problem. Rewrite the ending of the story so that Mae and her husband work together to handle his frustrations with life.

Zora Neale Hurston

(1901?–1960) was born in Eatonville, Fla., to John Hurston, a carpenter and Baptist preacher, and Lucy Ann Potts Hurston, a former country school teacher. In 1918 Zora Neale Hurston graduated from Morgan Academy and entered Howard University, where she studied under poet Georgia Douglas Johnson (see Chapter 5) and philosophy professor Alain Locke. Hurston's first short story, "John Redding Goes to Sea" (1921), was published in *Stylus*, a Howard University literary magazine. The story brought her to the attention of sociologist Charles S. Johnson, who encouraged Hurston to move to New York City. Johnson published many of Hurston's stories in his magazine *Opportunity: A Journal of Negro Life*. Hurston was an active participant in the Harlem Renaissance, the black literary and cultural movement of the 1920s, associating with such writers as W. E. B. Du Bois, Langston Hughes, Countee Cullen, and Claude McKay. She received a scholarship to Barnard College where she majored in anthropology, earning a B.A. degree in 1928. From 1927 to 1931, with the financial assistance of Charlotte Osgood Mason, Hurston traveled throughout the South collecting African American folklore—stories, songs, lies, customs, superstitions, and jokes.

In 1934 her first novel, *Jonah's Gourd Vine*, was published. In 1936 and 1938 Hurston received Guggenheim Fellowships to collect folklore. Throughout her writing career Hurston held a variety of jobs, including teaching, writing for a newspaper, and housekeeping. Even with these jobs, a patron, and the publication of numerous short stories, musical reviews, and novels, Hurston was frequently without money. In 1960 Hurston died in poverty and was buried in a segregated cemetery in Fort Pierce, Fla. In 1973, Alice Walker had a tombstone erected on her grave.

Hurston's work represents a part of African American culture that would have been lost had she not recorded it in written form. Her stories and novels capture the life and spirit of the common people. "Sweat" first appeared in the sole issue of *Fire!!* (November, 1926), a Harlem literary journal. Her other works include *Mules and Men* (1935), *Their Eyes Were Watching God* (1937), *Tell My Horse* (1938), *Moses, Man of the Mountain* (1939), *Dust Tracks on the Road* (autobiography, 1942), *Seraph on the Suwanee* (1948), *I Love Myself When I Am Laughing . . . & Then Again When I Am Looking Mean & Impressive* (ed. Alice Walker, 1979).

Sweat

ZORA NEALE HURSTON

I

It was eleven o'clock of a Spring night in Florida. It was Sunday. Any other night, Delia Jones would have been in bed for two hours by this time. But she was a washwoman, and Monday morning meant a great deal to her. So she collected the soiled clothes on Saturday when she returned the clean things. Sunday night after church, she sorted and put the white things to soak. It saved her almost a half-day's start. A great hamper in the bedroom held the clothes that she brought home. It was so much neater than a number of bundles lying around.

She squatted on the kitchen floor beside the great pile of clothes, sorting them into small heaps according to color, and humming a song in a mournful key, but wondering through it all where Sykes, her husband, had gone with her horse and buckboard.

Just then something long, round, limp and black fell upon her shoulders and slithered to the floor beside her. A great terror took hold of her. It softened her knees and dried her mouth so that it was a full minute before she could cry out or move. Then she saw that it was the big bull whip her husband liked to carry when he drove.

She lifted her eyes to the door and saw him standing there bent over with laughter at her fright. She screamed at him.

"Sykes, what you throw dat whip on me like dat? You know it would skeer me—looks just like a snake, an' you knows how skeered Ah is of snakes."

"Course Ah knowed it! That's how come Ah done it." He slapped his leg with his hand and almost rolled on the ground in his mirth. "If you such a big fool dat you got to have a fit over a earth worm or a string, Ah don't keer how bad Ah skeer you."

"You ain't got no business doing it, Gawd knows it's a sin. Some day Ah'm gointuh drop dead from some of yo' foolishness. 'Nother thing, where you been wid mah rig? Ah feeds dat pony. He ain't fuh you to be drivin' wid no bull whip."

"You sho' is one aggravatin' nigger woman!" he declared and stepped into the room. She resumed her work and did not answer him at once. "Ah done tole you time and again to keep them white folks' clothes outa dis house."

He picked up the whip and glared at her. Delia went on with her work.

She went out into the yard and returned with a galvanized tub and set it on the washbench. She saw that Sykes had kicked all of the clothes together again, and now stood in her way truculently, his whole manner hoping, *praying*, for an argument. But she walked calmly around him and commenced to re-sort the things.

"Next time, Ah'm gointer kick 'em outdoors," he threatened as he struck a match along the leg of his corduroy breeches.

Delia never looked up from her work, and her thin, stooped shoulders sagged further.

"Ah ain't for no fuss t'night Sykes. Ah just come from taking sacrament at the church house."

He snorted scornfully. "Yeah, you just come from de church house on a Sunday night, but heah you is gone to work on them clothes. You ain't nothing but a hypocrite. One of them amen-corner Christians—sing, whoop, and shout, then come home and wash white folks' clothes on the Sabbath."

He stepped roughly upon the whitest pile of things, kicking them helter-skelter as he crossed the room. His wife gave a little scream of dismay, and quickly gathered them together again.

"Sykes, you quit grindin' dirt into these clothes! How can Ah git through by Sat'day if Ah don't start on Sunday?"

"Ah don't keer if you never git through. Anyhow, Ah done promised Gawd and a couple of other men, Ah ain't gointer have it in mah house. Don't gimme no lip neither, else Ah'll throw 'em out and put mah fist up side yo' head to boot."

Delia's habitual meekness seemed to slip from her shoulders like a blown scarf. She was on her feet; her poor little body, her bare knuckly hands bravely defying the strapping hulk before her.

"Looka heah, Sykes, you done gone too fur. Ah been married to you fur fifteen years, and Ah been takin' in washin' fur fifteen years. Sweat, sweat, sweat! Work and sweat, cry and sweat, pray and sweat!"

"What's that got to do with me?" he asked brutally.

"What's it got to do with you, Sykes? Mah tub of suds is filled yo' belly with vittles more times than yo' hands is filled it. Mah sweat is done paid for this house and Ah reckon Ah kin keep on sweatin' in it."

She seized the iron skillet from the stove and stuck a defensive pose, which act surprised him greatly, coming from her. It cowed him and he did not strike her as he usually did.

"Naw you won't," she panted, "that ole snaggle-toothed black woman you runnin' with ain't comin' heah to pile up on *mah* sweat and blood. You ain't paid for nothin' on this place, and Ah'm gointer stay right heah till Ah'm toted out foot foremost."

"Well, you better quit gittin' me riled up, else they'll be totin' you out sooner than you expect. Ah'm so tired of you Ah don't know whut to do. Gawd! How Ah hates skinny wimmen!"

A little awed by this new Delia, he sidled out of the door and slammed the back gate after him. He did not say where he had gone, but she knew too well. She knew very well that he would not return until nearly daybreak also. Her work over, she went on to bed but not to sleep at once. Things had come to a pretty pass!

She lay awake, gazing upon the debris that cluttered their matrimonial trail. Not an image left standing along the way. Anything like flowers had long ago been drowned in the salty stream that had been pressed from her heart. Her tears, her sweat, her blood. She had brought love to the union and he had brought a longing after the flesh. Two months after the wedding, he had given her the first brutal beating. She had the memory of his numerous trips to Orlando with all of his wages when he had returned to her penniless, even before the first year had passed. She was young and soft then, but now she thought of her knotty, muscled limbs, her harsh knuckly hands, and drew herself up into an unhappy little ball in the middle of the big feather bed. Too late now to hope for love, even if it were not Bertha it would be someone else. This case differed from the others only in that she was bolder than the others. Too late for everything except her little home. She had built it for her old days, and planted one by one the trees and flowers there. It was lovely to her, lovely.

Somehow, before sleep came, she found herself saying aloud: "Oh well, whatever goes over the Devil's back, is got to come under his belly. Sometime or ruther, Sykes, like everybody else, is gointer reap his sowing." After that she was able to build a spiritual earthworks against her husband. His shells could no longer reach her. AMEN. She went to sleep and slept until he announced his presence in bed by kicking her feet and rudely snatching the covers away.

"Gimme some kivah heah, an' git yo' damn foots over on yo' own side! Ah oughter mash you in you' mouf fuh drawing dat skillet on me."

Delia went clear to the rail without answering him. A triumphant indifference to all that he was or did.

II

The week was as full of work for Delia as all other weeks, and Saturday found her behind her little pony, collecting and delivering clothes.

It was a hot, hot day near the end of July. The village men on Joe Clarke's porch even chewed cane listlessly. They did not hurl the cane-knots as usual. They let them dribble over the edge of the porch. Even conversation had collapsed under the heat.

"Heah come Delia Jones," Jim Merchant said, as the shaggy pony came 'round the bend of the road toward them. The rusty buckboard was heaped with baskets of crisp, clean laundry.

"Yep," Joe Lindsay agreed. "Hot or col', rain or shine, jes'ez reg'lar ez de weeks roll roun' Delia carries 'em an' fetches 'em on Sat'day."

"She better if she wanter eat," said Moss. "Syke Jones ain't wuth de shot an' powder hit would tek tuh kill 'em. Not to *huh* he ain't."

"He sho' ain't," Walter Thomas chimed in. "It's too bad, too, cause she wuz a right pretty li'l trick when he got huh. Ah'd uh mah'ied huh mahself if he hadnter beat me to it."

Delia nodded briefly at the men as she drove past.

"Too much knockin' will ruin *any* 'oman. He done beat huh 'nough tuh kill three women, let 'lone change they looks," said Elijah Moseley. "How Syke kin stommuck dat big black greasy Mogul he's layin' roun' wid, gits me. Ah swear dat eight-rock couldn't kiss a sardine can Ah done thowed out de back do' 'way las' yeah."

"Aw, she's fat, thass how come. He's allus been crazy 'bout fat women," put in Merchant. "He'd a' been tied up wid one long time ago if he could a' found one tuh have him. Did Ah tell yuh 'bout him come sidlin' roun' *mah* wife—bringin' her a basket uh peecans outa his yard fuh a present? Yessir, mah wife! She tol' him tuh take 'em right straight back home, 'cause Delia works so hard ovah dat washtub she reckon everything on de place taste lak sweat an' soapsuds. Ah jus' wisht Ah'd a' caught 'im 'roun' dere! Ah'd a' made his hips ketch on fiah down dat shell road."

"Ah know he done it, too. Ah sees 'im grinnin' at every 'oman dat passes," Walter Thomas said. "But even so, he useter eat some mighty big hunks uh humble pie tuh git dat li'l 'oman he got. She wuz ez pritty ez a speckled pup! Dat wuz fifteen years ago. He useter be so skeered uh losin' huh, she could make him do some parts of a husband's duty. Dey never wuz de same in de mind."

"There oughter be a law about him," said Lindsay. "He ai't fit tuh carry guts tuh a bear."

Clarke spoke for the first time. "Tain't no law on earth dat kin make a man be decent if it ain't in 'im. There's plenty men dat takes a wife lak dey do a joint uh sugar-cane. It's round, juicy an' sweet when dey gits it. But dey squeeze an' grind, squeeze an' grind an' wring tell dey wring every drop uh pleasure dat's in 'em out. When dey's satisfied dat dey is wrung dry, dey treats 'em jes' lak dey do a cane-chew. Dew thows 'em away. Dey knows whut dey is doin' while dey is at it, an' hates theirselves fuh it but they keeps on hangin' after huh tell she's empty. Den dey hates huh fuh bein' a cane-chew an' in de way."

"We oughter take Syke an' dat stray 'oman uh his'n down in Lake Howell swamp an' lay on de rawhide till they cain't say Lawd a' mussy. He allus wuz uh ovahbearin niggah, but since dat white 'oman from up north done teached 'im how to run a automobile, he done got too beggety to live—an' we oughter kill 'im," Old Man Anderson advised.

A grunt of approval went around the porch. But the heat was melting their civic virtue and Elijah Moseley began to bait Joe Clarke.

"Come on, Joe, git a melon outa dere an' slice it up for yo' customers. We'se all sufferin' wid de heat. De bear's done got *me*!''

"Thass right, Joe, a watermelon is jes' whut Ah needs tuh cure de eppizudicks," Walter Thomas joined forces with Moseley. "Come on dere, Joe. We all is steady customers an' you ain't set us up in a long time. Ah chooses dat long, bowlegged Floridy favorite."

"A god, an' be dough. You all gimme twenty cents and slice away," Clarke retorted. "Ah needs a col' slice m'self. Heah, everybody chip in. Ah'll lend y'all mah meat knife."

The money was all quickly subscribed and the huge melon brought forth. At that moment, Sykes and Bertha arrived. A determined silence fell on the porch and the melon was put away again.

Merchant snapped down the blade of his jackknife and moved toward the store door.

"Come on in, Joe, an' gimme a slab uh sow belly an' uh pound uh coffee— almost fuhgot 'twas Sat'day. Got to git on home." Most of the men left also.

Just then Delia drove past on her way home, as Sykes was ordering magnificently for Bertha. It pleased him for Delia to see.

"Git whutsoever yo' heart desires, Honey. Wait a minute, Joe. Give huh two bottles uh strawberry soda-water, uh quart parched ground-peas, an' a block uh chewin' gum."

With all this they left the store, with Sykes reminding Bertha that this was his town and she could have it if she wanted it.

The men returned soon after they left, and held their watermelon feast.

"Where did Syke Jones git da 'oman from nohow?" Lindsay asked.

"Ovah Apopka. Guess dey musta been cleanin' out de town when she lef'. She don't look lak a thing but a hunk uh liver wid hair on it."

"Well, she sho' kin squall," Dave Carter contributed. "When she gits ready tuh laff, she jes' opens huh mouf an' latches it back tuh de las' notch. No ole granpa alligator down in Lake Bell ain't got nothin' on huh."

III

Bertha had been in town three months now. Sykes was still paying her room-rent at Della Lewis'—the only house in town that would have taken her in. Sykes took her frequently to Winter Park to "stomps."[1] He still assured her that he was the swellest man in the state.

"Sho' you kin have dat l'l ole house soon's Ah git dat 'oman outa dere. Everything b'longs tuh me an' you sho' kin have it. Ah sho' 'bominates uh skinny 'oman. Lawdy, you sho' is got one portly shape on you! You kin git *anything* you wants. Dis is *mah* town an' you sho' kin have it."

Delia's work-worn knees crawled over the earth in Gethsemane and up the rocks of Calvary many, many times during these months. She avoided the villagers and meeting places in her efforts to be blind and deaf. But Bertha nullified this to a degree, by coming to Delia's house to call Sykes out to her at the gate.

Delia and Sykes fought all the time now with no peaceful interludes. They slept and ate in silence. Two or three times Delia had attempted a timid friendliness, but she was repulsed each time. It was plain that the breaches must remain agape.

The sun had burned July to August. The heat streamed down like a million hot arrows, smiting all things living upon the earth. Grass withered, leaves browned, snakes went blind in shedding and men and dogs went mad. Dog days!

Delia came home one day and found Sykes there before her. She wondered, but started to go on into the house without speaking, even though he was standing in the kitchen door and she must either stoop under his arm or ask him to move. He made no room for her. She noticed a soap box beside the steps, but paid no particular attention to it, knowing that he must have brought it there. As she was stooping to pass under his outstretched arm, he suddenly pushed her backward, laughingly.

"Look in de box dere Delia, Ah done brung yuh somethin'!"

She nearly fell upon the box in her stumbling, and when she saw what it held, she all but fainted outright.

"Syke! Syke, mah Gawd! You take dat rattlesnake 'way from heah! You *gottah*. Oh, Jesus, have mussy!"

"Ah ain't got tuh do nuthin' uh de kin'—fact is Ah ain't got tuh do nothin' but die. Tain't no use uh you puttin' on airs makin' out lak you skeered uh dat snake—he's gointer stay right heah tell he die. He wouldn't bite me cause Ah knows how tuh handle 'im. Nohow he wouldn't risk breakin' out his fangs 'gin *yo* skinny laigs."

---

[1]*stomps:* parties.

"Naw, now Syke, don't keep dat thing 'round tryin' tuh skeer me tuh death. You knows Ah'm even feared uh earth worms. Thass de biggest snake Ah evah did see. Kill 'im Syke, please.'

"Doan ast me tuh do nothin' fuh yuh. Goin' 'round tryin' tuh be so damn asterperious. Naw, Ah ain't gonna kill it. Ah think uh damn sight mo' uh him dan you! Dat's a nice snake an' anybody doan lak 'im kin jes' hit de grit.''

The village soon heard that Sykes had the snake, and came to see and ask questions.

"How de hen-fire did you ketch dat six-foot rattler, Syke?'' Thomas asked.

"He's full uh frogs so he cain't hardly move, thass how Ah eased up on 'm. But Ah'm a snake charmer an' knows how tuh handle 'em. Shux, dat ain't nothin'. Ah could ketch one eve'y day if Ah so wanted tuh.''

"Whut he needs is a heavy hick'ry club leaned real heavy on his head. Dat's de bes' way tuh charm a rattlesnake.''

"Naw, Walt, y'all jes' don't understand dese diamon' backs lak Ah do,'' said Sykes in a superior tone of voice.

The village agreed with Walter, but the snake stayed on. His box remained by the kitchen door with its screen wire covering. Two or three days later it had digested its meal of frogs and literally came to life. It rattled at every movement in the kitchen or the yard. One day as Delia came down the kitchen steps she saw his chalky-white fangs curved like scimitars hung in the wire meshes. This time she did not run away with averted eyes as usual. She stood for a long time in the doorway in a red fury that grew bloodier for every second that she regarded the creature that was her torment.

That night she broached the subject as soon as Sykes sat down to the table.

"Syke, Ah wants you tuh take dat snake 'way fum heah. You done starved me an' Ah put up widcher, you done beat me an Ah took dat, but you done kilt all mah insides bringin' dat varmint heah.''

Sykes poured out a saucer full of coffee and drank it deliberately before he answered her.

A whole lot Ah keer 'bout how you feels inside uh out. Dat snake ain't goin' no damn wheah till Ah gits ready fuh 'im tuh go. So fur as beatin' is concerned, yuh ain't took near all dat you gointer take ef yuh stay 'round *me*.''

Delia pushed back her plate and got up from the table. "Ah hates you, Sykes,'' she said calmly. "Ah hates you tuh de same degree dat Ah useter love yuh. Ah done took an' took till mah belly is full up tuh mah neck. Dat's de reason Ah got mah letter fum de church an' moved mah membership tuh Woodbridge—so Ah don't haftuh take no sacrament wid yuh. Ah don't wantuh see yuh 'round me atall. Lay 'round wid dat 'oman all yuh wants tuh, but gwan 'way fum me an' mah house. Ah hates yuh lak uh suck-egg dog.''

Sykes almost let the huge wad of corn bread and collard greens he was chewing fall out of his mouth in amazement. He had a hard time whipping himself up to the proper fury to try to answer Delia.

"Well, Ah'm glad you does hate me. Ah'm sho' tiahed uh you hangin' ontuh me. Ah don't want yuh. Look at yuh stringey ole neck! Yo' rawbony laigs an' arms is enough tuh cut uh man tuh death. You looks jes' lak de devvul's doll-baby tuh *me*. You cain't hate me no worse dan Ah hates you. Ah been hatin' *you* fuh years."

"Yo' ole black hide don't look lak nothin' tuh me, but uh passle uh wrinkled up rubber, wid yo' big ole yeahs flappin' on each side lak uh paih uh buzzard wings. Don't think Ah'm gointuh be run 'way fum mah house neither. Ah'm goin' tuh de white folks 'bout *you,* mah young man, de very nex' time you lay yo' han's on me. Mah cup is done run ovah." Delia said this with no signs of fear and Sykes departed from the house, threatening her, but made not the slightest move to carry out any of them.

That night he did not return at all, and the next day being Sunday, Delia was glad she did not have to quarrel before she hitched up her pony and drove the four miles to Woodbridge.

She stayed to the night service—"love feast"—which was very warm and full of spirit. In the emotional winds her domestic trials were borne far and wide so that she sang as she drove homeward,

> *Jurden water, black an' col*
> *Chills de body, not de soul*
> *An' Ah wantah cross Jurden in uh calm time.*

She came from the barn to the kitchen door and stopped.

"What's de mattah, ol' Satan, you ain't kickin' up yo' racket?" She addressed the snake's box. Complete silence. She went on into the house with new hope in its birth struggles. Perhaps her threat to go to the white folks had frightened Sykes! Perhaps he was sorry! Fifteen years of misery and suppression had brought Delia to the place where she would hope *anything* that looked towards a way over or through her wall of inhibitions.

She felt in the match-safe behind the stove at once for a match. There was only one there.

"Dat niggah wouldn't fetch nothin' heah tuh save his rotten neck, but he kin run thew whut Ah brings quick enough. Now he done toted off nigh on tuh haff uh box uh matches. He done had dat 'oman heah in mah house, too."

Nobody but a woman could tell how she knew this even before she struck the match. But she did and it put her into a new fury.

Presently she brought in the tubs to put the white things to soak. This time she decided she need not bring the hamper out of the bedroom; she would go in there and do the sorting. She picked up the pot-bellied lamp and went in. The room was small and the hamper stood hard by the foot of the white iron bed. She could sit and reach through the bedposts—resting as she worked.

"*Ah wantah cross Jurden in uh calm time.*" She was singing again. The mood of the "love feast" had returned. She threw back the lid of the basket almost gaily. Then, moved by both horror and terror, she sprang back toward the door. *There lay the snake in the basket!* He moved sluggishly at first, but even as she turned round and round, jumped up and down in an insanity of fear, he began to stir vigorously. She saw him pouring his awful beauty from the basket upon the bed, then she seized the lamp and ran as fast as she could to the kitchen. The wind from the open door blew out the light and the darkness added to her terror. She sped to the darkness of the yard, slamming the door after her before she thought to set down the lamp. She did not feel safe even on the ground, so she climbed up in the hay barn.

There for an hour or more she lay sprawled upon the hay a gibbering wreck.

Finally she grew quiet, and after that came coherent thought. With this stalked through her a cold, bloody rage. Hours of this. A period of introspection, a space of retrospection, then a mixture of both. Out of this an awful calm.

"Well, Ah done de bes' Ah could. If things ain't right, Gawd knows tain't mah fault."

She went to sleep—a twitch sleep—and woke up to a faint gray sky. There was a loud hollow sound below. She peered out. Sykes was at the wood-pile, demolishing a wire-covered box.

He hurried to the kitchen door, but hung outside there some minutes before he entered, and stood some minutes more inside before he closed it after him.

The gray in the sky was spreading. Delia descended without fear now, and crouched beneath the low bedroom window. The drawn shade shut out the dawn, shut in the night. But the thin walls held back no sound.

"Dat ol' scratch is woke up now!" She mused at the tremendous whirr inside, which every woodman knows, is one of the sound illusions. The rattler is a ventriloquist. His whirr sounds to the right, to the left, straight ahead, behind, close under foot—everywhere but where it is. Woe to him who guesses wrong unless he is prepared to hold up his end of the argument! Sometimes he strikes without rattling at all.

Inside, Sykes heard nothing until he knocked a pot lid off the stove while trying to reach the match-safe in the dark. He had emptied his pockets at Bertha's.

The snake seemed to wake up under the stove and Sykes made a quick leap into the bedroom. In spite of the gin he had had, his head was clearing now.

"May Gawd!" he chattered, "ef Ah could on'y strack uh light!"

The rattling ceased for a moment as he stood paralyzed. He waited. It seemed that the snake waited also.

"Oh, fuh de light! Ah thought he'd be too sick"—Sykes was muttering to himself when the whirr began again, closer, right underfoot this time. Long before this, Sykes' ability to think had been flattened down to primitive instinct and he leaped—onto the bed.

Outside Delia heard a cry that might have come from a maddened chimpanzee, a stricken gorilla. All the terror, all the horror, all the rage that man possibly could express, without a recognizable human sound.

A tremendous stir inside there, another series of animal screams, the intermittent whirr of the reptile. The shade torn violently down from the window, letting in the red dawn, a huge brown hand seizing the window stick, great dull blows upon the wooden floor punctuating the gibberish of sound long after the rattle of the snake had abruptly subsided. All this Delia could see and hear from her place beneath the window, and it made her ill. She crept over to the four-o'clocks and stretched herself on the cool earth to recover.

She lay there. "Delia, Delia!" She could hear Sykes calling in a most despairing tone as one who expected no answer. The sun crept on up, and he called. Delia could not move—her legs had gone flabby. She never moved, he called, and the sun kept rising.

"Mah Gawd!" She heard him moan, "Mah Gawd fum Heben!" She heard him stumbling about and got up from her flower-bed. The sun was growing warm. As she approached the door she heard him call out hopefully, "Delia, is dat you Ah heah?"

She saw him on his hands and knees as soon as she reached the door. He crept an inch or two toward her—all that he was able, and she saw his horribly swollen neck and his one open eye shining with hope. A surge of pity too strong to support bore her away from that eye that must, could not, fail to see the tubs. He would see the lamp. Orlando with its doctors was too far. She could scarcely reach the chinaberry tree, where she waited in the growing heat while inside she knew the cold river was creeping up and up to extinguish that eye which must know by now that she knew.

Thinking About the Story

1. Delia sweats while she earns a living washing clothes. Some of the townspeople say that they would not want to eat food from Delia's house because it would taste like sweat. Discuss the amount of "sweat" that Delia has contributed to saving her marriage. What toll has this "sweat" taken on Delia's physical and mental health?

2. Several times in the story, Delia expresses herself through African American folk proverbs or religious statements. Select two of these expressions and explain how they foreshadow events that occur in the story.

3. The townspeople are all aware that Sykes treats Delia unfairly. Select specific statements or actions by the townspeople that illustrate their reactions to Sykes and Delia's relationship.

4. After Sykes has been bitten by the snake, Delia hears Sykes call her name several times. Why does she choose not to respond to his calls for help? Since she does not respond, is Delia partly responsible for Sykes's death? Why or why not?

Reading/Writing Connections

1. In a journal entry write about your response to Sykes scaring Delia with the snake. What could Delia have done to cope with her fears and her husband's actions?

2. Rewrite the ending of the story so that instead of Sykes being bitten by the snake, Delia is bitten. Write a new ending to the story in which Sykes finds Delia dying in their bedroom. How would he feel? What would he say to Delia?

Gwendolyn Brooks

(b. 1917) was born in Topeka, Kans., to David Anderson and Keziah Corinne Wims Brooks. When Gwendolyn Brooks entered elementary school, she was subjected to ridicule by other African American children because of the darkness of her skin and her lack of athletic abilities. Brooks turned to writing poetry as an escape from intraracial prejudice. Both of her parents supported her writing. In 1930 when she was thirteen, her poem "Eventide" was published in *American Childhood* magazine. While she was in high school, her poetry was published in the *Chicago Defender* newspaper. During the 1930s, Brooks corresponded with Harlem Renaissance poet James Weldon Johnson and shared some of her poetry with Langston Hughes. Both men encouraged Brooks to continue writing. By the time she graduated from Wilson Junior College in 1936, Brooks had a large collection of poetry, including seventy-five poems that had been published in the *Chicago Defender*. Brooks' first poetry collection, *A Street in Bronzeville* (1945), brought her national attention. In 1950 *Annie Allen* won the Pulitzer Prize. Since the 1950s Brooks has continued to publish books of poetry, conduct poetry workshops for young people, and teach poetry at the university level. She has been honored at the national and international levels for her poetry. In 1962, at the request of President John F. Kennedy, Brooks read at a Library of Congress poetry festival. In 1968 the governor of Illinois, Otto Kerner, appointed Brooks poet laureate of Illinois. In 1973 she was appointed honorary consultant in American letters to the Library of Congress. On January 3, 1980, she read her works at the White House with Robert Hayden and nineteen other distinguished poets. In 1985 Brooks was named poetry consultant to the Library of Congress.

Brooks' mastery of poetic techniques and her themes of racial identity and equality have signaled her as one of the most distinguished American poets of the twentieth century. Her poetry forms a bridge between the academic poets of the 1940s and the black militant writers of the 1960s. Her poetry collections include *The Bean Eaters* (1960), *In the Mecca* (1968), *Riot* (1969), *Beckoning* (1975), *Primer for Blacks* (1980) and *The Near-Johannesburg Boy, and Other Poems* (1986).

The Bean Eaters

GWENDOLYN BROOKS

They eat beans mostly, this old yellow pair.
Dinner is a casual affair.
Plain chipware on a plain and creaking wood,
Tin flatware.

Two who are Mostly Good.   5
Two who have lived their day,
But keep on putting on their clothes
And putting things away.

And remembering . . .
Remembering, with twinklings and twinges,   10
As they lean over the beans in their rented back room that
is full of beads and receipts and dolls and clothes,
tobacco crumbs, vases and fringes.

Thinking About the Poem

1. What type of relationship does the couple have? Use specific information from the poem to support your opinion.

2. Referring to words and phrases from the poem, discuss the economic situation of the couple.

3. What influence has the couple's economic situation had on their relationship?

4. The couple's room is described as being ". . . full of beads and receipts and dolls and clothes, / tobacco crumbs, vases and fringes." What do these items tell you about the life that the couple has shared together?

Reading/Writing Connections

1. Write an essay in which you compare and contrast the housing conditions, the food, and life in general between the couple in "The Bean Eaters" and Jeff and Jennie Patton in Arna Bontemps' "A Summer Tragedy" (see Chapter 2).

2. In your journal describe the items that you hope to have around you when you are older. Why are these items important to you? What would these items say about you to other people?

"The Builders" (also *"The Family"*) by Jacob Lawrence. Medium: Serigraph. Photographer, Chris Eden. Reprinted by permission of Francine Seders Gallery, Seattle, Washington.

7

PASSING DOWN HERITAGE

Africans were torn from their homeland and brought to a country that further dehumanized them by declaring that they were only to be beasts of burden. Many of these same men and women, more than 200 years ago, began using literature to express their plight. They left a rich heritage for those generations that were to follow.

The early African Americans, whose indigenous language, culture, and music had long since disappeared, developed new music based on Biblical texts. The spirituals or sorry songs, as W.E.B. Du Bois called them, coupled with folktales and other imaginative devices, led to another oral tradition prevalent in the African American culture—the sermon as spoken by black preachers.

The rich literary heritage left by those fathers and mothers snatched from their homeland serves as a guidepost for their sons and daughters of today who continue the legacy of telling the story of a proud people.

An African American sermon written in the form of a poem, a poem about strong black women, a story about a boy who attempted to snatch an old woman's purse, a poem in celebration of a people, a story about a teacher and her students, and a poem about people who wear masks in order to hide their true feelings—these are some of the literary experiences you will share as you read the selections in this chapter.

James Weldon Johnson   (1871–1938) was born in Jacksonville, Fla. Educated at Atlanta and Columbia universities, Johnson was a teacher, poet, novelist, and musician. He also served as a United States diplomat in Venezuela and Nicaragua. After a brief career as a teacher, he and his brother, John Rosamond, went to New York City to write music for the stage. From 1920 to 1930, Johnson served as executive secretary of the National Association for the Advancement of Colored People. The association awarded him the Spingarn Medal in 1925. He taught literature at Fisk University in Tennessee and was a visiting professor at New York University. His publications include *The Autobiography of an Ex-Coloured Man* (1912), *Fifty Years and Other Poems* (1917), *God's Trombones, or Seven Negro Sermons in Verse* (1927), *St. Peter Relates an Incident of the Resurrection Day* (1935), *The Book of American Negro Poetry* (1922; expanded, 1931), *Black Manhattan* (1930), and his autobiography, *Along This Way* (1933). He and his brother edited two collections of spirituals. Johnson was considered a "true Renaissance man."

The Creation

JAMES WELDON JOHNSON

A Negro Sermon

And God stepped out on space,
And He looked around and said,
"I'm lonely—
I'll make me a world."

And far as the eye of God could see   5
Darkness covered everything,
Blacker than a hundred midnights
Down in a cypress swamp.

Then God smiled,
And the light broke,   10
And the darkness rolled up on one side,
And the light stood shining on the other,
And God said, *"That's good!"*

Then God reached out and took the light in His hands,
And God rolled the light around in His hands,   15
Until He made the sun;
And He set that sun a-blazing in the heavens.
And the light that was left from making the sun
Got gathered up in a shining ball
And flung against the darkness,   20
Spangling the night with the moon and stars.
Then down between
The darkness and the light
He hurled the world;
And God said, *"That's good!"*   25

Then God himself stepped down—
And the sun was on His right hand,
And the moon was on His left;
The stars were clustered about His head,
And the earth was under His feet.   30
And God walked, and where He trod
His footsteps hollowed the valleys out
And bulged the mountains up.

Then He stopped and looked and saw
That the earth was hot and barren.   35
So God stepped over to the edge of the world
And He spat out the seven seas;
He batted His eyes, and the lightnings flashed;
He clapped His hands, and the thunders rolled;
And the waters above the earth came down,   40
The cooling waters came down.

Then the green grass sprouted,
And the little red flowers blossomed,
The pine-tree pointed his finger to the sky,
And the oak spread out his arms;   45
The lakes cuddled down in the hollows of the ground,
And the rivers ran down to the sea;
And God smiled again,
And the rainbow appeared,
And curled itself around His shoulder.   50

Then God raised His arm and He waved His hand
Over the sea and over the land,
And He said, "*Bring forth! Bring forth!*"
And quicker than God could drop His hand,
Fishes and fowls   55
And beast and birds
Swam the rivers and the seas,
Roamed the forests and the woods,
And split the air with their wings,
And God said, "*That's good!*"   60

Then God walked around
And God looked around
On all that He had made.
He looked at His sun,
And He looked at His moon,   65
And He looked at His little stars;
He looked on His world
With all its living things,
And God said, "*I'm lonely still.*"

Then God sat down   70
On the side of a hill where He could think;
By a deep, wide river He sat down;
With His head in His hands,
God thought and thought,
Till He thought, "*I'll make me a man!*"   75

Up from the bed of the river
God scooped the clay;
And by the bank of the river
He kneeled Him down;
And there the great God Almighty,   80
Who lit the sun and fixed it in the sky,
Who flung the stars to the most far corner of the night,
Who rounded the earth in the middle of His hand—
This Great God,
Like a mammy bending over her baby,   85
Kneeled down in the dust
Toiling over a lump of clay
Till He shaped it in His own image;

Then into it He blew the breath of life,
And man became a living soul.   90
Amen. Amen.

Thinking About the Poem

1. Taken from a collection of poems entitled *God's Trombones*, "The Creation" tells a Biblical story. What technique does Johnson use to make the poem similar to a sermon?

2. What are some of the descriptive words and phrases Johnson uses to make the poem effective?

3. The opening lines of the poem treat God as if he has human qualities. What are some of these qualities?

Reading/Writing Connections

1. Write an essay in which you describe a favorite stanza for a friend who has not yet read the poem.

2. This poem, in the form of a sermon, is written in free verse. Using the free-verse style, write a poem on a theme of your own choosing.

3. In your journal, write about the religious or spiritual values depicted in the poem.

Alice Walker   (b. 1944) was born in Eatonton, Ga. She attended Spelman College in Atlanta and graduated from Sarah Lawrence College in 1965. Her first volume of poetry, *Once*, was published in 1968. She published *Good Night, Willie Lee, I'll See You In The Morning* in 1979. Walker has written short stories, poetry, essays, and novels. She has edited the works of Zora Neale Hurston and Langston Hughes. Her honors include the Rosenthal Award of the American Academy of Arts and Letters for her collection of short stories entitled *In Love and Trouble* (1973); the Lillian Smith Award of the Southern Regional Council for her poems collected in *Revolutionary Petunias* (1973); and a Guggenheim Fellowship (1977–1978). She received a Pulitzer Prize and the American Book Award for her novel *The Color Purple* (1982). Her latest novel is *Possessing the Secret of Joy* (1992).

Walker, who often writes about women who survive cruelty and adversity, considers herself a "womanist." She currently lives on a ranch in northern California.

Women

ALICE WALKER

They were women then
My mama's generation
Husky of voice—stout of
Step
With fists as well as   5
Hands
How they battered down
Doors
And ironed
Starched white   10
Shirts
How they led
Armies
Headragged Generals
Across mined   15
Fields
Booby-trapped
Ditches
To discover books
Desks   20
A place for us
How they knew what we
Must know
Without knowing a page
Of it   25
Themselves.

Thinking About the Poem

1. Alice Walker writes about women of her mother's generation. What are some of the characteristics of these women?

2. Walker uses military metaphors in describing the women of her mother's generation. Locate them in the poem and discuss their effect with the class.

3. Discuss some women of today who you think exhibit some of the same qualities as the women in the poem.

Reading/Writing Connections

1. Write a character sketch about a woman who you feel exemplifies the qualities mentioned in the poem.

2. In an essay, describe how your mother, female guardian, or friend has helped you to be who you are.

3. In your journal, write a poem about someone in your life who has made it possible for you to achieve a certain goal.

Langston Hughes

Langston Hughes (1902–1967) is recognized not only as a leading African American poet, but also as a fine writer of fiction, nonfiction, and drama. Hughes was one of the few African American writers of his era who made a living solely on his literary efforts. His stories about Jesse B. Semple, his popular fictional hero of Harlem, came to be known as the Simple tales; eventually five volumes of the tales written during the 1950s were compiled. Also a master of the short story, Hughes' short story collections include *Laughing to Keep from Crying* (1952) and *Something in Common* (1963). Hughes also edited anthologies, including *An African Treasure* (1960) and *The Best Short Stories by Negro Writers* (1967). (For further biographical information, see pages 32 and 148.)

Thank You, M'am

LANGSTON HUGHES

She was a large woman with a large purse that had everything in it but a hammer and nails. It had a long strap, and she carried it slung across her shoulder. It was about eleven o'clock at night, dark, and she was walking alone, when a boy ran up behind her and tried to snatch her purse. The strap broke with the sudden single tug the boy gave it from behind. But the boy's weight and the weight of the purse combined caused him to lose his balance. Instead of taking off full blast as he had hoped, the boy fell on his back on the sidewalk and his legs flew up. The large woman simply turned around and kicked him right square in his blue-jeaned sitter. Then she reached down, picked the boy up by his shirt front, and shook him until his teeth rattled.

After that the woman said, "Pick up my pocketbook, boy, and give it here."

She still held him tightly. But she bent down enough to permit him to stoop and pick up her purse. Then she said, "Now ain't you ashamed of yourself?"

Firmly gripped by his shirt front, the boy said, "Yes'm."

The woman said, "What did you want to do it for?"

The boy said, "I didn't aim to."

She said, "You a lie!"

By that time two or three people passed, stopped, turned to look, and some stood watching.

"If I turn you loose, will you run?" asked the woman.

"Yes'm," said the boy.

"Then I won't turn you loose," said the woman. She did not release him.

"Lady, I'm sorry," whispered the boy.

"Um-hum! Your face is dirty. I got a great mind to wash your face for you. Ain't you got nobody home to tell you to wash your face?"

"No'm," said the boy.

"Then it will get washed this evening," said the large woman, starting up the street, dragging the frightened boy behind her.

He looked as if he were fourteen or fifteen, frail and willow-wild, in tennis shoes and blue jeans.

The woman said, "You ought to be my son. I would teach you right from wrong. Least I can do right now is to wash your face. Are you hungry?"

"No'm," said the being-dragged boy. "I just want you to turn me loose."

"Was I bothering *you* when I turned that corner?" asked the woman.

"No'm."

"But you put yourself in contact with *me*," said the woman. "If you think that that contact is not going to last awhile, yot another thought coming. When I get through with you, sir, you are going to remember Mrs. Luella Bates Washington Jones."

Sweat popped out on the boy's face and he began to struggle. Mrs. Jones stopped, jerked him around in front of her, put a half nelson about his neck, and continued to drag him up the street. When she got to her door, she dragged the boy inside, down a hall, and into a large kitchenette-furnished room at the rear of the house. She switched on the light and left the door open. The boy could hear other roomers laughing and talking in the large house. Some of their doors were open, too, so he knew he and the woman were not alone. The woman still had him by the neck in the middle of her room.

She said, "What is your name?"

"Roger," answered the boy.

"Then, Roger, you go to that sink and wash your face," said the woman, whereupon she turned him loose—at last. Roger looked at the door—looked at the woman—looked at the door—*and went to the sink.*

"Let the water run till it gets warm," she said. "Here's a clean towel."

"You gonna take me to jail?" asked the boy, bending over the sink.

"Not with that face, I would not take you nowhere," said the woman. "Here I am trying to get home to cook me a bite to eat, and you snatch my pocketbook! Maybe you ain't been to your supper either, late as it be. Have you?"

"There's nobody home at my house," said the boy.

"Then we'll eat," said the woman. "I believe you're hungry—or been hungry—to try to snatch my pocketbook!"

"I want a pair of blue suede shoes," said the boy.

"Well, you didn't have to snatch *my* pocketbook to get some suede shoes," said Mrs. Luella Bates Washington Jones. "You could of asked me."

"Ma'am?"

The water dripping from his face, the boy looked at her. There was a long pause. A very long pause. After he had dried his face, and not knowing what else to do, dried it again, the boy turned around, wondering what next. The door was open. He could make a dash for it down the hall. He could run, run, run, *run!*

The woman was sitting on the daybed. After a while she said, "I were young once and I wanted things I could not get."

There was another long pause. The boy's mouth opened. Then he frowned, not knowing he frowned.

The woman said, "Um-humm! You thought I was going to say *but*, didn't you? You thought I was going to say, *but I didn't snatch people's pocketbooks.* Well, I wasn't going to say that." Pause. Silence. "I have done things, too, which I would not tell you, son—neither tell God, if He didn't already know. Everybody's got something in common. so you set down while I fix us something to eat. You might run that comb through your hair so you will look presentable."

In another corner of the room behind a screen was a gas plate and an icebox. Mrs. Jones got up and went behind the screen. The woman did not watch the boy to see if he was going to run now, nor did she watch her purse, which she left behind her on the daybed. But the boy took care to sit on the far side of the room, away from the purse, where he thought she could easily see him out of the corner of her eye if she wanted to. He did not trust the woman *not* to trust him. And he did not want to be mistrusted now.

"Do you need somebody to go to the store," asked the boy, "maybe to get some milk or something?"

"Don't believe I do," said the woman, "unless you just want sweet milk yourself. I was going to make cocoa out of this canned milk I got here."

"That will be fine," said the boy.

She heated some lima beans and ham she had in the icebox, made the cocoa, and set the table. The woman did not ask the boy anything about where he lived, or his folks, or anything else that would embarrass him. Instead, as they ate, she told him about her job in a hotel beauty shop that stayed open late, what the work was like, and how all kinds of women came in and out, blondes, redheads, and Spanish. Then she cut him a half of her ten-cent cake.

"Eat some more, son," she said.

When they were finished eating, she got up and said, "Now here, take this ten dollars and buy yourself some blue suede shoes. And next time, do not make the mistake of latching onto *my* pocketbook *nor nobody else's*—because shoes got by devilish ways will burn your feet. I got to get my rest now. But from here on in, son, I hope you will behave yourself."

She led him down the hall to the front door and opened it. "Good night! Behave yourself, boy!" she said, looking out into the street as he went down the steps.

The boy wanted to say something other than, "Thank you, m'am," to Mrs. Luella Bates Washington Jones, but although his lips moved, he couldn't even say that as he turned at the foot of the barren stoop and looked up at the large woman in the door. Then she shut the door.

Thinking About the Story

1. Mrs. Jones has qualities that have helped her survive in her poor environment. What are some of these qualities? Discuss them with your classmates.

2. The woman is described as being large; do you think this fact made it easier to control the boy? The boy said he was sorry. Do you believe him? Discuss with your classmates by using evidence either implied or stated in the story.

3. Mrs. Jones said she had done things that she would not tell the boy or anyone else. Do you think her background made it possible for her better to handle and to understand Roger?

Reading/Writing Connections

1. Re-read the story's ending and then write one that is different.

2. At the end of the story, Roger could not tell Mrs. Jones how he felt. Pretend that you are Roger and write Mrs. Jones a letter expressing your feelings for what she did for you.

3. Mrs. Jones says "shoes got by devilish ways will burn your feet." Write an essay explaining what you believe she means by the statement.

Margaret Walker (b. 1915), daughter of a Methodist minister, was born in Birmingham, Ala. She studied at Northwestern University and later at the University of Iowa, from which she received a Ph.D. degree in creative writing for her historical novel *Jubilee* (1965), the first novel about the Civil War to be written from a slave's point of view. She has taught English at such historical African American colleges as Livingston College in North Carolina and at West Virginia State College. Her poem "For My People" was published in *Poetry* magazine in 1937. In that same year, she moved to Chicago where she became a member of the Federal Writers' Project and a close associate of Richard Wright. Walker received a Rosenwald Fellowship in 1944. For *Jubilee*, she received a Houghton-Mifflin Literary Fellowship Award in 1966. Since 1968, she has served as the director of the Institute for the Study of History, Life, and Culture of Black People at Jackson State College in Jackson, Mississippi.

For My People

MARGARET WALKER

For my people everywhere singing their slave songs repeatedly: their dirges and their ditties and their blues and jubilees, praying their prayers nightly to an unknown god, bending their knees humbly to an unseen power;

For my people lending their strength to the years, to the gone years and the now years and the maybe years, washing ironing cooking scrubbing sewing mending hoeing plowing digging planting pruning patching dragging along never gaining never reaping never knowing and never understanding;

For my playmates in the clay and dust and sand of Alabama backyards playing baptizing and preaching and doctor and jail and soldier and school and mama and cooking and playhouse and concert and store and hair and Miss Choomby and company;

For the cramped bewildered years we went to school to learn to know the reasons why and the answers to and the people who and the places where and the days when, in memory of the bitter hours when we discovered we were black and poor and small and different and nobody cared and nobody wondered and nobody understood;

For the boys and girls who grew in spite of these things to be man and woman, to laugh and dance and sing and play and drink their wine and religion and success, to marry their playmates and bear children and then die of consumption and anemia and lynching;

For my people thronging 47th Street in Chicago and Lenox Avenue in New York and Rampart Street in New Orleans, lost disinherited dispossessed and happy people filling the cabarets and taverns and other people's pockets needing bread and shoes and milk and land and money and something— something all our own;

For my people walking blindly spreading joy, losing time being lazy, sleeping when hungry, shouting when burdened, drinking when hopeless, tied and shackled and tangled among ourselves by the unseen creatures who tower over us omnisciently and laugh;

For my people blundering and groping and floundering in the dark of churches

259

and schools and clubs and societies, associations and councils and committees and conventions, distressed and disturbed and deceived and devoured by money-hungry glory-craving leeches, preyed on by facile force of state and fad and novelty, by false prophet and holy believer;

For my people standing staring trying to fashion a better way from confusion, from hypocrisy and misunderstanding, trying to fashion a world that will hold all the people, all the faces, all the adams and eves and their countless generations;

Let a new earth rise. Let another world be born. Let a bloody peace be written in the sky. Let a second generation full of courage issue forth; let a people loving freedom come to growth. Let a beauty full of healing and a strength of final clenching be the pulsing in our spirits and our blood. Let the martial songs be written, let the dirges disappear. Let a race of men now rise and take control.

Thinking About the Poem

1. This free-verse poem appears to summarize African American life in both urban and rural areas. Select those stanzas that give such descriptions and discuss them with the class.

2. The poet uses a literary device called **alliteration**. In stanza eight, locate the alliteration and discuss it with the class.

3. How would you describe stanza nine? What is the poet's attitude toward her people?

Reading/Writing Connections

1. If this poem is ultimately about inclusion rather than exclusion, write an essay in which you explain this truth.

2. One writer has said that literature is a mirror by which we all are reflected. Write an essay agreeing or disagreeing with this statement. Use information from "For My People" as a basis for your position.

3. Write a free-verse poem of your own based on the following statement from stanza ten: "Let a second generation full of courage issue forth; let a people loving freedom come to growth."

Mary Elizabeth Vroman

(1923–1967) was born in Buffalo, N.Y. and raised in the British West Indies. She was a graduate of Alabama State University. "See How They Run" and "And Have Not Charity," two of her short stories, were published in the *Ladies' Home Journal*. Her only adult novel, *Esther*, was published in 1963 and her young-adult novel, *Harlem Summer*, was published the year she died from complications of a surgery. In 1953, her short story "See How They Run" was made into a film by MGM entitled *Bright Road*. Ms. Vroman was the first African American woman to be granted membership in the Screen Writers Guild.

See How They Run

MARY ELIZABETH VROMAN

A bell rang. Jane Richards squared the sheaf of records decisively in the large manila folder, placed it in the right-hand corner of her desk, and stood up. The chatter of young voices subsided, and forty-three small faces looked solemnly and curiously at the slight young figure before them. The bell stopped ringing.

I wonder if they're as scared of me as I am of them. She smiled brightly.

"Good morning, children, I am Miss Richards." As if they don't know— the door of the third-grade room had a neat new sign pasted above it with her name in bold black capitals; and anyway, a new teacher's name is the first thing that children find out about on the first day of school. Nevertheless she wrote it for their benefit in large white letters on the blackboard.

"I hope we will all be happy working and playing together this year." Now why does that sound so trite? "As I call the roll will you please stand, so that I may get to know you as soon as possible, and if you like to you may tell me something about yourselves, how old you are, where you live, what your parents do, and perhaps something about what you did during the summer."

Seated, she checked the names carefully. "Booker T. Adams."

Booker stood, gangling and stoop-shouldered: he began to recite tiredly. "My name is Booker T. Adams, I'se ten years old." Shades of Uncle Tom! "I live on Painter's Path." He paused, the look he gave her was tinged with something very akin to contempt. "I didn't do nothing in the summer," he said deliberately.

"Thank you, Booker." Her voice was even. "George Allen." Must remember to correct that stoop. . . . Where is Painter's Path? . . . How to go about correcting those speech defects? . . . Go easy, Jane, don't antagonize them. . . . They're clean enough, but this is the first day. . . . How can one teacher do any kind of job with a load of forty-three? . . . Thank heaven the building is modern and well built even though it is overcrowded, not like some I've seen—no potbellied stove.

"Sarahlene Clover Babcock." Where do these names come from? . . . Up from slavery. . . . How high is up. Jane smothered a sudden desire to giggle. Outside she was calm and poised and smiling. Clearly she called the names, listening with interest, making a note here and there, making no corrections—not yet.

She experienced a moment of brief inward satisfaction: I'm doing very well, this is what is expected of me . . . Orientation to Teaching . . . Miss Murray's voice beat a distant tattoo in her memory. Miss Murray with the Junoesque figure and the moon face . . . "The ideal teacher personality is one which, combining in itself all the most desirable qualities, expresses itself with quiet assurance in its endeavor to mold the personalities of the students in the most desirable patterns." . . . Dear dull Miss Murray.

She made mental estimates of the class. What a cross section of my people they represent, she thought. Here and there signs of evident poverty, here and there children of obviously well-to-do parents.

"My name is Rachel Veronica Smith. I am nine years old. I live at Six-oh-seven Fairview Avenue. My father is a Methodist minister. My mother is a housewife. I have two sisters and one brother. Last summer Mother and Daddy took us all to New York to visit my Aunt Jen. We saw lots of wonderful things. There are millions and millions of people in New York. One day we went on a ferryboat all the way up the Hudson River—that's a great big river as wide across as this town, and—"

The children listened wide-eyed. Jane listened carefully. She speaks good English. Healthy, erect, and even perhaps a little smug. Immaculately well dressed from the smoothly braided hair, with two perky bows, to the shiny brown oxfords . . . Bless you, Rachel, I'm so glad to have you.

"—and the buildings are all very tall, some of them nearly reach the sky."

"Haw-haw"—this from Booker, cynically.

"Well, they are too." Rachel swung around, fire in her eyes and insistence in every line of her round, compact body.

"Ain't no building as tall as the sky, is dere, Miz Richards?"

Crisis No. 1. Jane chose her answer carefully. As high as the sky . . . mustn't turn this into a lesson in science . . . all in due time. "The sky is a long way out, Booker, but the buildings in New York are very tall indeed. Rachel was only trying to show you how very tall they are. In fact, the tallest building in the whole world is in New York City."

"They call it the Empire State Building," interrupted Rachel, heady with her new knowledge and Jane's corroboration.

Booker wasn't through. "You been dere, Miz Richards?"

"Yes, Booker, many times. Someday I shall tell you more about it. Maybe Rachel will help me. Is there anything you'd like to add, Rachel?"

"I would like to say that we are glad you are our new teacher, Miss Richards." Carefully she sat down, spreading her skirt with her plump hands, her smile angelic.

Now I'll bet me a quarter her reverend father told her to say that. "Thank you, Rachel."

The roll call continued. . . . Tanya, slight and pinched, with the toes showing through the very white sneakers, the darned and faded but clean blue dress, the gentle voice like a tinkling bell, and the beautiful sensitive face. . . . Boyd and Lloyd, identical in their starched overalls, and the slightly vacant look. . . . Marjorie Lee, all of twelve years old, the well-developed body moving restlessly in the childish dress, the eyes too wise, the voice too high. . . . Joe Louis, the intelligence in the brilliant black eyes gleaming above the threadbare clothes. Lives of great men all remind us—Well, I have them all . . . Frederick Douglass, Franklin Delano, Abraham Lincoln, Booker T., Joe Louis, George Washington. . . . What a great burden you bear, little people, heirs to all your parents' stillborn dreams of greatness. I must not fail you. The last name on the list . . . C. T. Young. Jane paused, small lines creasing her forehead. She checked the list again.

"C. T., what is your name? I only have your initials on my list."

"Dat's all my name, C. T. Young."

"No, dear, I mean what does C. T. stand for? Is it Charles or Clarence?"

"No'm, jest C. T."

"But I can't put that in my register, dear."

Abruptly Jane rose and went to the next room. Rather timidly she waited to speak to Miss Nelson, the second-grade teacher, who had the formidable record of having taught all of sixteen years. Miss Nelson was large and smiling.

"May I help you, dear?"

"Yes, please. It's about C. T. Young. I believe you had him last year."

"Yes, and the year before that. You'll have him two years too."

"Oh? Well, I was wondering what name you registered him under. All the information I have is C. T. Young."

"That's all there is, honey. Lots of these children only have initials."

"You mean . . . can't something be done about it?"

"What?" Miss Nelson was still smiling, but clearly impatient.

"I . . . well . . . thank you." Jane left quickly.

Back in Room 3 the children were growing restless. Deftly Jane passed out the rating tests and gave instructions. Then she called C. T. to her. He was as small as an eight-year-old, and hungry-looking, with enormous guileless eyes and a beautifully shaped head.

"How many years did you stay in the second grade, C. T.?"

"Two."

"And in the first?"

"Two."

"How old are you?"

"'Leven."

"When will you be twelve?"

"Nex' month."

And they didn't care . . . nobody ever cared enough about one small boy to give him a name.

"You are a very lucky little boy, C. T. Most people have to take the name somebody gave them whether they like it or not, but you can choose your very own."

"Yeah?" The dark eyes were belligerent. "My father named me C. T. after hisself, Miz Richards, an dat's my name."

Jane felt unreasonably irritated. "How many children are there in your family, C. T.?"

"'Leven."

"How many are there younger than you?" she asked.

"Seven."

Very gently. "Did you have your breakfast this morning, dear?"

The small figure in the too-large trousers and the too-small shirt drew itself up to full height. "Yes'm, I had fried chicken, and rice, and coffee, and rolls, and oranges too."

Oh, you poor darling. You poor proud lying darling. Is that what you'd like for breakfast?

She asked, "Do you like school, C. T.?"

"Yes'm," he told her suspiciously.

She leafed through the pile of records. "Your record says you haven't been coming to school very regularly. Why?"

"I dunno."

"Did you ever bring a lunch?"

"No'm, I eats such a big breakfast, I doan git hungry at lunchtime."

"Children need to eat lunch to help them grow tall and strong, C. T. So from now on you'll eat lunch in the lunchroom"—an after-thought: Perhaps it's important to make him think I believe him—"and from now on maybe you'd better not eat such a big breakfast."

Decisively she wrote his name at the top of what she knew to be an already too large list. "Only those in absolute necessity," she had been told by Mr. Johnson, the kindly, harassed principal. "We'd like to feed them all, so many are underfed, but we just don't have the money." Well, this was absolute necessity if she ever saw it.

"What does your father do, C. T.?"

"He work at dat big factory cross-town, he make plenty money, Miz Richards." The record said "Unemployed."

"Would you like to be named Charles Thomas?"

The expressive eyes darkened, but the voice was quiet. "No'm."

"Very well." Thoughtfully Jane opened the register; she wrote firmly C. T. Young.

October is a witching month in the Southern United States. The richness of the golds and reds and browns of the trees forms an enchanted filigree through which the lilting voices of children at play seem to float, embodied like so many nymphs of Pan.

Jane had played a fast-and-furious game of tag with her class and now she sat quietly under the gnarled old oak, watching the tireless play, feeling the magic of the sun through the leaves warmly dappling her skin, the soft breeze on the nape of her neck like a lover's hands, and her own drowsy lethargy. Paul, Paul my darling . . . how long for us now? She had worshiped Paul Carlyle since they were freshmen together. On graduation day he had slipped the small circlet of diamonds on her finger. . . . "A teacher's salary is small, Jane. Maybe we'll be lucky enough to get work together, then in a year or so we can be married. Wait for me, darling, wait for me!"

But in a year or so Paul had gone to war, and Jane went out alone to teach. . . . Lansing Creek—one year . . . the leaky roof, the potbellied stove, the water from the well . . . Maryweather Point—two years . . . the tight-lipped spinster principal with the small, vicious soul. . . . Three hard lonely years and then she had been lucky.

The superintendent had praised her. "You have done good work, Miss—ah—Jane. This year you are to be placed at Centertown High—that is, of course, if you care to accept the position."

Jane had caught her breath. Centertown was the largest and best equipped of all the schools in the county, only ten miles from home and Paul—for Paul had come home, older, quieter, but still Paul. He was teaching now more than a hundred miles away, but they went home every other weekend to their families and each other. . . . "Next summer you'll be Mrs. Paul Carlyle, darling. It's hard for us to be apart so much. I guess we'll have to be for a long time till I can afford to support you. But, sweet, these little tykes need us so badly." He had held her close, rubbing the nape of the neck under the soft curls. "We have a big job, those of us who teach," he had told her, "a never-ending and often thankless job, Jane, to supply the needs of these kids who lack so much." Dear, warm, big, strong, gentle Paul.

They wrote each other long letters, sharing plans and problems. She wrote him about C. T. "I've adopted him, darling. He's so pathetic and so determined to prove that he's not. He learns nothing at all, but I can't let myself believe that he's stupid, so I keep trying."

"Miz Richards, please, ma'am." Tanya's beautiful amber eyes sought hers timidly. Her brown curls were tangled from playing, her cheeks a bright red under the tightly stretched olive skin. The elbows jutted awkwardly out of the sleeves of the limp cotton dress, which could not conceal the finely chiseled bones in their pitiable fleshlessness. As always when she looked at her, Jane thought, What a beautiful child! So unlike the dark, gaunt, morose mother, and the dumpy, pasty-faced father who had visited her that first week. A fairy's changeling. You'll make a lovely angel to grace the throne of God, Tanya! Now what made me think of that?

"Please, ma'am, I'se sick."

Gently Jane drew her down beside her. She felt the parchment skin, noted the unnaturally bright eyes. Oh, dear God, she's burning up! "Do you hurt anywhere, Tanya?"

"My head, ma'am and I'se so tired." Without warning she began to cry.

"How far do you live, Tanya?"

"Two miles."

"You walk to school?"

"Yes'm."

"Do any of your brothers have a bicycle?"

"No'm."

"Rachel!" Bless you for always being there when I need you. "Hurry, dear, to the office and ask Mr. Johnson please to send a big boy with a bicycle to take Tanya home. She's sick."

Rachel ran.

"Hush now, dear, we'll get some cool water, and then you'll be home in a little while. Did you feel sick this morning?"

"Yes'm, but Mot Dear sent me to school anyway. She said I just wanted to play hooky." Keep smiling, Jane. Poor, ambitious, well-meaning parents, made bitter at the seeming futility of dreaming dreams for this lovely child . . . willing her to rise above the drabness of your own meager existence . . . too angry with life to see that what she needs most is your love and care and right now medical attention.

Jane bathed the child's forehead with cool water at the fountain. Do the white schools have a clinic? I must ask Paul. Do they have a lounge or a couch where they can lay one wee sick head? Is there anywhere in this town free medical service for one small child . . . born black?

The boy with the bicycle came. "Take care of her now, ride slowly and carefully, and take her straight home. . . . Keep the newspaper over your head, Tanya, to keep out the sun, and tell your parents to call the doctor." But she knew they wouldn't because they couldn't.

The next day Jane went to see Tanya.

"She's sho' nuff sick, Miz Richards," the mother said. "She's always been a puny child, but this time she's took real bad, throat's all raw, talk all out her haid las' night. I been using a poultice and some herb brew but she ain't got no better."

"Have you called a doctor, Mrs. Fulton?"

"No'm, we cain't afford it, an' Jake, he doan believe in doctors nohow."

Jane waited till the tide of high bright anger welling in her heart and beating in her brain had subsided. When she spoke her voice was deceptively gentle. "Mrs. Fulton, Tanya is a very sick little girl. She is your only little girl. If you love her, I advise you to have a doctor for her, for if you don't . . . Tanya may die."

The wail that issued from the thin figure seemed to have no part in reality.

Jane spoke hurriedly. "Look, I'm going into town. I'll send a doctor out. Don't worry about paying him. We can see about that later." Impulsively she put her arms around the taut, motionless shoulders. "Don't you worry, honey, it's going to be all right."

There was a kindliness in the doctor's weather-beaten face that warmed Jane's heart, but his voice was brusque. "You sick, girl? Well?"

"No, sir. I'm not sick" What long sequence of events has caused even the best of you to look on even the best of us as menials? "I am a teacher at Centertown High. There's a little girl in my class who is very ill. Her parents are very poor. I came to see if you would please go to see her."

He looked at her, amused.

"Of course I'll pay the bill, Doctor," she added hastily.

"In that case . . . well . . . where does she live?"

Jane told him. "I think it's diphtheria, Doctor."

He raised his eyebrows. "Why?"

Jane sat erect. Don't be afraid, Jane! You're as good a teacher as he is a doctor, and you made an A in that course in childhood diseases. "High fever, restlessness, sore throat, headache, croupy cough, delirium. It could, of course, be tonsilitis or scarlet fever, but that cough—well, I'm only guessing, of course," she finished lamely.

"Humph." The doctor's face was expressionless. "Well, we'll see. Have your other children been inoculated?"

"Yes, sir, Doctor, if the parents ask, please tell them that the school is paying for your services."

This time he was wide-eyed.

The lie haunted her. She spoke to the other teachers about it the next day at recess.

"She's really very sick, maybe you'd like to help?"

Mary Winters, the sixth-grade teacher, was the first to speak. "Richards, I'd like to help, but I've got three kids of my own, and so you see how it is?"

Jane saw.

"Trouble with you, Richards, is you're too emotional." This from Nelson. "When you've taught as many years as I have, my dear, you'll learn not to bang your head against a stone wall. It may sound hardhearted to you, but one just can't worry about one child more or less when one has nearly fifty.''

The pain in the back of her eyes grew more insistent. "I can," she said.

"I'll help, Jane," said Marilyn Andrews, breathless, bouncy, newlywed Marilyn.

"Here's two bucks. It's all I've got, but nothing's plenty for me." Her laughter pealed echoing down the hall.

"I've got a dollar, Richards"—this from mousy, severe, little Miss Mitchell—"though I'm not sure I agree with you."

"Why don't you ask the high-school faculty?" said Marilyn. "Better still, take it up in teachers' meeting."

Mr. Johnson has enough to worry about now," snapped Nelson. Why, she's mad, thought Jane, mad because I'm trying to give a helpless little tyke a chance to live, and because Marilyn and Mitchell helped.

The bell rang. Wordlessly Jane turned away. She watched the children troop in noisily, an ancient nursery rhyme running through her head:

Three blind mice,
  three blind mice,
See how they run,
  see how they run.
They all ran after
  the farmer's wife
She cut off their tails
  with a carving knife,
Did you ever see
  such a sight in your life
As three blind mice?

Only this time it was forty-three mice. Jane giggled. Why, I'm hysterical, she thought in surprise. The mice thought the sweet-smelling farmer's wife might have bread and a wee bit of cheese to offer poor blind mice; but the farmer's wife didn't like poor, hungry, dirty blind mice. So she cut off their tails. Then they couldn't run any more, only wobble. What happened then? Maybe they starved, those that didn't bleed to death. Running round in circles. Running where, little mice?

She talked to the high-school faculty, and Mr. Johnson. All together, she got eight dollars.

The following week she received a letter from the doctor:

Dear Miss Richards:
    I am happy to inform you that Tanya is greatly improved, and with

careful nursing will be well enough in about eight weeks to return to school. She is very frail, however, and will require special care. I have made three visits to her home. In view of the peculiar circumstances, I am donating my services. The cost of the medicines, however, amounts to the sum of fifteen dollars. I am referring this to you as you requested. What a beautiful child!

Yours sincerely,
Jonathan H. Sinclair, M.D.

P.S. She had diphtheria.

Bless you forever and ever, Jonathan H. Sinclair, M.D. For all your long Southern heritage, "a man's a man for a' that . . . and a' that!"

Her heart was light that night when she wrote to Paul. Later she made plans in the darkness. You'll be well and fat by Christmas, Tanya, and you'll be a lovely angel in my pageant. . . . I must get the children to save pennies. . . . We'll send you milk and oranges and eggs, and we'll make funny little get-well cards to keep you happy.

But by Christmas Tanya was dead!

The voice from the dark figure was quiet, even monotonous. "Jake an' me, we always work so hard, Miz Richards. We didn't neither one have no schooling much when we was married—our folks never had much money, but we was happy. Jake, he tenant farm. I tuk in washing—we plan to save and buy a little house and farm of our own someday. Den the children come. Six boys, Miz Richards all in a hurry We both want the boys to finish school, mabbe go to college. We try not to keep them out to work the farm, but sometimes we have to. Then come Tanya. Just like a little yellow rose she was, Miz Richards, all pink and gold . . . and her voice like a silver bell. We think when she grow up an' finish school she take voice lessons—be like Marian Anderson. We think mabbe by then the boys would be old enough to help. I was kinda feared for her when she get sick, but then she start to get better. She was doing so well, Miz Richards. Den it get cold, an' the fire so hard to keep all night long, an' eben the newspapers in the cracks doan keep the win' out, an' I give her all my kivvers; but one night she jest tuk to shivering an' talking all out her haid—sat right up in bed, she did. She call your name onc't or twice, Miz Richards, then she say, 'Mot Dear, does Jesus love me like Miz Richards say in Sunday school?' I say, 'Yes, honey.' She say, 'Effen I die will I see Jesus?' I say, 'Yes, honey, but you ain't gwine die.' But she did, Miz Richards . . . jest smiled an' laid down—jest smiled an' laid down."

It is terrible to see such hopeless resignation in such tearless eyes. . . . One little mouse stopped running. . . . You'll make a lovely angel to grace the throne of God, Tanya!

Jane did not go to the funeral. Nelson and Rogers sat in the first pew. Everyone on the faculty contributed to a beautiful wreath. Jane preferred not to think about that.

C. T. brought a lovely potted rose to her the next day. "Miz Richards, ma'am, do you think this is pretty enough to go on Tanya's grave?"

"Where did you get it, C. T.?"

"I stole it out Miz Adams's front yard, right out of that li'l glass house she got there. The door was open, Miz Richards, she got plenty, she won't miss this li'l one."

You queer little bundle of truth and lies. What do I do now? Seeing the tears blinking back in the anxious eyes, she said gently, "Yes, C. T., the rose is nearly as beautiful as Tanya is now. She will like that very much."

"You mean she will know I put it there, Miz Richards? She ain't daid at all?"

"Maybe she'll know, C. T. You see, nothing that is beautiful ever dies as long as we remember it."

So you loved Tanya, a little mouse? The memory of her beauty is yours to keep now forever and always, my darling. Those things money can't buy. They've all been trying, but your tail isn't off yet, is it, brat? Not by a long shot. Suddenly she laughed aloud.

He looked at her wonderingly. "What you laughing at, Miz Richards?"

"I'm laughing because I'm happy, C. T.," and she hugged him.

Christmas with its pageantry and splendor came and went. Back from the holidays, Jane had an oral English lesson.

"We'll take this period to let you tell about your holidays, children."

On the weekend that Jane stayed in Centertown she visited different churches, and taught in the Sunday schools when she was asked. She had tried to impress on the children the reasons for giving at Christmastime. In class they had talked about things they could make for gifts, and ways they could save money to buy them. Now she stood by the window, listening attentively, reaping the fruits of her labors.

"I got a bicycle and a catcher's mitt."

"We all went to a party and had ice cream and cake."

"I got—"

"I got—"

"I got—"

Score one goose egg for Jane. She was suddenly very tired. "It's your turn, C. T." Dear God, please don't let him lie too much. He tears my heart. The children never laugh. It's funny how polite they are to C. T. even when they know he's lying. Even that day when Boyd and Lloyd told how they had seen him take food out of the garbage cans in front of the restaurant, and he said he was taking it to some poor hungry children, they didn't laugh. Sometimes children have a great deal more insight than grownups.

C. T. was talking. "I didn't get nothin' for Christmas, because Mamma was sick, but I worked all that week before for Mr. Bondel what owns the store on Main Street. I ran errands an' swep' up an' he give me three dollars, and so I bought Mamma a real pretty handkerchief an' a comb, an' I bought my father a tie pin, paid a big ole fifty cents for it too . . . an' I bought my sisters an' brothers some candy an' gum an' I bought me this whistle. Course I got what you give us, Miz Richards" (she had given each a small gift) "an' Mamma's white lady give us a whole crate of oranges, an' Miz Smith what live nex' door give me a pair of socks. Mamma she was so happy she made a cake with eggs an' butter an' everything; an' then we ate it an' had a good time."

Rachel spoke wonderingly, "Didn't Santa Claus bring you anything at all?"

C. T. was the epitome of scorn. "Ain't no Santa Claus," he said and sat down.

Jane quelled the age-old third-grade controversy absently, for her heart was singing. C. T. . . . C. T., son of my own heart, you are the bright new hope of a doubtful world, and the gay new song of a race unconquered. Of them all—Sarahlene, sole heir to the charming stucco home on the hill, all fitted for gracious living; George, whose father is a contractor; Rachel, the minister's daughter; Angela, who has just inherited ten thousand dollars—of all of them who got, you, my dirty little vagabond, who have never owned a coat in your life, because you say you don't get cold; you, out of your nothing, found something to give, and in the dignity of giving found that it was not so important to receive. . . . Christ child, look down in blessing on one small child made in Your image and born black!

Jane had problems. Sometimes it was difficult to maintain discipline with forty-two children. Busy as she kept them, there were always some not busy enough. There was the conference with Mr. Johnson.

"Miss Richards, you are doing fine work here, but sometimes your room is a little . . . well—ah—well, to say the least, noisy. You are new here, but we have always maintained a record of having fine discipline here at this school. People have said that it used to be hard to tell whether or not there were children in the building. We have always been proud of that. Now take Miss Nelson. She is an excellent disciplinarian." He smiled. "Maybe if you ask her she will give you her secret. Do not be too proud to accept help from anyone who can give it, Miss Richards."

"No, sir, thank you, sir, I'll do my best to improve, sir." Ah, you dear, well-meaning, shortsighted, round, busy little man. Why are you not more concerned about how much the children have grown and learned in these past four months than you are about how much noise they make? I know Miss Nelson's secret. Spare not the rod and spoil not the child. Is that what you want me to do? Paralyze these kids with fear so that they will be afraid to move? afraid to question? afraid to grow? Why is it so fine for people not to know there are children in the building? Wasn't the building built for children? In her room Jane locked the door against the sound of the playing children, put her head on the desk, and cried.

Jane acceded to tradition and administered one whipping docilely enough, as though used to it; but the sneer in his eyes that had almost gone returned to haunt them. Jane's heart misgave her. From now on I positively refuse to impose my will on any of these poor children by reason of my greater strength. So she had abandoned the rod in favor of any other means she could find. They did not always work.

There was a never-ending drive for funds. Jane had a passion for perfection. Plays, dances, concerts, bazaars, suppers, parties, followed one on another in staggering succession.

"Look here, Richards," Nelson told her one day, "it's true that we need a new piano, and that science equipment, but, honey, these drives in a colored school are like the poor: with us always. It doesn't make too much difference if Suzy forgets her lines, or if the ice cream is a little lumpy. Cooperation is fine, but the way you tear into things you won't last long."

"For once in her life Nelson's right, Jane," Elise told her later. "I can understand how intense you are because I used to be like that; but, pet, Negro teachers have always had to work harder than any others and till recently have always got paid less, so for our own health's sake, we have to let up wherever possible. Believe me, honey, if you don't learn to take it easy, you're going to get sick."

Jane did. Measles!

"Oh, no," she wailed, "not in my old age!" But she was glad of the rest. Lying in her own bed at home, she realized how very tired she was.

Paul came to see her that weekend and sat by her bed, and read aloud to her the old classic poems they both loved so well. They listened to their favorite radio programs. Paul's presence was warm and comforting. Jane was reluctant to go back to work.

What to do about C. T. was a question that daily loomed larger in Jane's consciousness. Watching Joe Louis's brilliant development was a thing of joy, and Jane was hard pressed to find enough outlets for his amazing abilities. Jeanette Allen was running a close second, and even Booker, so long a problem, was beginning to grasp fundamentals, but C. T. remained static.

"I always stays two years in a grade, Miz Richards," he told her blandly. "I does better the second year.

"I don't keer." His voice had been cheerful. Maybe he really is slow, Jane thought. But one day something happened to make her change her mind.

C. T. was possessed of an unusually strong tendency to protect those he considered to be poor or weak. He took little Johnny Armstrong, who sat beside him in class, under his wing. Johnny was nearsighted and nondescript, his one outstanding feature being his hero-worship of C. T. Johnny was a plodder. Hard as he tried, he made slow progress at best.

The struggle with multiplication tables was a difficult one, in spite of all the little games Jane devised to make them easier for the children. On this particular day there was the uneven hum of little voices trying to memorize. Johnny and C. T. were having a whispered conversation about snakes.

Clearly Jane heard C. T.'s elaboration. "Man, my father caught a moccasin long as that blackboard, I guess, an' I held him while he was live right back of his ugly head—so."

Swiftly Jane crossed the room. "C. T. and Johnny, you are supposed to be learning your tables. The period is nearly up and you haven't even begun to study. Furthermore, in more than five months you haven't even learned the two-times table. Now you will both stay in at the first recess to learn it, and every day after this until you do."

Maybe I should make up some problems about snakes, Jane mused, but they'd be too ridiculous. . . . Two nests of four snakes—Oh, well, I'll see how they do at recess. Her heart smote her at the sight of the two little figures at their desks, listening wistfully to the sound of the children at play, but she busied herself and pretended not to notice them. Then she heard C. T.'s voice:

"Lissen, man, these tables is easy if you really want to learn them. Now see here. Two times one is two. Two times two is four. Two times three is six. If you forgit, all you got to do is add two like she said."

"Sho' nuff, man?"

"Sho'. Say them with me . . . two times one—" Obediently Johnny began to recite. Five minutes later they came to her. "We's ready, Miz Richards."

"Very well. Johnny, you may begin."

"Two times one is two. Two times two is four. Two times three is . . . Two times three is—"

"Six," prompted C. T.

In sweat and pain, Johnny managed to stumble through the two-times table with C. T.'s help.

"That's very poor, Johnny, but you may go for today. Tomorrow I shall expect you to have it letter perfect. Now it's your turn, C. T."

C. T.'s performance was a fair rival to Joe Louis's. Suspiciously she took him through in random order.

"Two times nine?"

"Eighteen."

"Two times four?"

"Eight."

"Two times seven?"

"Fourteen."

"C. T., you could have done this long ago. Why didn't you?"

"I dunno. . . . May I go to play now, Miz Richards?"

"Yes, C. T. Now learn your three-times table for me tomorrow."

But he didn't, not that day or the day after that or the day after that. . . . Why doesn't he? Is it that he doesn't want to? Maybe if I were as ragged and deprived as he I wouldn't want to learn either.

Jane took C. T. to town and bought him a shirt, a sweater, a pair of dungarees, some underwear, a pair of shoes and a pair of socks. Then she sent him to the barber to get his hair cut. She gave him the money so he could pay for the articles himself and figure up the change. She instructed him to take a bath before putting on his new clothes, and told him not to tell anyone but his parents that she had bought them.

The next morning the class was in a dither.

"You seen C. T.?"

"Oh, boy, ain't he sharp!"

"C.T., where'd you get them new clothes?"

"Oh, man, I can wear new clothes any time I feel like it, but I can't be bothered with being a fancypants all the time like you guys."

C. T. strutted in new confidence, but his work didn't improve.

Spring came in its virginal green gladness and the children chafed for the out-of-doors. Jane took them out as much as possible on nature studies and excursions.

C. T. was growing more and more mischievous, and his influence began to spread throughout the class. Daily his droll wit became more and more edged with impudence. Jane was at her wit's end.

"You let that child get away with too much, Richards," Nelson told her. "What he needs is a good hiding."

One day Jane kept certain of the class in at the first recess to do neglected homework, C. T. among them. She left the room briefly. When she returned C. T. was gone.

"Where is C. T.?" she asked.

"He went out to play, Miz Richards. He said couldn't no ole teacher keep him in when he didn't want to stay."

Out on the playground C. T. was standing in a swing gently swaying to and fro, surrounded by a group of admiring youngsters. He was holding forth.

"I gets tired of stayin' in all the time. She doan pick on nobody but me, an' today I put my foot down. From now on', I say, 'I ain't never goin' to stay in, Miz Richards.' Then I walks out." He was enjoying himself immensely. Then he saw her.

"You will come with me, C. T." She was quite calm except for the telltale veins throbbing in her forehead.

"I ain't comin'." The sudden fright in his eyes was veiled quickly by a nonchalant belligerence. He rocked the swing gently.

She repeated, "Come with me, C. T."

The children watched breathlessly.

"I done told you I ain't coming', Miz Richards." His voice was patient as though explaining to a child. "I ain't . . . comin' . . . a . . . damn . . . tall!"

Jane moved quickly, wrenching the small but surprisingly strong figure from the swing. Then she bore him bodily, kicking and screaming, to the building.

The children relaxed, and began to giggle. "Oh boy! Is he goin' to catch it!" they told one another.

Panting, she held him, still struggling, by the scruff of his collar before the group of teachers gathered in Marilyn's room. "All right, now you tell me what to do with him!" she demanded. "I've tried everything." The tears were close behind her eyes.

"What'd he do?" Nelson asked.

Briefly she told them.

"Have you talked to his parents?"

"Three times I've had conferences with them. They say to beat him."

"That, my friend, is what you ought to do. Now he never acted like that with me. If you'll let me handle him, I'll show you how to put a brat like that in his place."

"Go ahead," Jane said wearily.

Nelson left the room, and returned with a narrow but sturdy leather thong. "Now, C. T."—she was smiling, tapping the strap in her open left palm— "go to your room and do what Miss Richards told you to."

"I ain't gonna, an' you can't make me." He sat down with absurd dignity at a desk.

Still smiling, Miss Nelson stood over him. The strap descended without warning across the bony shoulders in the thin shirt. The whip became a dancing demon, a thing possessed, bearing no relation to the hand that held it. The shrieks grew louder. Jane closed her eyes against the blurred fury of a singing lash, a small boy's terror and a smiling face.

Miss Nelson was not tired. "Well, C. T.?"

"I won't, Yer can kill me but I won't!"

The sounds began again. Red welts began to show across the small arms and through the clinging sweat-drenched shirt.

"Now will you go to your room?"

Sobbing and conquered, C. T. went. The seated children stared curiously at the little procession. Jane dismissed them.

In his seat C. T. found pencil and paper.

"What's he supposed to do, Richards?" Jane told her.

"All right, now write!"

C. T. stared at Nelson through swollen lids, a curious smile curving his lips. Jane knew suddenly that come hell or high water, C.T. would not write. I mustn't interfere. Please, God, don't let her hurt him too badly. Where have I failed so miserably? . . . Forgive us our trespasses. The singing whip and the shrieks became a symphony from hell. Suddenly Jane hated the smiling face with an almost unbearable hatred. She spoke, her voice like cold steel.

"That's enough, Nelson."

The noise stopped.

"He's in no condition to write now anyway."

C. T. stood up. "I hate you. I hate you all. You're mean and I hate you." Then he ran. No one followed him. Run, little mouse! They avoided each other's eyes.

"Well, there you are," Nelson said as she walked away. Jane never found out what she meant by that.

The next day C. T. did not come to school. The day after that he brought Jane the fatal homework, neatly and painstakingly done, and a bunch of wild flowers. Before the bell rang, the children surrounded him. He was beaming.

"Did you tell yer folks you got a whipping, C. T.?"

"Naw! I'd 'a' only got another."

"Where were you yesterday?"

"Went fishin'. Caught me six cats long as your haid, Sambo."

Jane buried her face in the sweet-smelling flowers. Oh, my brat, my wonderful resilient brat. They'll never get your tail, will they?

It was seven weeks till the end of term, when C. T. brought Jane a model wooden boat.

Jane stared at it. "Did you make this? It's beautiful, C. T."

"Oh, I make them all the time . . . an' airplanes an' houses too. I do 'em in my spare time," he finished airily.

"Where do you get the models, C. T.?" she asked.

"I copies them from pictures in the magazines."

Right under my nose . . . right there all the time, she thought wonderingly. "C. T., would you like to build things when you grow up? Real houses and ships and planes?"

"Reckon I could, Miz Richards," he said confidently.

The excitement was growing in her.

"Look, C. T. You aren't going to do any lessons at all for the rest of the year. You're going to build ships and houses and airplanes and anything else you want to."

"I am, huh?" He grinned. "Well, I guess I wasn't goin' to get promoted nohow."

"Of course if you want to build them the way they really are, you might have to do a little measuring, and maybe learn to spell the names of the parts you want to order. All the best contractors have to know things like that, you know."

"Say, I'm gonna have real fun, huh? I always said lessons wussent no good nohow. Pop say too much study eats out yer brains anyway."

The days went by. Jane ran a race with time. The instructions from the model companies arrived. Jane burned the midnight oil planning each day's work.

Learn to spell the following words: ship, sail, steamer—boat, anchor, airplane wing, fly.

Write a letter to the lumber company, ordering some lumber.

The floor of our model house is ten inches long. Multiply the length by the width and you'll find the area of the floor in square inches.

Read the story of Columbus and his voyages.

Our plane arrives in Paris in twenty-eight hours. Paris is the capital city of a country named France across the Atlantic Ocean.

Long ago sailors told time by the sun and the stars. Now, the earth goes around the sun—.

Work and pray, Jane, work and pray!

C. T. learned. Some things vicariously, some things directly. When he found that he needed multiplication to plan his models to scale, he learned to multiply. In three weeks he had mastered simple division.

Jane bought beautifully illustrated stories about ships and planes. He learned to read.

He wrote for and received his own materials.

Jane exulted.

The last day! Forty-two faces waiting anxiously for report cards. Jane spoke to them briefly, praising them collectively, and admonishing them to obey the safety rules during the holidays. Then she passed out the report cards.

As she smiled at each childish face, she thought, I've been wrong. The long arm of circumstance, environment and heredity is the farmer's wife that seeks to mow you down, and all of us who touch your lives are in some way responsible for how successful she is. But you aren't mice, my darlings. Mice are hated, hunted pests. You are normal, lovable children. The knife of the farmer's wife is doubled-edged for you, because you are Negro children, born mostly in poverty. But you are wonderful children, nevertheless, for you wear the bright protective cloak of laughter, the strong shield of courage, and the intelligence of children everywhere. Some few of you may indeed become as the mice—but most of you shall find your way to stand fine and tall in the annals of man. There's a bright new tomorrow ahead. For every one of us whose job it is to help you grow that is insensitive and unworthy, there are hundreds who daily work that you may grow straight and whole. If it were not so, our world could not long endure.

She handed C. T. his card.

"Thank you, ma'm."

"Aren't you going to open it?"

He opened it dutifully. When he looked up his eyes were wide with disbelief. "You didn't make no mistake?"

"No mistake, C. T. You're promoted. You've caught up enough to go to the fourth grade next year."

She dismissed the children. They were a swarm of bees released from a hive. " 'By, Miss Richards." . . . "Happy holidays, Miss Richards."

C. T. was the last to go.

"Well, C. T.?"

"Miz Richards, you remember what you said about a name being important?"

"Yes, C. T."

"Well, I talked to Mamma, and she said if I wanted a name it would be all right, and she'd go to the courthouse about it."

"What name have you chosen, C. T.?" she asked.

"Christopher Turner Young."

"That's a nice name, Christopher," she said gravely.

"Sho' nuff, Miz Richards?"

"Sure enough, C. T."

"Miz Richards, you know what?"

"What, dear?"

"I love you."

She kissed him swiftly before he ran to catch his classmates.

She stood at the window and watched the running, skipping figures, followed by the bold mimic shadows. I'm coming home, Paul. I'm leaving my forty-two children, and Tanya there on the hill. My work with them is finished now. The laughter bubbled up in her throat. But Paul, oh Paul. See how straight they run!

Thinking About the Story

1. Booker T. Adams, like many of his fellow students, speaks a nonstandard variety of English. The new teacher says to herself that she must "correct" his speech defects. Do you think his speech is deficient? Why? Why not? What should the teacher do to help him with his nonstandard dialect? Discuss these issues with your classmates.

2. How would you describe Miss Richards? What kind of person do you think she is?

3. What is C. T.'s attitude about learning at the beginning of the story? At the end?

Reading/Writing Connections

1. "What a burden you bear, little people, heirs to all your parents' stillborn dreams of greatness." Paraphrase this statement made by Miss Richards and briefly explain what you think she means.

2. The author says that sometimes children have a great deal more insight than grownups. Do you agree or disagree with this statement? Write an essay supporting your belief; use examples from your reading, history, or personal experience.

3. In the last paragraph of the story, Miss Richards says, "My work with them is finished now. . . . See how straight they run!" Pretend you are Miss Richards and write a letter to Paul describing your feelings about the children and your accomplishments with them.

Paul Laurence Dunbar (1872–1906) was born in Dayton, Ohio, where he was educated. He began writing verse as a youth. He held several positions as a high-school student—editor in chief of the school newspaper, president of the literary society, and class poet. Dunbar was the first African American poet to win national recognition and acceptance by the larger American public. He sold his first book of poems, *Oak and Ivy*, in 1893. He published *Majors and Minors* in 1895, and in 1896 Dodd, Mead and Company published his volume of poetry entitled *Lyrics of Lowly Life*. It became an instant success. His poems and short stories appeared in many well-known American magazines. The poems he wrote in standard American English he called *major*; those in dialect he called *minor*. He wrote the *minor* poems in dialect as a way to get his works published. Although these poems were well received by white Americans, they—in effect—confirmed many stereotypes about African Americans. Dunbar is best known today for his poems written in standard English. He wrote numerous stories and four novels before he died at the age of thirty-four.

We Wear the Mask

PAUL LAURENCE DUNBAR

We wear the mask that grins and lies,
It hides our cheeks and shades our eyes,—
This debt we pay to human guile;
With torn and bleeding hearts we smile,
And mouth with myriad subtleties.   5

Why should the world be over-wise,
In counting all our tears and sighs?
Nay, let them only see us, while
    We wear the mask.

We smile, but, O great Christ, our cries   10
To thee from tortured souls arise.
We sing, but oh, the clay is vile
Beneath our feet, and long the mile;
But let the world dream otherwise,
    We wear the mask.   15

Thinking About the Poem

1. The first line of the poem begins with "We"; who are the "We" in the poem?

2. What kind of mask do people in this poem wear? Discuss your opinion with your classmates.

3. Masks are used either to disguise or to hide one's true feelings or self. Discuss with your classmates ways in which people you know hide their true feelings.

Reading/Writing Connections

1. Dunbar wrote this poem following the many years of slavery in America. Write an essay describing how "wearing masks" from the Reconstruction period through the 1950s might have saved African Americans from humiliation and, in many cases, from death.

2. In your writing journal, explain how disguising one's feelings may prove to be self-defeating.

3. Lines one and two of the poem make a statement about the conditions of African Americans one hundred years ago. Write an essay about that statement; is it as accurate today as it was when Dunbar wrote "We Wear the Mask" at the end of the nineteenth century?

"The Black Jamaican" by Calvin Jones. Medium: Conté crayon with acrylic appliqué. Reprinted by permission of Isobel Neal Gallery, Chicago, Illinois.

8

OF DREAMERS AND REVOLUTIONARIES

"Brethren, arise, arise! Strike for your lives and liberties. Now is the day and the hour. . . . Rather die free men than live to be slaves. Let your motto be resistance! Resistance! RESISTANCE!"

—Henry Highland Garnet (1843)

The desire and the push for freedom and dignity by African American women and men did not begin with the civil rights movement of the 1960s. The revolt led by Nat Turner in 1831 against slavery signaled a turning point in how blacks perceived themselves and were perceived by their slave owners. Although blacks continued to be subjected to the most inhumane acts, the slaves kept their dignity intact. Important to note is that the first revolutionary to die in the war between England and the colonies in 1770 was a former slave, Crispus Attucks.

African Americans from their earliest days in America protested against discrimination and segregation. Their experiences in this country have been chronicled by men and women who have used the pen, not the sword, to focus attention on their plight and their quest for freedom and respect.

In recent decades, black pride and an increased interest in their African American heritage have encouraged black writers to create literature reflecting their own identity. The Civil Rights Movement, the Black Arts Movement, and the taking of African/Muslim names heightened in the 1960s. During this time, poetry became the major vehicle for transporting the ideas of protest. Amiri Baraka was in the vanguard of the new black aesthetic—defining it as follows: the reason for all black artistic expression is the achievement of change in all areas that are social, political, and moral. Selections by key "revolutionary" black writers of this important part of the African American literary tradition are included in this chapter.

Mari Evans was born in Toledo, Ohio. She attended public schools in Toledo and enrolled at the University of Toledo where she studied fashion design. Evans' father was a strong influence in her writing career. He saved her first printed story, written when she was in fourth grade, and included his own proud comments. From 1968 to 1973, Evans was a producer, writer, and director of "The Black Experience" at WTTV, Channel 4, in Indianapolis. In addition, she has served as a consultant with the National Endowment for the Arts (1969–1970), a director of the Literary Advisory Panel for the Indiana Arts Commission (1976–1977), and a member of the board of directors of the First World Foundation. Evans has combined her writing career with an academic one, teaching at Indiana University, Purdue University, Washington University, Cornell University, Spelman College, and the State University of New York at Albany.

Evans writes short fiction, political essays, poetry, and theatre pieces. She uses her strong writing skills to present authentic voices from African American communities. Her published works and play productions include *I Am a Black Woman* (1970), *I Look at Me!* (1973), *River of My Song* (1977), *Eyes* (1979), *Nightstar: 1973–1978* (1981), and *A Dark and Splendid Mass* (1992). She also edited *Black Women Writers (1950–1980): A Critical Evaluation* (1984).

Vive Noir!

i

am going to rise
en masse
from Inner City
        sick   5
          of newyork ghettos
          chicago tenements
        l a's slums
weary
     of exhausted lands   10
     sagging privies
     saying yessuh yessah
     yesSIR
     in an assortment
     of geographical dialects i   15
have seen my last
broken down plantation
even from a
distance
     i   20
will load all my goods
in '50 Chevy pickups '53
Fords fly United and '66
caddys i
     have packed in   25
     the old man and the old lady and
     wiped the children's noses

Vive Noir!: Long Live Black!

I'm tired
of hand me downs
shut me ups   30
pin me ins
keep me outs
messing me over have
just had it
baby   35
from
you . . .
i'm
gonna spread out
over America   40
intrude
my proud blackness
all
over the place
i have wrested wheat fields   45
from the forests

turned rivers
from their courses

leveled mountains
at a word   50
festooned the land with
bridges
gemlike
on filaments of steel
moved   55
glistening towersofBabel in place
like blocks
sweated a whole
civilization
. . . for you   60
now
i'm
gonna breathe fire
through flaming nostrils BURN
a place for   65
me

in the skyscrapers and the
schoolrooms on the green
lawns and the white
beaches   70
   i'm
gonna wear the robes and
sit on the benches
make the rules and make
the arrests say   75
who can and who
can't
   baby you don't stand
   a
   chance   80
i'm
 gonna put black angels
 in all the books and a black
 Christchild in Mary's arms i'm
 gonna make black bunnies black   85
fairies black santas black
nursery rhymes and
    black
 ice cream
   i'm   90
gonna make it a
 crime
  to be anything BUT black
  pass the coppertone

gonna make white   95
a twentyfourhour
lifetime
J.O.B.
  an' when all the coppertone's gone . . . . ?

Thinking About the Poem

1. From line 1 to line 37, "Vive Noir!" sounds similar to Ntozake Shange's poem "one thing i dont need" on page 155. In what ways are the two poems similar to each other?

2. There is very little punctuation in this poem. Sentences start with lowercase letters and there are no commas or periods. Evans uses ellipses three times and a question mark once. How does the limited use of punctuation and the placement of the words on the lines affect the overall feeling of the poem?

3. The speaker in the poem refers to himself or herself with a lowercase *i*. Who is the speaker? How would you describe the speaker based on descriptions or images presented in the poem?

4. Throughout the poem the speaker is talking to someone whom he/she refers to as "baby" and "you." To whom do you think the speaker is addressing the poem? What is the speaker's attitude toward this person or group?

5. What is the relationship between the title "Vive Noir!" and the content presented in this poem?

Reading/Writing Connections

1. In an essay discuss the poetic techniques that are similar and different in "Vive Noir!" and Ntozake Shange's "one thing i dont need." Which poetic techniques are used in each poem? How are they used in the poems? What do they contribute to the meaning of each poem?

2. Reread the last five lines of the poem. What do you think the speaker is saying about a person being white? If you changed the word *white* to *black*, how would that change the meaning of the sentence? Put your response into a writing journal entry.

Nikki Giovanni

Nikki Giovanni (b. 1943) was born Yolande Cornelia Giovanni, Jr., in Knoxville, Tenn., to Gus Giovanni, a social worker, and Yolande Giovanni, a supervisor for the welfare department. A strong influence in Giovanni's life was her maternal grandmother, Louvenia Terrell Watson. Giovanni lived with her grandmother during her sophomore and junior years in high school. Her grandmother instilled in her a responsibility for other African Americans.

While attending Fisk University, Giovanni edited *Elan,* the campus literary magazine, participated in the Fisk Writers Workshop under the direction of author John O. Killens, and became politically active. In 1964 she founded a chapter of the Student Non-Violent Coordinating Committee (SNCC), a civil rights organization on the Fisk campus. Giovanni graduated *magna cum laude* with honors in history in 1967. For a short time, Giovanni attended graduate school at the University of Pennsylvania School of Social Work and the School of Fine Arts at Columbia University. During this time, Giovanni was active in a number of arts and culture programs in African American communities. Her experiences developed into her first two poetry collections: *Black Feeling, Black Talk* (1967) and *Black Judgement* (1968). These two volumes brought Giovanni national attention. In 1968 she received a National Foundation for the Arts grant and began her university teaching career. She has taught at Queen's College, Rutgers University, and Livingston College; currently she teaches at Virginia Polytechnic and State University.

Along with Haki Madhubuti (Don L. Lee) and Sonia Sanchez, Giovanni has been recognized as one of the three leading figures in black poetry between 1968 and 1971. Due in part to her international travels in the mid-1970s and 1980s, her work has moved from black nationalism toward a more humanist world view. Giovanni has published poetry collections, dialogues, an autobiography, and essays, including *Spin a Soft Black Song: Poems for Children* (1971), *My House: Poems* (1972), *A Dialogue: James Baldwin and Nikki Giovanni* (1973), *A Poetic Equation: Conversations Between Nikki Giovanni and Margaret Walker* (1974). *Cotton Candy on a Rainy Day* (1978), *Those Who Ride the Night Winds* (1983), and *Sacred Cows . . . and Other Edibles* (1988).

Nikki-Roasa

NIKKI GIOVANNI

childhood remembrances are always a drag
if you're Black
you always remember things like living in Woodlawn
with no inside toilet
and if you become famous or something   5
they never talk about how happy you were to have your mother
all to yourself and
how good the water felt when you got your bath from one of those
big tubs that folk in chicago barbecue in
and somehow when you talk about home   10
it never gets across how much you
understood their feelings
as the whole family attended meetings about Hollydale
and even though you remember
your biographers never understand   15
your father's pain as he sells his stock
and another dream goes
and though you're poor it isn't poverty that
concerns you
and though they fought a lot   20
it isn't your father's drinking that makes any difference
but only that everybody is together and you
and your sister have happy birthdays and very good christ-
masses and I really hope no white person ever has cause to
write about me because they never understand Black love   25
is Black wealth and they'll probably talk about my hard
childhood and never understand that all the while I was
quite happy

Nikki-Roasa: also published under the title "Nikki-Rosa," this poem was originally entitled
"Nikki-Roasa" by the author, that name being a childhood nickname.

Thinking About the Poem

1. Giovanni does not use formal punctuation, capitalization, or stanza breaks in her free-verse poem. Instead, she uses line breaks to indicate where you should pause. Select four lines which you believe end with important words. Why do you think these words are important? Would their significance change if they were not the last words?

2. Do you agree or disagree with the speaker when the speaker says in lines 24–26 that a "white person" would not understand that "Black love is Black wealth"? Why or why not?

3. In lines 18 and 19 the speaker says "and though you're poor it isn't poverty that / concerns you." What things do you think concern the speaker? Why would these things be more important than poverty?

4. The poem begins with the line "childhood remembrances are always a drag" and ends with the words "all the while I was quite happy." Is there a contradiction between these two thoughts? Use words and phrases from the poem to support your answer.

Reading/Writing Connections

1. When we view the experiences that others have, it is easy for us to see them one way while those who are living through those experiences will see them another way. Remember an occasion that made you happy. In your journal write about that occasion, explaining why you consider it a happy one and why others might not.

2. Write your own free-verse poem, about an everyday event that makes you happy. Try to capture the feeling of the event. You do not need to use standard punctuation, capitalization, or stanza breaks in your poem. End your lines where you want a pause—with words that you feel are important.

William Edward Burghardt Du Bois   (1868–1963) one

of the most important leaders of black protest in the United States, was born in Great Barrington, Mass. Du Bois was raised by his mother, a New Englander of Dutch-African descent. She was an inspirational force in his life, encouraging him to excel in his studies. Du Bois began his writing and public speaking career while attending Fisk University. He then went to Harvard, becoming the first African American to receive a Ph.D. in American history.

Du Bois believed that the problems of African Americans could not be understood without systematic investigation and intelligent understanding. In 1899 he published *The Philadelphia Negro: A Social Study,* the first systematic sociological study of a large number of African Americans in any major city of the United States. One of the founders of the National Association for the Advancement of Colored People (NAACP), Du Bois edited its journal, *The Crisis,* from 1910 until 1930. After many years of affiliation with that organization, he parted with it, disagreeing on ideologies.

A strong proponent of civil rights for African Americans and dedicated to principle and truth, this prolific writer of books, essays, and speeches is a major revolutionary African American writer. As an intellectual and scholar, Du Bois traveled internationally, writing and speaking on the conditions of African Americans in the United States. In 1961, Du Bois—disappointed with the lack of progress in civil rights for blacks and the system of government in this country—moved to Ghana and later became a citizen of that African country.

The following is a selected list of his works: *The Suppression of the African Slave-Trade to the United States of America, 1638–1870* (1896); *The Souls of Black Folk: Essays and Sketches* (1905), *The Quest for the Silver Fleece* (1911), *The Gift of Black Folk: The Negroes in the Making of America* (1924), *Africa: Its Place in Modern History* (1930), *Dusk of Dawn: An Essay Toward an Autobiography of a Race Concept* (1940), *In Battle for Peace: The Story of My 83rd Birthday* (1952), and *The Autobiography of W. E. B. Du Bois: A Soliloquy on Viewing My Life From the Last Decade of Its First Century,* edited by Herbert Aptheker (1968).

The Immediate Program of the American Negro

W. E. B. DU BOIS

The immediate program of the American Negro means nothing unless it is mediate to his great ideal and the ultimate ends of his development. We need not waste time by seeking to deceive our enemies into thinking that we are going to be content with a half loaf, or by being willing to lull our friends into a false sense of our indifference and present satisfaction.

The American Negro demands equality—political equality, industrial equality and social equality; and he is never going to rest satisfied with anything less. He demands this in no spirit of braggadocio and with no obsequious envy of others, but as an absolute measure of self-defense and the only one that will assure to the darker races their ultimate survival on earth.

Only in a demand and a persistent demand for essential equality in the modern realm of human culture can any people show a real pride of race and a decent self-respect. For any group, nation or race to admit for a moment the present monstrous demand of the white race to be the inheritors of the earth, the arbiters of mankind and the sole owners of a heritage of culture which they did not create, nor even improve to any greater extent than the other great division of men—to admit such pretense for a moment is for the race to write itself down immediately as indisputably inferior in judgment, knowledge and common sense.

The equality in political, industrial and social life which modern men must have in order to live, is not to be confounded with sameness. On the contrary, in our case, it is rather insistence upon the right of diversity;—upon the right of a human being to be a man even if he does not wear the same cut of vest, the same curl of hair or the same color of skin. Human equality does not even entail, as is sometimes said, absolute equality of opportunity; for certainly the natural inequalities of inherent genius and varying gift make this a dubious phrase. But there is a more and more clearly recognized minimum of opportunity and maximum of freedom to be, to move and to think, which the modern world denies to no being which it recognizes as a real man.

These involve both negative and positive sides. They call for freedom on the one hand and power on the other. The Negro must have political freedom; taxation without representation is tyranny. American Negroes of today are ruled by tyrants who take what they please in taxes and give what they please in law and administration, in justice and in injustice; and the great mass of black people must stand helpless and voiceless before a condition which has time and time again caused other peoples to fight and die.

The Negro must have industrial freedom. Between the peonage of the rural South, the oppression of shrewd capitalists and the jealousy of certain trade unions, the Negro laborer is the most exploited class in the country, giving more hard toil for less money than any other Americans, and have less voice in the conditions of his labor.

In social intercourse every effort is being made today from the President of the United States and the so-called Church of Christ down to saloons and boot-blacks to segregate, strangle and spiritually starve Negroes so as to give them the least possible chance to know and share civilization.

These shackles must go. But that is but the beginning. The Negro must have power; the power of men, the right to do, to know, to feel and to express that knowledge, action and spiritual gift. He must not simply be free from the political tyranny of white folk, he must have the right to vote and to rule over the citizens, white and black, to the extent of his proven foresight and ability. He must have a voice in the new industrial democracy which is building and the power to see to it that his children are not in the next generation trained to be the mudsills of society. He must have the right to social intercourse with his fellows. There was a time in the atomic individualistic group when ''social intercourse'' meant merely calls and tea-parties; today social intercourse means theatres, lectures, organizations, churches, clubs, excursions, travel, hotels,—it means in short Life; to bar a group from such methods of thinking, living and doing is to bar them from the world and bid them create a new world;—a task to which no single group is to-day equal; it is to crucify them and taunt them with not being able to live.

What now are the practical steps which must be taken to accomplish these ends?

First of all before taking steps the wise man knows the object and end of his journey. There are those who would advise the black man to pay little or no attention to where he is going so long as he keeps moving. They assume that God or his vice-gerent the White Man will attend to the steering. This is arrant nonsense. The feet of those that aimlessly wander land as often in hell as in heaven. Conscious self-realization and self-direction is the watchword of modern man, and the first article in the program of any group that will survive must be the great aim, equality and power among men.

The practical steps to this are clear. First we must fight obstructions; by continual and increasing effort we must first make American courts either build up a body of decisions which will protect the plain legal rights of American citizens or else make them tear down the civil and political rights of all citizens in order to oppress a few. Either result will bring justice in the end. It is lots of fun and most ingenious just now for courts to twist law so as to say I shall not live here or vote there, or marry the woman who wishes to marry me. But when tomorrow these decisions throttle all freedom and overthrow the foundation of democracy and decency there is going to be some judicial house cleaning.

We must *secondly* seek in legislature and congress remedial legislation; national aid to public school education, the removal of all legal discriminations based simply on race and color, and those marriage laws passed to make the seduction of black girls easy and without legal penalty.

Third, the human contact of human beings must be increased; the policy which brings into sympathetic touch and understanding, men and women, rich and poor, capitalist and laborer, Asiatic and European, must bring into closer contact and mutual knowledge the white and black people of this land. It is the most frightful indictment of a country which dares to call itself civilized that it has allowed itself to drift into a state of ignorance where ten million people are coming to believe that all white people are liars and thieves, and the whites in turn to believe that the chief industry of Negroes is raping white women.

Fourth, only the publication of the truth repeatedly and incisively and uncompromisingly can secure that change in public opinion which will correct these awful lies. THE CRISIS, our record of the darker races, must have a circulation of 35,000 chiefly among colored folk but of at least 250,000 among all men who believe in men. It must not be a namby-pamby box of salve, but a voice that thunders fact and is more anxious to be true than pleasing. There should be a campaign of tract distribution—short well-written facts and arguments—rained over this land by millions of copies, particularly in the South, where the white people know less about the Negro than in any other part of the civilized world. The press should be utilized—the 400 Negro weeklies, the great dailies and eventually the magazines, when we get magazine editors who will lead public opinion instead of following afar with resonant brays. Lectures, lantern-slides and moving pictures, co-operating with a bureau of information and eventually becoming a Negro encyclopedia, all these are efforts along the line of making human beings realize that Negroes are human.

Such is the program of work against obstructions. Let us now turn to constructive effort. This may be summed up under (1) economic co-operation, (2) a revival of art and literature, (3) political action, (4) education, and (5) organization.

Under economic co-operation we must strive to spread the idea among colored people that the accumulation of wealth is for social rather than individual ends. We must avoid, in the advancement of the Negro race, the mistakes of ruthless exploitation which have marked modern economic history. To this end we must seek not simply home ownership, small landholding and saving accounts, but also all forms of co-operation, both in production and distribution, profit sharing, building and loan associations, systematic migration from mob rule and robbery, to freedom and enfranchisement, the emancipation of women and the abolition of child labor.

In art and literature we should try to loose the tremendous emotional wealth of the Negro and the dramatic strength of his problems through writing, the stage, pageantry and other forms of art. We should resurrect forgotten ancient Negro art and history, and we should set the black man before the world as both a creative artist and a strong subject for artistic treatment.

In political action we should organize the votes of Negroes in such congressional districts as have any number of Negro voters. We should systematically interrogate candidates on matters vital to Negro freedom and uplift. We should train colored voters to reject the bribe of office and to accept only decent legal enactments both for their own uplift and for the uplift of laboring classes of all races and both sexes.

In education we must seek to give colored children free public school training. We must watch with grave suspicion the attempt of those who, under the guise of vocational training, would fasten ignorance and menial service on the Negro for another generation. Our children must not in large numbers, be forced into the servant class; for menial service is still, in the main, little more than an antiquated survival of impossible conditions. It has always been as statistics show, a main cause of bastardy and prostitution and despite its many marvelous exceptions it will never come to the light of decency and honour until the house servant becomes the Servant in the House. It is our duty then, not drastically but persistently, to seek out colored children of ability and genius, to open up to them broader, industrial opportunity and above all, to find that Talented Tenth[1] and encourage it by the best and most exhaustive training in order to supply the Negro race and the world with leaders, thinkers and artists.

For the accomplishment of all these ends we must organize. Organization among us already has gone far but it must go much further and higher. Organization is sacrifice. It is sacrifice of opinions, of time, of work and of money, but it is, after all, the cheapest way of buying the most priceless of gifts—freedom and efficiency. I thank God that most of the money that supports the National Association for the Advancement of Colored People comes from black hands; a still larger proportion must so come, and we must not only support but control this and similar organizations and hold them unwaveringly to our objects, our aims and our ideals.

---

[1]*Talented Tenth:* A term Du Bois created to describe the intellectual top ten percent of African Americans who would be leaders, thinkers, and artists of the race.

Thinking About the Essay

1. Du Bois opens his essay, written in 1914, by stating that "The American Negro demands equality—political equality, industrial equality and social equality." Why is it necessary for African Americans to have equality in each of these areas?

2. To accomplish the goal of equality, Du Bois presents four practical steps that must be followed. Identify these steps and establish the connections between them and Du Bois' three aspects of equality.

3. Du Bois argues against providing African American children with only vocational training. He states that African Americans will not have "decency and honour until the house servant becomes the Servant in the House." What does Du Bois mean by this statement?

4. Describe the tone of Du Bois' essay. Use specific words, phrases, or sentences from the essay to illustrate your description. What specific audience do you think Du Bois had in mind when he was writing this essay? Is the tone of the essay appropriate for the audience he was trying to reach? Why or why not?

Reading/Writing Connections

1. After reading another source of information on the conditions of African Americans in the United States in the early 1900s, write an essay in which you discuss either the political, economic, or social position of African Americans. Use examples from Du Bois' essay and from your other sources of information to support your opinion.

2. Write a letter to Du Bois in which you describe to what degree African Americans have obtained political, economic, and social equality in the United States.

3. Du Bois supported the development of what he called the "Talented Tenth," the intellectual top ten percent of African Americans who would be "leaders, thinkers and artists," as opposed to Booker T. Washington's support of vocational training for all African Americans as a way for African Americans to establish their rightful place in the United States. In your journal write an entry in which you discuss the strengths and weaknesses of each position.

Amiri Baraka (LeRoi Jones)   (b. 1934) was born in Newark, N.J. After graduating from high school, Baraka enrolled at Howard University, graduating at the age of nineteen. Beginning his career as a poet, he brought his African American identity as well as radical political issues to his writing, rejecting traditional poetic forms. As part of his rejection of the white-dominated culture in the 1960s, he changed his name to a Muslim name, Imamu Ameer Baraka; later he shortened it to Amiri Baraka. His literary works at that time reflected a black nationalist stance.

One of the founders of the Black Arts Movement, Baraka produced a series of one-act plays during the early 1960s—powerful dramas about race relations that enjoyed successful off-Broadway runs. His other works include *Blues People: Negro Music in White America* (1963), *The Systems of Dante's Hell* (1965), essays, and two volumes of poetry. A powerful figure in the African American literary tradition, his more recent publications include *Reggae or Not* (1982), a poetry collection, and *The Autobiography of LeRoi Jones-Amiri Baraka* (1984).

Preface to a
Twenty Volume Suicide
Note

(For Kellie Jones, Born 16 May, 1959)

AMIRI BARAKA

Lately, I've become accustomed to the way
The ground opens up and envelops me
Each time I go out to walk the dog.
Or the broad edged silly music the wind
Makes when I run for a bus . . .   5

Things have come to that.

And now, each night I count the stars,
And each night I get the same number.
And when they will not come to be counted,
I count the holes they leave.   10

Nobody sings anymore.

And then last night, I tiptoed up
To my daughter's room and heard her
Talking to someone, and when I opened
The door, there was no one there . . .   15
Only she on her knees, peeking into

Her own clasped hands.

Thinking About the Poem

1. What are the poet's feelings and what is his attitude about life as expressed in stanzas one and two of the poem?

2. Discuss the **irony** in the title of this poem. What do you think the speaker's attitude about suicide is as you read the poem's last stanza?

3. Baraka writes in free verse. What techniques does he use in "Preface to a Twenty Volume Suicide Note" to achieve poetic effects?

Reading/Writing Connections

1. In the last stanza of the poem, the speaker tells of finding his daughter on her knees, peeking into her clasped hands, and talking to someone he does not see. In your journal, write about whom you think the girl is speaking to.

2. Imagining you are the poet, Amiri Baraka, write a letter to your daughter, Kellie, after she becomes an adult. Explain why you wrote "Preface to a Twenty Volume Suicide Note," published in 1961, and dedicated it to her.

3. The line "Nobody sings anymore" expresses the poet's impression of the world. In your journal, describe what you think the meaning of that is. You may research Baraka's life and the 1960s or you may use examples from your personal background, events, literature, or history to illustrate your points.

Haki Madhubuti (Don L. Lee) (b. 1942) was reared in Detroit and educated in Chicago. He is the director of the Institute of Positive Education and the editor of Third World Press. He has served as poet-in-residence at Cornell, Howard, and Central State universities and at the University of Illinois at Chicago. He is currently a professor of English at Chicago State University.

Among his many published books are *Think Black* (1967), *Black Pride* (1968), *Don't Cry, Scream* (1969), *Dynamite Voices: Black Poets of the 1960s* (1971), *See That the River Turns: The Impact of Gwendolyn Brooks* (1987), *Killing Memory, Seeking Ancestors* (1987), and *Black Men: Obsolete, Single, Dangerous? The Afrikan American Family in Transition* (1990).

Assassination

it was wild.
the
bullet hit high.
        (the throat-neck)
& from everywhere: 5
       the motel, from under bushes and cars,
       from around corners and across streets,
       out of the garbage cans and from rat holes
       in the earth
they came running.   10
with
guns
drawn
they came running
toward the King—   15
       all of them
       fast and sure—
as if
the King
was going to fire back.   20
they came running,
fast and sure,   .
in the
wrong
direction.   25

Thinking About the Poem

1. The speaker does not state who "they" are in the poem. Who do you think "they" are? Give reasons for your answer.

2. In "Assassination," the victim is simply referred to as "the King." What is the significance of the poet not mentioning Martin Luther King, Jr., by his full name?

3. The speaker states "they came running, fast and sure,/in the/ wrong/direction." What is ironic about this statement? What do you believe was the right direction?

Reading/Writing Connections

1. King was in Memphis supporting striking workers (garbage collectors) and organizing a Poor People's Campaign in that city when he was assassinated at a motel. Take on the persona of one of the motel maids or janitors present the day of the assassination and in your journal write an account of that day and your reactions.

2. The Reverend Jesse Jackson was one of the people standing on the motel balcony with King when he was shot in 1968. Assume you are Jackson and, in your journal, write how the assassination of King affected you and the Civil Rights Movement.

3. It is said that the dreamer has been slain but the dream has not died. Write an essay explaining what you think this statement means. Use examples from your reading, from history, or from your personal experience or background.

4. Write a free-verse or traditional poem about another assassination, such as that of Malcolm X.

Martin Luther King, Jr.   (1929–1968) was born in Atlanta, Ga.

He attended Washington High School where he participated in basketball and football. He studied hard and was able to skip two grades. King had a gift for public speaking; his choice of words and his delivery won him a speaking contest in Atlanta. Later he became a Baptist minister and the main leader of the civil rights movement in the United States during the 1950s and 1960s.

King was president of the Southern Christian Leadership Conference and co-pastor of the Ebenezer Baptist Church in Atlanta. He was a leader in the Montgomery, Ala., "walk for freedom" movement that resulted in the desegregation of public transportation in that city. In 1963, he was *Time* magazine's Man of the Year. He received the Nobel Peace Prize in 1964. King was assassinated on April 4, 1968, in Memphis, Tenn. His most famous speech that follows was delivered on August 28, 1963, at the Lincoln Memorial in Washington, D.C.

I Have a Dream

MARTIN LUTHER KING, JR.

I am happy to join with you today in what will go down in history as the greatest demonstration for freedom in the history of our nation.

Five score years ago a great American in whose symbolic shadow we stand today signed the Emancipation Proclamation. This momentous decree is a great beacon light of hope to millions of Negro slaves who had been seared in the flames of withering injustice. It came as a joyous daybreak to end the long night of their captivity. But 100 years later the Negro still is not free. One hundred years later the life of the Negro is still badly crippled by the manacles of segregation and the chains of discrimination. One hundred years later the Negro lives on a lonely island of poverty in the midst of a vast ocean of material prosperity. One hundred years later the Negro is still languished in the corners of American society and finds himself in exile in his own land. So we've come here today to dramatize a shameful condition.

In a sense we've come to our nation's capital to cash a check. When the architects of our Republic wrote the magnificent words of the Constitution and the Declaration of Independence, they were signing a promissory note to which every American was to fall heir. This note was a promise that all men—yes, black men as well as white men—would be guaranteed the unalienable rights of life, liberty, and the pursuit of happiness. It is obvious today that America has defaulted on this promissory note insofar as her citizens of color are concerned. Instead of honoring this sacred obligation, America has given the Negro people a bad check which has come back marked "insufficient funds."

But we refuse to believe that the bank of justice is bankrupt. We refuse to believe that there are insufficient funds in the great vaults of opportunity of this nation. So we've come to cash this check, a check that will give us upon demand the riches of freedom and the security of justice.

We have also come to this hallowed spot to remind America of the fierce urgency of now. This is no time to engage in the luxury of cooling off or to take the tranquilizing drug of gradualism. Now is the time to make real the promises of democracy. Now is the time to rise from the dark and desolate valley of segregation to the sunlit path of racial justice. Now is the time to lift our nation from the quicksands of racial injustice to the solid rock of brotherhood.

Now is the time to make justice a reality for all of God's children. It would be fatal for the nation to overlook the urgency of the moment. This sweltering summer of the Negro's legitimate discontent will not pass until there is an invigorating autumn of freedom and equality—1963 is not an end but a beginning. Those who hope that the Negro needed to blow off steam and will now be content will have a rude awakening if the nation returns to business as usual.

There will be neither rest nor tranquility in America until the Negro is granted his citizenship rights. The whirlwinds of revolt will continue to shake the foundations of our nation until the bright day of justice emerges. And that is something that I must say to my people who stand on the worn threshold which leads into the palace of justice. In the process of gaining our rightful place we must not be guilty of wrongful deeds. Let us not seek to satisfy our thirst for freedom by drinking from the cup of bitterness and hatred.

We must forever conduct our struggle on the high plane of dignity and discipline. We must allow our creative protests to degenerate into physical violence. Again and again we must rise to the majestic heights of meeting physical force with soul force. The marvelous new militancy which has engulfed the Negro community must not lead us to distrust all white people, for many of our white brothers, as evidenced by their presence here today, have come to realize that their destiny is tied up with our destiny.

They have come to realize that their freedom is inextricably bound to our freedom. We cannot walk alone. And as we walk we must make the pledge that we shall always march ahead. We cannot turn back. There are those who are asking the devotees of civil rights, "When will you be satisfied?" We can never be satisfied as long as the Negro is the victim of the unspeakable horrors of police brutality.

We can never be satisfied as long as our bodies, heavy with the fatigue of travel, cannot gain lodging in the motels of the highways and the hotels of the cities.

We cannot be satisfied as long as the Negro's basic mobility is from a smaller ghetto to a larger one. We can never be satisfied as long as our children are stripped of their adulthood and robbed of their dignity by signs stating "For Whites Only."

We cannot be satisfied as long as the Negro in Mississippi cannot vote and the Negro in New York believes he has nothing for which to vote.

No, no, we are not satisfied and we will not be satisfied until justice rolls down like waters and righteousness like a mighty stream.

I am not unmindful that some of you have come here out of great trials and tribulation. Some of you have come fresh from narrow jail cells. Some of you have come from areas where your quest for freedom left you battered by the storms of persecution and staggered by the winds of police brutality. You have been the veterans of creative suffering.

Continue to work with the faith that unearned suffering is redemptive. Go back to Mississippi, go back to Alabama, go back to South Carolina, go back to Georgia, go back to Louisiana, go back to the slums and ghettos of our Northern cities, knowing that somehow this situation can and will be changed. Let us not wallow in the valley of despair.

I say to you today, my friends, though, even though we face the difficulties of today and tomorrow, I still have a dream. It is a dream deeply rooted in the American dream. I have a dream that one day this nation will rise up, live out the true meaning of its creed: "We hold these truths to be self-evident, that all men are created equal."

I have a dream that one day on the red hills of Georgia sons of former slaves and the sons of former slave-owners will be able to sit down together at the table of brotherhood. I have a dream that one day even the state of Mississippi, a state sweltering with the heat of injustice, sweltering with the heat of oppression, will be transformed into an oasis of freedom and justice.

I have a dream that my four little children will one day live in a nation where they will not be judged by the color of their skin but by the content of their character. I have a dream . . . I have a dream that one day in Alabama, with its vicious racists, with its governor having his lips dripping with the words of interposition and nullification, one day right there in Alabama little black boys and black girls will be able to join hands with little white boys and white girls as sisters and brothers.

I have a dream today . . . I have a dream that one day every valley shall be exalted, every hill and mountain shall be made low. The rough places will be made plain, and the crooked places will be made straight. And the glory of the Lord shall be revealed, and all flesh shall see it together. This is our hope. This is the faith that I go back to the South with. With this faith we will be able to hew out of the mountain of despair a stone of hope. With this faith we will be able to transform the jangling discords of our nation into a beautiful symphony of brotherhood. With this faith we will be able to work together, to pray together, to struggle together, to go to jail together, to stand up for freedom together, knowing that we will be free one day.

This will be the day when all of God's children will be able to sing with new meaning, "My country, 'tis of thee, sweet land of liberty, of thee I sing. Land where my fathers died, land of the pilgrim's pride, from every mountain side, let freedom ring." And if America is to be a great nation, this must become true. So let freedom ring from the prodigious hilltops of New Hampshire. Let freedom ring from the mighty mountains of New York. Let freedom ring from the heightening Alleghenies of Pennsylvania. Let freedom ring from the snow-capped Rockies of Colorado. Let freedom ring from the curvacious slopes of California.

But not only that. Let freedom ring from Stone Mountain of Georgia. Let freedom ring from Lookout Mountain of Tennessee. Let freedom ring from every hill and molehill of Mississippi, from every mountain side. Let freedom ring . . . .

When we allow freedom to ring—when we let it ring from every city and every hamlet, from every state and every city, we will be able to speed up that day when all of God's children, black men and white men, Jews and Gentiles, Protestants and Catholics, will be able to join hands and sing in the words of the old Negro spiritual, "Free at last, Free at last, Great God a-mighty, We are free at last."

Thinking About the Speech

1. King says his dream is "deeply rooted in the American dream." How would you describe the "American dream"?

2. King uses figurative language throughout his speech. For example, he says, "With this faith we will be able to hew out of the mountain of despair a stone of hope." "Mountain of despair" is a metaphor. What do you think this phrase means?

3. King often said Mahatma Gandhi served as his model for bringing about social change in the United States. Research Gandhi (India's foremost religious and political leader of the early decades of the twentieth century) and discuss the similarities of his methods with those used by King in the Civil Rights Movement.

Reading/Writing Connections

1. "I Have a Dream" and "The Creation" (see Chapter 7) use an oratorical style. King was trained as a minister and James Weldon Johnson wrote "The Creation" in the form of a sermon. Reread "The Creation" and write an essay comparing King's and Johnson's style.

2. If King were still alive, what do you think would be his reaction to the lives of African Americans today? Write a poem, story, essay, or drama in which you describe his reaction. You may wish to use some literary devices, such as metaphor or repetition.

3. Assume you have a particular desire for the improvement of something about your school or community. What might that be? Write a speech in which you explain that dream. You may wish to imitate King's style.

"Family Tree," quilt by Wini McQueen. See copyright page for further information.

Glossary of Key Literary Terms

Alliteration   A repetition of consonant sounds at the beginning of words or within words, as in Robert Hayden's phrase "some in silks and some in shackles." *Example*: "Runagate Runagate," p. 11, line 17.

Anecdote   A short narrative of an entertaining and presumably true incident. This device is used by, among others, writers of biography and autobiography.

Ballad   A story told in verse, usually with a refrain, strong rhythm, and rhyme, originally meant to be sung. Ballads are often about physical courage resulting in death (for example, ballads about John Henry; for a non-ballad form of his story, see "The Steel Drivin' Man," pp. 73–75). *Folk ballads* deal with the common people; they are anonymous and have been preserved through *oral tradition*.

Blues   A vocal and instrumental music developed by African Americans. The blues grew out of the *spirituals* (religious songs) and work songs of the slaves. Blues sometimes contain a *call-and-response* pattern (an African pattern of exchange between singer or storyteller and audience).

Couplet   Two consecutive lines of poetry that rhyme and are written in the same *meter* (i.e., the same pattern of stressed and unstressed syllables).

Folktale   A short narrative passed down to succeeding generations through *oral tradition*. (Folktales are also referred to as *folklore*.)

Free verse   Poetry that does not have a fixed *rhyme scheme*, meter, line length, or *stanza* form. *Example*: Alice Walker's "Women" (p. 249).

Harlem Renaissance   The flowering of African American creativity in New York City's Harlem in the 1920s. The four principal writers to achieve recognition during this period were Claude McKay, Jean Toomer, Countee Cullen, and Langston Hughes. The Harlem Renaissance was not only a literary movement, but a general cultural expression in music and art as well as writing.

Heroic couplet   A pair of rhyming iambic pentameter lines; the favorite verse form of the eighteenth-century *neoclassical* poets. (An *iamb* consists of one unstressed syllable followed by one stressed syllable; a line of five iambs is an *iambic pentameter*.)

Hyperbole   The use of obvious, extravagant exaggeration for emphasis or comic effect. *Example*: Amiri Baraka's "Preface to a Twenty Volume Suicide Note" (p. 305).

Irony   When a writer or speaker says one thing but means something different (even the opposite of what is said).

Italian sonnet   A 14-line poem in iambic pentameter, organized into two parts: an *octave*, consisting of the first eight lines and rhyming *abba, abba,* and a *sestet,* the remaining six lines, which may have a number of different *rhyme schemes* (for example, cd, cd, cd; cde, cde; cdd, cdd, and so on). The octave establishes a theme or poses a problem that is developed or resolved in the sestet. *Example*: Countee Cullen's ''From the Dark Tower'' (p. 25).

Metaphor   Implied comparison between two unlike things or actions. *Example*: ''The only wreath of household love'' in Frances Watkins Harper's ''The Slave Mother'' (p. 3).

Mythology   Anonymous narrative, usually transmitted orally, that explains in supernatural terms the origin of life, religious beliefs, or natural forces, or that recounts the deeds of traditional heroes.

Neoclassical   Adjective form of *neoclassicism*, the dominant literary movement in England from the late seventeenth through the eighteenth century. Neoclassicists sought to revive the artistic ideals of ancient Greece and Rome. *Example*:   Phillis Wheatley's ''On Being Brought from Africa to America'' (pp. 6–7).

Oral tradition   The myths, folktales, histories, and other narratives that are passed on by the spoken, not the written, word. The experts in oral performance, the storytellers, of Africa pass on the oral tradition today as they have since ancient times. Called *griots* (grē′ō) in West Africa, these revered storytellers serve as singers, poets, historians, and teachers, and use their memories rather than written words to preserve the oral tradition. In *Roots*, Alex Haley writes about the griot whom he visited in a village in The Gambia, who retold the history—the story—of Kunta Kinte, Haley's great-great-great-great-grandfather.

Persona   The personality or voice created by the author, through which a story is told. The persona may be the narrator, the ''I'' in a first-person narrative, as in ''Sonny Blues'' by James Baldwin (pp. 93–119).

Quatrain   A *stanza* of four lines, rhymed or unrhymed; also a poem consisting of four lines only.

Rhyme scheme   The pattern of rhymes in a *stanza* or an entire poem.

Setting   The time and place in which the action of a narrative occurs. The setting is usually conveyed to the reader by description.

Shakespearean sonnet   A 14-line poem in iambic pentameter, with three quatrains and a concluding couplet. The *rhyme scheme* is usually *abab, cdcd, efef, gg*. Each quatrain deals with a single thought, and the poem is summed up or resolved in the couplet. *Example*: Claude McKay's "If We Must Die" (p. 29).

Simile   A figure of speech that uses "like," "as," or "as if," to compare two unlike things or actions, as in McKay's poem "If We Must Die": "If we must die, let it not be *like* hogs/Hunted and penned in an inglorious spot."

Spirituals   The religious songs of American slaves. The rhythms of spirituals appear to have elements in common with African music. W.E.B. Du Bois called spirituals "sorrow songs."

Stanza   A section or division of a poem; specifically a grouping of lines into a recurring pattern determined by the number of lines, their meter, and their *rhyme scheme*.

Tone   The reflection in a work of the author's attitude toward his or her subject, characters, and readers.

Index of Literary Selections and Authors

Credits

Envoi

On The Pulse of Morning

MAYA ANGELOU

This poem was written for and delivered at President Bill Clinton's inauguration in Washington, D.C., on January 20, 1993.

A Rock, A River, A Tree
Hosts to species long since departed,
Marked the mastodon.
The dinosaur, who left dry tokens
Of their sojourn here
On our planet floor,
Any broad alarm of their hastening
    doom
Is lost in the gloom of dust and ages.

But today, the Rock cries out to us,
    clearly, forcefully,
Come, you may stand upon my
Back and face your distant destiny,
But seek no haven in my shadow.
I will give you no more hiding place
    down here.

You, created only a little lower than
The angels, have crouched too long in
The bruising darkness,
Have lain too long
Face down in ignorance.
Your mouths spilling words

Armed for slaughter.
The Rock cries out today, you may
    stand on me,
But do not hide your face.

Across the wall of the world,
A River sings a beautiful song,
Come rest here by my side.
Each of you a bordered country,
Delicate and strangely made proud,
Yet thrusting perpetually under siege.
Your armed struggles for profit

Have left collars of waste upon
My shore, currents of debris upon my
    breast.
Yet, today I call you to my riverside,
If you will study war no more. Come,
Clad in peace and I will sing the
    songs
The Creator gave to me when I and the
Tree and the stone were one.
Before cynicism was a bloody sear
    across your
Brow and when you yet knew you
    still
Knew nothing.
The River sings and sings on.

There is a true yearning to respond to
The singing River and the wise Rock.
So say the Asian, the Hispanic, the
    Jew
The African and Native American,
    the Sioux,
The Catholic, the Muslim, the
    French, the Greek
The Irish, the Rabbi, the Priest, the
    Sheikh,
The Gay, the Straight, the Preacher,
The privileged, the homeless, the
    Teacher.
They hear. They all hear
The speaking of the Tree.

Today, the first and last of every Tree
Speaks to humankind. Come to me,
    here beside the River.
Plant yourself beside me, here beside
    the River.

Each of you, descendant of some
    passed
On traveler, has been paid for.
You, who gave me my first name, you
Pawnee, Apache and Seneca, you
Cherokee Nation, who rested with me,
    then
Forced on bloody feet, left me to the
    employment of
Other seekers—desperate for gain,
Starving for gold.
You, the Turk, the Swede, the German,
    the Scot
You the Ashanti, the Yoruba, the Kru,
    bought
Sold, stolen, arriving on a nightmare
Praying for a dream.
Here, root yourselves beside me.
I am the Tree planted by the River,
Which will not be moved.
I, the Rock, I the River, I the Tree
I am yours—your Passages have been
    paid.
Lift up your faces, you have a piercing
    need
For this bright morning dawning for
    you.
History, despite its wrenching pain,
Cannot be unlived, and if faced
With courage, need not be lived
    again.

Lift up your eyes upon
The day breaking for you.
Give birth again
To the dream.

Women, children, men,
Take it into the palms of your hands.
Mold it into the shape of your most
Private need. Sculpt it into
The image of your most public self.
Lift up your hearts
Each new hour holds new chances
For new beginnings.
Do not be wedded forever
To fear, yoked eternally
To brutishness.

The horizon leans forward,
Offering you space to place new steps
    of change.
Here, on the pulse of this fine day
You may have the courage
To look up and out upon me, the
Rock, the River, the Tree, your
    country.
No less to Midas than the mendicant.
No less to you now than the mastodon
    then.

Here on the pulse of this new day
You may have the grace to look up
    and out
And into your sister's eyes, into
Your brother's face, your country
And say simply
Very simply
With hope
Good morning.